Addressing Problematic
Sexual Behaviors in Children

Addressing Problematic Sexual Behaviors in Children

How We Can Help

Genevieve Naquin

ROWMAN & LITTLEFIELD
Lanham • Boulder • New York • London

Published by Rowman & Littlefield
An imprint of The Rowman & Littlefield Publishing Group, Inc.
4501 Forbes Boulevard, Suite 200, Lanham, Maryland 20706
www.rowman.com

86-90 Paul Street, London EC2A 4NE

British Library Cataloguing in Publication Information Available

Library of Congress Cataloging-in-Publication Data

ISBN 978-1-5381-9789-9 (cloth)
ISBN 978-1-5381-9790-5 (paperback)
ISBN 978-1-5381-9791-2 (ebook)

∞™ The paper used in this publication meets the minimum requirements of American
National Standard for Information Sciences—Permanence of Paper for Printed Library
Materials, ANSI/NISO Z39.48-1992.

Brief Contents

Preface   xiii

Introduction to the Research   xvii

Some Things to Note Before We Get Started   xxix

PART I: CURRICULUM   **1**

  1 Building Rapport   3

  2 The Foundation of Treatment: Safety Planning, Boundaries,
          and Types of Touch   11

  3 Body Awareness   23

  4 Client History   37

  5 Ownership   45

  6 Healthy Relationships and Appropriate Sexuality   53

  7 Empathy and Awareness   69

  8 Future Safety and Finishing Strong   79

PART II: ADDITIONAL CONSIDERATIONS   **83**

  9 Multisystem Involvement   85

10 Common Characteristics, Barriers, and Challenges When Working With Children Exhibiting Problematic Sexual Behaviors Who Are Twelve Years of Age and Younger 109

11 Furthering the Field 141

Appendix: Activity Worksheets and Examples 149

References 177

Index 187

About the Author 201

Contents

Preface   **xiii**

Introduction to the Research   **xvii**

Some Things to Note Before We Get Started   **xxix**
    Definitions at a Glance   xxix
    Development   xxxi
        Children Zero to Four Years of Age   xxxiii
        Children Five to Nine Years of Age   xxxvi
        Children Ten to Twelve Years of Age   xxxvii
    Treatment Steps   xxxix

PART I: CURRICULUM   **1**

1 Building Rapport   **3**
    Building Trust   4
        Building Rapport Age Considerations   4
        Building Rapport With Clients   5
        Building Rapport With the Family   6
        Rapport-Building Activities   7

**2 The Foundation of Treatment: Safety Planning,
    Boundaries, and Types of Touch**   **11**
    Basics of a Safety Plan   12
    The Safety Plan   13
    Boundaries   14
        Physical Boundaries   14
        Emotional/Mental Boundaries   16
        Practicing Boundaries and Body Rights   17

Types of Touch   18
  Safe/Good Touch   18
  Unsafe/Bad Touch   18
  Sexual/Secret Touch   19
  Further Learning Related to Touch   19

3 Body Awareness   **23**
Checking In   23
  Feelings Chart Check-in   24
  Puppet Check-in   25
Emotional Recognition and Regulation   26
  Feelings Chain   26
  Locus of Control   28
Building Coping Skills and Interventions   29
  Mindfulness Cards for Deep Breathing   30
Let's Talk About Body Parts   31
  Normalizing Body Parts   32
  Safety!   33
  How to Teach Kids About Body Parts   33
  The Puberty Talk   34
  Healthy Masturbation   35

4 Client History   **37**
Gathering Client History   38
  Ways to Help a Shy Client Open Up   39
  Life History and Sexual History Timeline   39
Trouble Thoughts   42
  Trouble Thoughts Activity   43

5 Ownership   **45**
Accountability   46
  The Staircase   47
  The Weed Activity   49
  The Flower Activity   50

6 Healthy Relationships and Appropriate Sexuality   **53**
Components of a Healthy Relationship   54
  CERTS   54
  Consent   54
  Equality   55
  Respect   55
  Trust   56
  Safety   56
  Follow-up Discussion   57

Components of Consent   58
  Freely Given   59
  Reversible   60
  Informed   60
  Enthusiastic   61
  Specific   61
Helpful Tools to Teach CERTS and FRIES   62
  Setting up the Flower Game   63
Safety in Relationships   63
Psychoeducation Related to Pornography   64
  For Those With Minimal Pornography Exposure   65
  For Those With Problematic Pornography Use   66
  Can We Stop Them?   67

7 **Empathy and Awareness**   **69**
Intent Versus Impact and Empathy Versus Sympathy   70
  Intent Versus Impact   70
  Empathy Versus Sympathy   71
Psychoeducation for Caregivers Regarding Empathy   72
  Listen   72
  Modeling   73
  Patience and Practice   73
Victim Awareness   73
  Psychoeducation Around Impacts   74

8 **Future Safety and Finishing Strong**   **79**
Safe-Play Plan   79
Treatment Review   80

PART II: ADDITIONAL CONSIDERATIONS   **83**

9 **Multisystem Involvement**   **85**
Let's Talk About School   86
  Where to Start Regarding School Engagement   87
  Individualized Education Programs and 504 Plans   89
  Safety Plans for School   90
Involvement in Extracurriculars   91
  Movement-Based Activities   92
  Non-Movement-Based Activities   94
Functioning within the Home   95
Community Partners   95
  Department of Human Services   96
  Wraparound Services   96

Intensive Care Coordination   101
Respite Services   102
Child Advocacy Centers   103
Survivor Therapist   105

**10 Common Characteristics, Barriers, and Challenges When
    Working With Children Exhibiting Problematic Sexual
    Behaviors Who Are Twelve Years of Age and Younger   109**
Common Characteristics, Barriers, and Issues Seen in
    Children With Problematic Sexual Behaviors   109
Attachment Challenges   110
Neurodivergence   111
Mental Health Challenges   112
Arousal in the Treatment Room   113
Pornography Use   114
Common Challenges That Come Up When Working With the
    Families of Children With Problematic Sexual Behaviors 116
Caregivers' Response   116
Technology Literacy   120
Lack of Knowledge Around Sexual Development   122
Caregiver's Own Trauma   124
Common Struggles and Issues Experienced When Working
    Within Larger Systems While Treating Problematic
    Sexual Behaviors   126
Mandatory Reporting   126
Lack of Discourse Around Sexuality as a Society   128
Lack of Training Specific to Working with Problematic
    Sexual Behaviors and Clinicians Working Outside of
    Their Scope of Practice   129
Who Should Work With Children That Are Engaging in
    Problematic Sexual Behaviors?   133
Conclusion   137
Ambiguity Around National Response, Certifications, and
    Protocol   137

11 Furthering the Field   141
Lack of Research   142
Race and Ethnicity   142
Girls and Gender-Diverse Children   144
Developmental Differences (Developmental Delays)   145
Assessments   146

Appendix: Activity Worksheets and Examples **149**
Boundaries 149
Boundaries Example 150
Types of Touch 151
Types of Touch Example 152
Feelings Faces 153
Feelings Faces Example 154
Feelings Chain 155
Feelings Chain Example 1 156
Feelings Chain Example 2 157
Trouble Thoughts 158
Trouble Thoughts: Mix and Match 159
Trouble Thoughts: Mix and Match Example 160
Staircase Activity 161
Staircase Activity Example 162
Weed Activity 163
Weed Activity Example 164
Flower Activity 165
Flower Activity Example 166
Rock and Ripple Activity 167
Rock and Ripple Activity Example 168
Letter of Growth 169
Safe-Play Plan 170
Treatment Review 173
Initial Treatment Safety Plan 175

References 177

Index 187

About the Author 201

Preface

Treatment for individuals who have perpetrated sexual abuse is often overlooked in the therapeutic field. When someone is struggling with mental health concerns, such as depression or anxiety, it can be an overwhelming and challenging experience. Thankfully, there is an abundance of qualified providers to turn to when needing support with these challenges. When it comes to treating sexual offending behaviors, the abundance of qualified clinicians discussed above, turns into a small trickle. Now, when it comes to treating *children* with problematic sexual behaviors, this trickle of qualified clinicians turns into a few drops. The sex offense treatment world is a specialized subset within the therapeutic field, so it's not surprising that this specialization yields a smaller number of qualified therapists than, say, therapists who specialize in anxiety. However, within this specialization we are seeing a need for additional specializations, like specializations in the treatment of female sexual offenders. An additional specialization the field is seeing an increased need for is clinicians who specialize in working with young children with problematic sexual behaviors.

There is research dedicated to the assessment and treatment of youth, over the age of twelve years, that have sexually acted out. Within the United States, youth ages twelve to eighteen have several avenues of resources when seeking services for harmful sexual behaviors, such as the backing of the juvenile justice system and all of the resources and financial support that comes with this system. However, for youth under the age of twelve years, we are seeing a serious dearth of resources. This age range often falls through the cracks, as problematic sexual behaviors in children twelve years and under are less likely to prompt intervention by law enforcement (Finkelhor et al., 2009). When we look at what is being done to assess, prevent, or treat problematic sexual behaviors within this age-group, the resources are few and far between. When children begin exhibiting troubling sexual behaviors, many, including clinicians, are unsure of what to do. These concerning behaviors may be ignored or minimized due to too few resources, a lack of providers working within this specialization, familial shame, lack of education around what normative and atypical sexual behaviors are for this age range, and the list goes on. This means that the child may never be provided with the appropriate resources to address these concerns unless they end up in our offices at an older age due to adjudication for a sexual offense. Hackett and colleagues (2013) mention this dynamic in their review of more than seven hundred cases involving UK adolescents who were referred to services for their sexually abusive behaviors. In reviewing their case files, they found that adolescents who later engaged in more invasive acts of sexual harm often had an earlier history of problematic sexual behaviors that went unaddressed.

Clinicians working in this subset of the field know that sexual abuse occurs at an alarming rate whether society chooses to acknowledge this or not. These harmful behaviors are not just perpetrated by adults, or adolescents, and if we are to help make the community safer, we must address the elephant in the room: children engage in harmful sexual behaviors too. If these behaviors are addressed early and effectively, children can overcome these struggles, and the future harm they pose to themselves, and to others, may be mitigated.

In my time working within this field, it has become clear that there is no, "one size fits all," approach to treatment. No two clients are exactly alike, and the field has evolved to agree with this line of thinking. Thanks to research, adolescents who have sexually offended are no longer engaging in treatment that reflects the treatment of adults who have sexually offended. It's clear that these are two distinct populations and should be treated as such. The same is true when comparing the treatment of adolescents and children who have engaged in sexually abusive behaviors, however, there are far fewer resources to guide clinicians in treating children. Unfortunately, this has led to clinicians treating children who are struggling with problematic sexual behaviors in the same way they would treat adolescents with these problematic sexual behaviors.

In 2002, Safer Society completed a nationwide survey of adult, adolescent, and child sexual abuse treatment programs. In reviewing this survey, McGrath et al. (2003) found that the majority of children programs treating problematic sexual behaviors utilized treatment elements that evolved from adult sexual offense–specific treatment work. Current literature points to a growing awareness that there are definite and distinct differences between young people who have engaged in harmful sexual behaviors and adults who have committed sexual offenses (Creeden, 2018, 2020; Hackett, 2014; McPherson et al., 2023). If the field continues moving away from treating adolescents like adults who have offended, why would we treat children this way?

To better understand why this might occur, I started to look for what other treatment curriculums or protocols were out there. Unsurprisingly, there are few. McPherson et al. (2023) conducted a literature review looking into effective assessment and intervention approaches used to respond to problematic sexual behaviors in young people. They found that the knowledge regarding research, resources, and understanding of how to best treat these children is limited, but awareness is growing. They also found that there is limited published research addressing the outcomes of assessment and intervention approaches, perhaps due to the lack of clarity around the root cause of these underlying behaviors (Elkovitch et al., 2009; McPherson et al., 2023). Though there is no singular causal factor or profile for children engaging in problematic sexual behaviors, the research clearly indicates adverse childhood experiences as a nearly universal impacting factor present in children engaging in these behaviors (Creeden, 2020; Vizard et al., 2007). These experiences, along with their engagement in problematic sexual behaviors, provide a strong indication for therapeutic intervention. Within this curriculum, I have done my best to review the literature, incorporate the research, and create a curriculum that can be used as a guide for treating these children.

This book is intended to combine several elements that can provide some structure and ideas for clinicians working with children under the age of twelve years who are engaging in problematic sexual behaviors. This book is based on the current treatment protocol I use when working with this population. This treatment protocol is based on current research, resources collected over the years, and trial and error. Additionally, after walking through the treatment curriculum I've created, I discuss the different systems I find myself working with, and within, when treating children with problematic sexual behaviors. The level of case management with these clients is often significant, and connecting these families to additional resources is common. I also discuss the barriers I've experienced when working with this population. I cover barriers and challenges ranging from systemic barriers all the way down to barriers present within the treatment room, and how I tend to address these challenges. Last, I discuss research areas in need of significant improvement and a few assessment tools and measures that may be helpful when working with these children and their families.

Introduction to the Research

Children under the age of twelve engage in problematic sexual behaviors; in fact, research approximates that children are responsible for about one-third of all child sexual abuse (Allardyce & Yates, 2018; Campbell et al., 2020; Finkelhor et al., 2009; Gray et al., 1999;). You may not know it if you were to look at the research out there, as it is relatively new and sparse. As Rasmussen (2002) sites, the research in this area of the field started in the late 1980s and early 1990s and remains comparatively untouched with unremarkable progress (Cantwell, 1988; Friedrich & Luecke, 1988; Glasgow et al., 1994; Hackett, 2014; Johnson, 1988; Johnson & Berry, 1989; Ray et al., 1995). This population, however, is beginning to garner more attention, as concerns over increased sexualized behavior problems in this age range have grown (Chaffin et al., 2008; Shawler et al., 2018). Swisher et al. (2008) note that, in recent decades, the number of children being referred to treatment for sexual behavior problems has increased. Though the exact causes of this increase are unknown, it is believed that it can be linked to more inclusive definitions of problematic sexual behaviors, an increase in understanding and, therefore, an increase in awareness and reports of these behaviors, and an actual increase in the frequency of these behaviors (Chaffin et al., 2008). A challenge in understanding what factors are responsible for the reported increase of these behaviors is also related to the challenges in tracking these behaviors. In the United States, children under the age of twelve years have relatively little contact with the juvenile justice system, thus, children engaging in problematic sexual behaviors often have no legal involvement; therefore, these behaviors are not systematically tracked in the same way they are for adults and adolescents (Silovsky et al., 2018).

In addition to an increase in referrals, there has been increased attention on this population to better understand how to treat these behaviors before they evolve into larger behavioral patterns that could lead to adolescent sexual offending, a progression that's discussed within several studies (Burton, 2000; Zolondek et al. 2001). Additionally, having a better understanding of how to treat these problems in childhood will ideally lead to a decrease in adult sexual offending behaviors. Studies have shown that up to half of adults who engage in sexual offending behaviors acknowledged a childhood or adolescent onset for these abusive behaviors (Abel et al., 1987; Hanson & Slater, 1988; Marshall et al. 1991). Approximately one-third to one-half of all child sexual abuse cases are committed by other youth (Campbell et al., 2020; Gray et al., 1999; Finkelhor et al., 2009), with a little under 30 percent of these cases committed by children who are twelve years old or under (DeLago et al., 2019; Office of Juvenile Justice Delinquency Prevention [OJJDP], 2022). Given the prevalence of kids twelve years old and under who are engaging in these behaviors, intervention is crucial and necessary. Silovsky and colleagues' (2018) study looked at the impacts that early intervention and treatment can have for this population. They found that treating these behaviors early on can have a profound impact on preventing child sexual abuse, as they found that problematic sexual behaviors can improve quickly with treatment, and these improvements were maintained even after treatment.

As we know, to prevent abuse, it must be discussed, and this may be one of the reasons there is such a deficiency in the research and resources regarding this topic. Sex and sexuality can be a difficult topic for some, but factor in the idea of discussing these topics with children, and acknowledging that children engage in sexual behaviors, and people balk at the idea. Children are curious beings and engage in normative sexual exploration, often through play; however, it is important to acknowledge the distinctions between normative sexual play and concerning sexual play.

Normative sexual play often involves "spontaneity, joy, laughter, embarrassment and sporadic levels of inhibition and disinhibition," whereas concerning sexual play often involves "dominance, coercion, threats and force," as well as emotional distress (Gil & Shaw, 2014, p. 19). Johnson and Berry (1989) further discuss the distinction between typical sexual development and sexually harmful behaviors by defining appropriate sexual exploration: "Appropriate childhood exploration is an information-gathering process of limited duration wherein children of similar ages explore, visually and/or tactilely, each other's bodies" (p. 186). Additionally, these behaviors are not inherently sexual, as many are related to concepts like curiosity and impulsivity rather than sexual gratification. Children engaging in these types of behaviors will participate on a voluntary basis and if caught and reprimanded, the behaviors generally diminish. Sexual behaviors of children are deemed problematic and in need of therapeutic intervention if,

(a) aggression, force, or coercion is involved; (b) it occurs between children of different ages, size, and development levels; (c) it occurs between children who do not know each other well; (d) it persists despite appropriate caregiver intervention, and/or it disrupts normal childhood activities; (e) it causes harm to the child or others; (f) it is accompanied by emotional distress; (g) it involves animals. (Silvosky & Bonner, 2004; Swisher et al., 2008, p. 51)

These types of behaviors are not developmentally normative and should be addressed immediately. Additionally, it is noted that these behaviors do not happen in a vacuum; therefore, understanding where they are coming from is also imperative to the treatment process.

In reviewing the research regarding preadolescents who engage in problematic sexual behaviors, there are several themes present when looking at the impacting factors that foster the development of these behaviors. Vizard et al. (2007) determined several psychosocial and behavioral characteristics that are common among this population. They determined that difficulties within the family environment were present for all young people in their sample and that "92% had suffered neglect, witnessed domestic violence, or experienced one form of abuse (sexual, physical, or emotional)" and "in the majority of cases this maltreatment began before they were six years old" (p. 62). All other forms of maltreatment, including emotional abuse, neglect, and physical abuse, were more likely to have started before the age of three years and "persisted for a number of years before any interventions were made" (p. 62). This early exposure to aggressive socialization and unhealthy relational dynamics may contribute to distorted beliefs around boundaries, which in turn may lead to an earlier onset of problematic sexual behaviors. Gray et al. (1999) also concluded that children who have engaged in sexually abusive behaviors have often been victims of sexual and physical maltreatment; however, they also acknowledge an environmental component in addition to the maltreatment. The research points to chronic distress within family systems as another impacting factor, citing "high rates of poverty, sexual abuse and perpetration within the extended family, and arrest for criminal behavior" (Gray et al., 1999, p. 602). Mesman et al. (2019) reviewed the appropriate literature and found that the research suggests that growing up in environments that model distress, domestic violence, physical abuse, and poor boundaries have been identified as impacting factors for children's engagement in problematic sexual behaviors. As one may guess, growing up in homes where there may be exposure to nudity, parental sexual activity, and/or pornography also increases the chances of children developing problematic sexual behaviors (Curwen et al., 2014; Friedrich et al., 2003; Levesque et al., 2010). Szanto and colleagues (2012) facilitated a study to identify the different types of trauma experiences linked to the later development of problematic sexual behaviors in kids. At the conclusion of this study, it was determined that sexual abuse was the most common form of abuse found among children in this population, as well as exposure to violence. The presence of multiple trauma experiences is correlated to the expression of problematic sexual behaviors in children (Finkelhor et al., 2007; Szanto et al., 2012).

The presence of the impacting factors above can help clinicians understand that children engaging in problematic sexual behaviors will need to engage in therapeutic work within a number of areas. Treatment will not solely focus on their problematic sexual behaviors; rather, it will focus on these behaviors in addition to exploring family dynamics and the relationships being modeled for them at home, trauma work around their own experiences of abuse and maltreatment, learning how to cope in chaotic or stressful environments, family therapy, and so on. Just as we would with all clients, we need to treat these children holistically, and research indicates and supports the importance of this. Sexually harmful behaviors in childhood stem from early trauma that has disrupted typical development in these children. So, what does the research say about the assessment, approach, and treatment of children engaging in these behaviors?

McPherson and colleagues (2023) highlight the challenges regarding the consistency, clarity, and context of assessing children who have engaged in problematic sexual behaviors. They identified considerable inconsistencies in their review of the literature with respect to assessment and intervention approaches for this population. They found two main assessment approaches: a forensically oriented approach and a developmentally oriented approach. A forensically oriented approach focuses on assessment via risk assessment tools; however, this would prove challenging for this population, as there are no assessment tools that I'm aware of that predict future sexual acting-out behaviors, or risk, for children under the age of eleven years. There are several risk assessment tools for youth aged twelve and older, such as the protective and risk observations for eliminating sexual offense recidivism (PROFESOR) and the estimate of risk of adolescent sexual offense recidivism (ERASOR), but these tools cannot be applied to children engaging in problematic sexual behaviors. It can be argued that even if these assessments were applicable to this younger age-group, they would not consider the developmental history of these children, thus a more holistic approach is favored.

A developmentally oriented approach to assessing risk allows for the clinician to incorporate a multitude of impacting factors. This approach is crucial due to the prevalence of trauma within this population and the impact that early childhood trauma can have on brain development. Blasingame (2018) highlights the impacts that child maltreatment can have on the brain, including long-term effects on the hippocampus that can impact mood regulation, memory, and learning, all of which will influence treatment. A developmentally oriented approach, when assessing risk, incorporates a more holistic view of the child. It considers the larger factors that impact a child, such as school, family, home dynamics, peers, extracurricular activities, and so on. Focusing on the whole child allows for a more trauma-informed approach that emphasizes growth, in addition to challenges, rather than providing a narrow focus on the problematic sexual behaviors themselves. Focusing exclusively on the problematic sexual behaviors would lead to a siloed assessment, thus impacting treatment and intervention. Just as assessment should consider developmental level and a holistic view of the child, so should treatment.

When engaging in case conceptualization, prior to treating the problematic sexual behaviors, understanding the present behaviors as being symptomatic of trauma can help create a lens in which to work from. I find that the "Trauma Outcome Process," explained by Rasmussen (2002), is a helpful model that can be used to assess how our clients have come to process their traumatic experiences. Knowing this can inform us of how to best move forward clinically. The trauma outcome process includes three premises: (1) there are three possible outcomes in how children respond to trauma, (2) victims have a choice about which of these outcomes to pursue, and (3) healing from the impacts of trauma is a dynamic process. The three behavioral response outcomes are (1) internalizing emotions that lead to self-destructive behaviors, (2) externalizing emotions that may lead to abusive behaviors, and (3) expressing emotions that aid in healing, as the child can understand and integrate their experiences (Rasmussen, 2002, p. 10). Understanding which behavioral responses our clients are engaging in dictates how to best proceed in the treatment process.

We are meeting with children who have engaged in problematic sexual behaviors, sometimes toward themselves (i.e., response 1: internalizing emotions that lead to self-destructive behaviors) and sometimes toward others (i.e., response 2: the externalization of emotions that lead to abusive behaviors). It is noted, however, that the three behavioral response outcomes are not mutually exclusive, and our clients may be enacting multiple responses at the same time, for example, enacting responses 1 and 2—engaging in excessive masturbation, as well as persistent attempts to touch the genitals of others. Once we, the clinicians, have a good understanding of how our client tends to process trauma, we can create a treatment plan and case conceptualization that includes working toward the goal of response 3: expressing, understanding, and integrating experiences. This is the ultimate goal for clients, as "being aware of feelings, thoughts, and body sensations enables individuals to make positive choices and engage in the adaptive option of recovery" (Rasmussen, 2002, p. 12).

Before the treatment planning process can begin, we first need to assess our clients and the outcome that they best fit into. To do this involves identifying the risk factors that may be present and how they have impacted the child's maladaptive response(s) to their trauma. The assessment must also address the emotional, behavioral, and cognitive outcomes from having experienced this trauma, and how aware the client is in the following areas: physical sensations, thoughts, feelings, motivations, and actions (Miller et al., 1975). Once these areas have been assessed, the clinician can identify the child's primary behavioral response to the trauma and how to best move forward. With this, treatment can begin.

When discussing how to treat problematic sexual behaviors specifically, the literature reflects a range of intervention approaches. In the last two decades, there has been growth in the development of good therapeutic practices for treating this population; however, evaluation outcomes regarding these practices and the effectiveness of specific treatment programs is still scarce (McPherson et al., 2023; Shlonsky et al., 2017). Though evaluation outcomes are hard to come by, there is still literature exploring the different modalities that have been used to treat young people with problematic sexual behaviors. In reviewing the literature, there are seven different intervention approaches aimed at treating this population. These seven approaches include cognitive behavioral therapy (CBT), behavioral approaches, strength-based approaches, multisystemic therapy, social learning approaches, specialist abuse-specific approaches, and holistic, developmental, and trauma-informed approaches (McPherson et al., 2023).

Though these seven distinct approaches have been identified in the literature, there has been no identifiable approach that is best suited for young children, as much of the research regarding therapeutic approaches and intervention focuses on adolescents, also discussed in the literature as "young people." The treatment of "young people" is discussed in some studies, like the study conducted by Jenkins et al. (2020), which supports the use of CBT when treating sexual behavior problems. Within this study, they sighted clinically significant reductions in problematic sexual behaviors of their participants, who ranged in age from eleven to eighteen years old with a median age of a little over fourteen years, when using problematic sexual behavior–cognitive behavioral therapy for adolescents (PSB-CBT-A). Other studies find unclear evidence regarding the use of CBT approaches when treating "young people" and whether these approaches result in improvements related to these behaviors (Sneddon et al., 2020). Multi-Systemic Therapy (MST), an integrative approach that includes a variety of components from other approaches, like family therapies and CBT, was identified as showing some promise for treating "young people" (Meiksans et al., 2017). Further research on the other five approaches is present in the literature, but again, we cannot extrapolate the findings, as this literature is predominantly focused on adolescents, not children engaging in problematic sexual behaviors.

There are a few reviews of the literature that focus specifically on the intervention approaches used to treat *children* with problematic sexual behaviors (Shlonsky et al., 2017). I was only able to identify two studies that focus on children ten years old and under, and both studies are from well over two decades ago. An additional study, from 2018, assessed the intervention of problematic sexual behavior–cognitive behavioral treatment (PSB-CBT) for youth between the ages of ten to fourteen. This study, conducted by Silovsky et al. (2018), evaluated the outcomes of several community-based programs treating youth with problematic sexual behaviors via PSB-CBT. Though this age range includes those above the age of twelve years, I include it here, as it specifically looked at youth who have had no prior court contact due to engagement in problematic sexual behaviors, which is what we tend to see with children ages twelve years old and under in the United States.

PSB-CBT utilizes group treatment for kids, as well as their caregivers, and has been developed to treat youth ages seven to twelve. It requires caregiver involvement, a necessary component of treating problematic sexual behaviors, as seen throughout the literature and discussed later in this literature review (Carpentier et al., 2006; Deblinger et al., 1996; 1999; DeLago et al., 2019; Griggs & Boldi, 1995; Heiman, 2002; Kenny et al., 2008; Pithers et al., 1998a; St. Amand et al., 2008). It is a strengths-based approach that focuses on utilizing CBT to teach youth about rules related to sexual behaviors and skills to aid with developing healthy relationships, engaging in appropriate coping, increasing impulse control, and increasing healthy decision-making. The PSB-CBT treatment manual used provided clinicians with a session format and guidelines, but the clinician was able to provide core components while adjusting it to meet the family and client where they were at. This study found that the youth and caregivers who participated in PSB-CBT to fidelity found that the problematic sexual behaviors "improved quickly, and gains were maintained post treatment" (Silovsky et al., 2018, p. 9).

The two studies from more than two decades ago were done by Bonner et al. (2000) and Pithers et al. (1998b), and they looked at the use of CBT versus dynamic play therapy (Bonner et al., 2020), and relapse prevention versus expressive therapy (Pithers et al., 1998b) when treating children exhibiting problematic sexual behaviors. They yielded findings that support the use of integrative models when treating this population because of the high level of complexity within these cases. Utilizing an integrative model that combines several approaches enables the clinician to best address the specific needs of each client while also ensuring they receive the information and skills necessary to discourage any future problematic sexual behaviors, comparable to PSB-CBT. In addition to integrating several therapeutic models, it can also be argued that "victim"- and "perpetrator"-specific treatment be integrated and incorporated into the treatment process, as these children often hold both identities having been the victim of maltreatment but also having perpetrated harmful sexual behaviors.

As discussed above, the factors that impact a child's engagement in problematic sexual behaviors often includes their own victimization and experiences of multiple traumas. Whether they have experienced sexual abuse, witnessed domestic violence, or live in a home with poor boundaries, they have internalized these dynamics and experiences. When children experience these kinds of trauma but do not have the skills to cope with such experiences, they may exhibit sexual behaviors and, at times, problematic sexual behaviors because they "lack the internal coping skills to handle their feelings in appropriate ways. . . . Lacking the words to communicate how they feel, they may act out their pain behaviorally and emotionally" (Katz, 1997, p. 6). To treat the child in a clinically sound and holistic way, we need to utilize approaches from both victim and perpetrator treatments.

The ability to use interventions and materials from several approaches, like CBT, dynamic play therapy, and relapse prevention, enables clinicians to address the problematic sexual behaviors while helping their client understand the root of these behaviors by processing their own experiences of trauma and any other impacting factors that are present. CBT can be utilized to provide appropriate psychoeducation to build skills and utilize interventions to prevent reenactments of unresolved emotional issues that impact our clients' engagement in problematic sexual behaviors, while play therapies and expressive therapies allow our clients to express their emotions about past maltreatment and trauma (Cunningham & MacFarlane, 1996; Gil, 1991; James, 1989). By using integrative modalities, clients can learn and utilize strategies that allow them to develop self-management and regulation skills to address impulsive behaviors and unhealthy thought patterns, while increasing healthy connection and social skills, and gaining tools to appropriately manage sexual feelings (Bonner et al., 2000; Burton et al., 1998; Cunningham & MacFarlane, 1996; Lane, 1997; Pithers & Gray, 1993; Pithers et al., 1998b). In addition to integrating therapeutic models, parental involvement in the treatment process is essential.

A 2008 meta-analysis by St. Amand et al. (2008) looked at "11 treatment outcome studies that evaluated 18 specific treatments" for addressing sexual behavior problems in children (p. 185). They found that the most effective treatment for children with problematic sexual behaviors involves utilizing several modalities, and that the elements most strongly related to a reduction in problematic sexual behaviors was parental involvement and training. They found that children who engage in CBT or trauma-focused (TF) CBT for their problematic sexual behaviors, and who have parents who participate in parent trainings that focus on sex education, abuse prevention, limit setting, and rules around sexual behaviors, are not likely to have further problematic sexual behaviors in the future. They concluded that the "primary agent of change" for children with sexual behavior problems is the involvement of parents or caregivers in the treatment process. They also found that the treatment element most strongly linked to a reduction of problematic sexual behaviors was parent behavior management skills.

Carpentier et al. (2006) engaged in a randomized trial of treating children with problematic sexual behaviors and found that working with children and their families via structured, psychoeducational, and cognitive-based therapy had great success regarding recidivism. They stated that after therapy, the rates of reengaging in problematic sexual behaviors were "indistinguishable from those of a comparison group of clinic children with common nonsexual behavior problems such as ADHD" (p. 486). Griggs and Boldi (1995) cited that the family's reaction to their child who's demonstrating problematic sexual behaviors can facilitate, or hinder, changing and redirecting these problematic behaviors. Their treatment of these problematic sexual behaviors should address healthy and appropriate rules around sexual behaviors, age-appropriate sexual education, and self-protection skills to minimize vulnerability and potential victimization. These findings are further supported by several studies done by Pithers and colleagues (Pithers & Gray, 1993; Pithers et al., 1998a), stating, "for children with sexual behavior problems, caring oversight is necessary to prevent further sexually problematic behavior" (Pithers et al., 1998, p. 405).

Farmer and Pollock's (2003) analysis of children who have been sexually abused and/or have engaged in problematic sexual behaviors found that there were four key elements related to successfully minimizing further problematic sexual behaviors and/or victimization in their sample. The four elements include adequate sex education, supervision, behavioral redirection, and understanding the underlying needs that the behaviors are serving. Caregivers played a significant role in each of these elements and were proven to be foundational in preventing further victimization or sexual acting-out behaviors. When able to provide age-appropriate education around sexual development, healthy relationships, and getting needs met in safe and nonsexualized ways, they were effective in addressing these behaviors. Though supervision is an important part of preventing repeated behaviors, they noted that simply providing supervision may limit opportunities to act out and/or prevent victimization, but it does not address the root of these behaviors, which is needed to generate long-lasting change.

In addition to adequate supervision and education, it can be argued that treatment addressing problematic sexual behaviors needs to integrate family involvement to adequately address past traumatic events. As we know, children engaging in these unwanted behaviors have experienced a range of traumatic events, some having taken place within the family or been perpetrated by immediate family members. Heiman (2002) acknowledges that for treatment to be comprehensive, and to address the roots of the larger systems at play, it should handle and aid in helping parents, or caregivers, develop specific skills to discuss and process past sexualized behaviors, build healthy home rules regarding sexual behaviors, and increase their skills in openly communicating topics within this subject. Combining both parent and child treatments leads to significantly greater reductions in externalizing behavioral symptoms, as opposed to parent-only or child-only treatments (Deblinger et al., 1996; 1999). Not only is parental involvement imperative to minimizing a child's future engagement in problematic sexual behaviors but it is also imperative to minimizing their risk of future victimization (DeLago et al., 2019).

Parental involvement in treatment acts as a protective factor in keeping children safe from possible future victimization. Kenny et al. (2008) discusses self-protection skills beginning in the home with the caregiver(s) and that the learning and modeling of these skills should continue throughout adolescence. This explicit learning can begin as early as age three, as this is when children are developmentally capable of learning the medical names of their genitalia (Kenny et al., 2008; Kurtuncu et al., 2015). Parents are also responsible for creating an environment that is communicative and open, so their child feels comfortable discussing this material. Open parent–child communication around themes related to sexuality, boundaries, healthy relationships, body rights, and so on, serves as a protective factor in reducing the child's risk of being victimized, or engaging in problematic behaviors that may victimize others (DeLago et al., 2019). Additionally, talking about this information will help children get their questions answered in a safe and healthy way, rather than seeking out answers on the internet or from misinformed peers. Normalizing these conversations can also help children feel comfortable discussing their sexual thoughts, feelings, or experiences, consensual or harmful, rather than behaving secretively or hiding their experiences. Education and communication are major pieces of prevention.

When discussing the importance of catching and treating these behaviors from an early age, prevention is a major reason. Treatment can be used as a tool for protecting vulnerable youth from future victimization. Elliott et al. (1995) interviewed ninety-one adults who had sexually offended children to better understand the methods that they used to target and abuse children, and what tools should be provided to children so they can be better protected from people engaging in sexually abusive behaviors. In their findings, they found that the majority of those who had offended coerced children by carefully testing their boundaries when it came to sexual topics and touching. They would create settings that normalized sexual topics by slowly pushing verbal and physical boundaries with these children. Briggs (2014) also identified this concern from an educator's lens, arguing that children engaging in problematic sexual behaviors within a school setting may attract attention from other children who are struggling with problematic sexual behaviors or older perpetrators, such as coaches or teachers, making them especially vulnerable to victimization. Therefore, teaching our clients appropriate boundaries and types of touch can protect against environments where individuals may push these boundaries or attempt to normalize inappropriate behaviors with them. Throughout treatment, children should also learn about red-flag behaviors, such as people asking them to keep conversations or activities secret. Children need to learn about these warning signs so they can better protect themselves when these red-flag moments occur and know when it is appropriate to get a trusted adult involved. Children gain increased protection from abuse by learning about and protecting their own boundaries, understanding how to respect the boundaries of others, and engaging in education about their own bodies and healthy sexuality (Briggs, 2014; DeLago et al., 2019; Ey & Mcinnes, 2017; Farmer & Pollock, 2003; Kenny et al., 2008; Kurtuncu et al., 2015).

Stone et al. (2013), as well as others, discuss how children who do not understand the correct names for body parts are more susceptible to abuse, as they are easier to trick and this ignorance can be exploited (Elliott et al., 1995; Kenny et al., 2008). Children should be supplied with age-appropriate education regarding privacy rules, especially including rules about their body parts, and sexual behaviors. Instilling rules that promote healthy boundaries and privacy, like being clothed while in the public areas at home, or closing the door while using the restroom, ensure that children can pick up on poor boundaries happening around them and seek out support in situations where boundaries are not being respected or followed. It is important to realize that these rules should be taught and modeled throughout the child's early life. In the research done by Kurtuncu et al. (2015), their study acknowledged that sexuality is present from the time a baby is born, and it is a misconception that sexuality suddenly appears during puberty. In fact, the "preschool period" (ages 0–6) is a "very critical period where learning is fastest, the child is affected the most from environmental factors, and the chance is highest that the child will maintain acquired attitudes, behavior and habits in the following years" (Kurtuncu et al., 2015, p. 2). Therefore, providing young children with information about their bodies, modeling how to have healthy boundaries, and learning about body safety and body rights can affect the attitudes and behaviors that children form, helping to keep themselves and others around them safe, even from a young age.

In discussing sexual education and children, there is a common and misinformed concern. Many believe that teaching children about their bodies, providing age-appropriate sexual health, and talking about sexual touch will lead to children engaging in inappropriate sexual behaviors. A review of existing sexual abuse education and body safety programs found that it is imperative for all children, whether they have been victims or perpetrators of sexual abuse or not, to learn self-protection skills. There is little evidence to support claims that engaging in these topics and providing education leads to negative side effects. In discussing these topics with kids, and providing them with age-appropriate education, the research is clear that the benefits from this education far outweigh any potential negative consequences (Kenny et al., 2008).

Children engaging in problematic sexual behaviors is not a new issue but one that has been long overlooked. We are beginning to see that rightful attention is being paid to this population and, in turn, best practices and prevention will follow. The research around how to best treat this population will continue, and I'm hopeful the attention paid to this diverse group of children will grow, but there is already a salient focal point present within the literature: *education.*

We, as clinicians, must educate ourselves so we can better educate our clients and their families. We must gain a better understanding of childhood sexuality to better comprehend and decipher typical versus atypical sexual behaviors. We must learn how to best support these children and their families, knowing that they may be experiencing high levels of distress. We must help children and their families process trauma, and the impacts this trauma has had on both an individual and familial level. We must help our clients learn about their bodies and boundaries and teach caregivers how to have these conversations. Last, we must provide our clients and their caregivers with education around safety and prevention. Education is the foundation from which every part of treatment should be derived.

Some Things to Note
Before We Get Started

Both sexuality and human development are broad topics and in no way do I intend to take you through a comprehensive review of each. That being said, it is important that I address sexual development before diving deeper into the work related to treating problematic sexual behaviors. In addition to discussing sexual development across childhood, it is also important that I define several key words and phrases to create a shared understanding of the topics discussed throughout this book.

DEFINITIONS AT A GLANCE

First, I'd like to define three phrases that I've seen used interchangeably: sexually reactive behaviors, sexually abusive behaviors, and problematic sexual behaviors. Each of these phrases may raise different connotations and elicit different responses, but once we take away our own feelings and preconceived notions, we can see how they relate.

These phrases fall along a continuum but are not in fact interchangeable, and to highlight this, I've defined them below. I've also provided a definition for "age-appropriate" sexual behaviors to better highlight normative behaviors versus "problematic" behaviors. While conducting research to define the phrases below, I found it incredibly challenging to find universal definitions across studies, even for phrases like "sexual abuse." Hackett (2014) acknowledged these challenges, writing, the "study of sexual abuse perpetrated by children and young people is fraught with definitional problems and complexities" (p. 12). Thus, the definitions I chose to use below highlight the definitions I found that have a higher level of overlap among the research I reviewed.

- **Sexually reactive behaviors.** While looking through the research, I've found that this definition varies. In the past, many definitions included the requirement for a "sexually reactive child" to have been sexual abused themselves. However, as we have progressed in the field, it has become clear that a child does not need to experience sexual abuse to engage in sexually reactive behaviors, rather they may be reacting to something they have been shown, or something they have witnessed. An example of varied definitions over the years is provided below, with the second definition representing more current understandings regarding sexual reactivity:
  ○ Friedrich (1990) defines sexual reactivity as sexualized behaviors and reactions that are directly linked to the experience of recent sexual abuse.
  ○ Tempest (2017) defines sexual reactivity as "when a child reacts in a sexual manner to things that happen. It can also identify developmental steps the child missed and dysfunctional coping and behaviors—those things that are significantly different than society's norms."
- **Sexually abusive behaviors.** The American Psychological Association (2023) defines sexual abuse as "any nonconsensual or exploitive sexual behavior or activity imposed on an individual without their consent." These behaviors are typically rooted in sexual gratification and/or sexual stimulation and endorse elements of coercion, aggression, force, violence, and so on.
- **Problematic sexual behavior.** Problematic sexual behaviors are deviations from normative or typical sexual behavior. The Association for the Treatment of Sexual Abusers (ATSA) Task Force defines problematic sexual behaviors as "children ages 12 and younger who initiate behaviors involving sexual body parts (i.e., genitals, anus, buttocks, or breasts) that are developmentally inappropriate or potentially harmful to themselves or others" (Chaffin et al., 2008, p. 200). These behaviors present as having problematic qualities, such as heightened frequency, hyper-focus, and past redirections or reprimands from adults have done little to decrease the behaviors. It is also noted that these behaviors are not necessarily linked to sexual gratification or stimulation; rather, they may be associated with self-soothing, curiosity, imitation, anxiety, and so on (Chaffin et al., 2008).
- **Age-appropriate sexual behavior.** This behavior is often referred to as typical or normative sexual behavior. These behaviors are seen as age-appropriate childhood exploration—that is, "an information gathering process of limited duration wherein children of similar ages explore visually and/or tactilely, each other's bodies" (Johnson & Berry, 1989, p. 186).
  ○ These behaviors are safe and reflect healthy sexual development. The behaviors occur between similarly aged peers that share similar developmental abilities. There is often a presence of curiosity, a desire to engage in experimentation, but these behaviors do not display any sort of nonconsensual characteristics (i.e., force, aggression, coercion, manipulation, and so on).

It is important to note that though age-appropriate sexual behaviors are seen as normative, it is still important to have discussions around boundaries and teach age-appropriate sexual education. For example, though it is considered an "age-appropriate sexual behavior" for a four-year-old to ask another four-year-old to see their privates, this would be a prime opportunity to discuss boundaries and ways we keep our bodies safe, including keeping private parts covered up and to ourselves. If this four-year-old continues to ask to see other peers' privates, after receiving age-appropriate education and redirection from an adult, that's when these behaviors would begin to move along the spectrum into concerning, and potentially problematic, sexual behaviors.

DEVELOPMENT

As mentioned in the literature review above, sexuality is present from the time a baby is born, and it is a misconception that sexuality suddenly appears during puberty (Kurtuncu et al., 2015). Understanding this allows us to better equip children, their caregivers, and ourselves with the appropriate information and education needed to help children develop a healthy understanding of age-appropriate sexuality. In discussing childhood sexual development, we can break it down into two larger age-groups: (1) the "preschool period," consisting of kids ages zero to six, and (2) the "school-age children," consisting of kids ages seven to twelve. For our purposes, we will further break these two groups into three, based on the widely recognized theories of developmental ages and stages defined by Erik Erickson's theory of emotional development, Jean Piaget's theory of cognitive development, and Lawrence Kohlberg's theory of moral development. These three groups will be broken down as (1) children ages zero to four years, (2) children ages five to nine years, and (3) children ages ten to twelve years. It is noted that there is an additional developmental stage that includes youth ages thirteen to eighteen that will not be explored, as our focus is on children ages twelve years and under. Youth who are thirteen years or older are often at an age where their sexually harmful behaviors are identified as illegal sexual behaviors and they become involved in the juvenile justice system after being charged with sexual offenses.

Within each of the developmental groups below, I will discuss normative sexual behaviors and knowledge and concerning or atypical sexual behaviors and knowledge. The information presented within these developmental categories was pulled from a variety of sources (Davies et al., 2000; El-Murr, 2017; Hackett, 2014; Mesman et al., 2019; Silovsky & Bonner, 2004). In reviewing the literature, I compared a number of "green-yellow-red" behavior lists, typical versus atypical behavior charts, and so on. After reviewing these resources, I created the lists below based on the information that was present across these varied resources. Within each developmental age, you will find "normative knowledge," "normative sexual behaviors," "concerning sexual behaviors," and "problematic sexual behaviors," each of which has been defined below. It is noted that the word "sexual" is used to describe sexual body parts, also known as private parts. I do not intend for this word to mean that these body parts are inherently sexual but rather to identify them as genitals—which is why I've placed it in quotes.

- **Normative sexual knowledge** is defined as knowledge about body parts that are considered "sexual" and behaviors involving these body parts that is deemed developmentally appropriate.
- **Atypical sexual knowledge** is defined as knowledge about body parts that are considered "sexual" and behaviors involving these body parts that is abnormally advanced for the child's developmental level.
- **Normative sexual behaviors** are defined as behaviors involving "sexual" body parts that are developmentally appropriate and do not cause harm to the child engaging in these behaviors, or others around the child.
- **Concerning sexual behaviors** is defined as behaviors involving "sexual" body parts that may start out as normative but begin to cause concern due to problematic elements like an increase in frequency, hyperfocus on behaviors, the child is not responding to redirection, and so on. These behaviors have not yet become harmful but appear to be headed in that direction.
- **Problematic sexual behaviors** are defined as "children ages 12 and younger who initiate behaviors involving sexual body parts (i.e., genitals, anus, buttocks, or breasts) that are developmentally inappropriate or potentially harmful to themselves or others" (Chaffin et al., 2008, p. 200).

Before getting into the details of the three developmental groups outlined above, I want to discuss general rules associated with healthy child sexual exploration. Generally, if a child is engaging in sexual behaviors that involve the following characteristics, the behaviors are not a cause for concern; rather, they are normative and, in most cases, do not require intensive redirection or intervention but do warrant a discussion around boundaries and safety (Chaffin et al., 2008):

- The sexual behaviors do not involve any force, coercion, threats, bribes, or manipulation.
- The sexual behaviors occur spontaneously and there are no concerns regarding the frequency in which they occur.
- The sexual behaviors do not cause distress or harm to the children involved.
- If there are sexual behaviors like the showing of genitals, these behaviors occur among children who are similarly aged.

- There are no significant emotional responses related to the sexual behaviors.
- The sexual behaviors are redirectable and often decrease with the appropriate intervention, such as verbal instructions from an adult to discontinue the behaviors.

Each of the age-groups discussed below share similarities and differences when it comes to normative, concerning, and problematic sexual behaviors. Though the behaviors and knowledge present within each of the age-groups vary, if sexual behaviors involve any of the following characteristics, there is due concern and the child exhibiting such behaviors should be connected with the appropriate therapeutic services as soon as possible.

- The sexual behaviors involve aggression, coercion, threat, trickery, manipulation, or force is involved.
- The sexual behaviors occur between children who are of different sizes, ages, or developmental levels.
- The sexual behaviors occur between children who do not know one another, have just met, or are not well acquainted with one another.
- The sexual behaviors continue despite adult intervention and redirection.
- The sexual behaviors cause harm to the child or others, physically or emotionally.
- The sexual behaviors involve animals.
- The sexual behaviors are connected to emotional distress.

Children Zero to Four Years of Age

Normative Sexual Knowledge

- Children begin understanding and distinguishing between genders around the age of three. Their understanding of gender, and the differences between genders, starts out based on visual factors, such as gender presentation via clothes. However, by the age of three to four years, children have an awareness of genital differences, showing basic understanding of the distinctions between the sexes.
  - Children between the ages of zero to five years do not yet have a strong understanding of gender roles, therefore displaying more behaviors that are associated within either gender, for example, boys wanting to dress up and wear dresses or girls taking their shirts off to flex, is normative.
- Normative sexual knowledge for this age-group is often limited to things they see around them, such as kissing, hugging, and cuddling. They often learn via their senses, thus, touching, feeling, seeing, hearing, and imitating what they've seen around them is normal.

- According to the National Center on the Sexual Behavior of Youth, approximately 25 percent of children in this age range report a more extensive understanding of adult sexual behavior (NCSBY, 2024).
- Preschool children have a vague understanding of pregnancy and birth.
- Children this age know the terms for sexual body parts but often use informal names like "pee-pee" instead of "penis."

Normative Sexual Behaviors

- Curiosity about sexual behaviors, body parts, and touch is typical. Curiosity is an important component of child sexual health exploration. It is noted that infants do not engage in self-touch for gratification or sexual purposes, rather this touching is in response to stimulation, and they may learn that touching these parts of the body leads to pleasurable sensations (Mesman et al., 2019).
  - Self-exploration:
    - this includes touching, rubbing, holding, or playing with one's own genitals. This exploration begins in infancy and can be seen during times when they are naked, like during baths and diaper changes.
    - according to Martinson (1981), boys begin discovering their penis between six to eight months of age, and girls begin discovering their vulvas between ten to eleven months of age.
  - Curiosity around and exploration of others' bodies:
    - this includes attempting to touch or look at the private parts of other children or familiar adults.
    - curiosity about the differences between the bodies of males and females.
    - interest around private parts and curiosity around what these private parts do.
  - Play:
    - engaging in exploratory play like doctor and patient, playing house and taking on parental roles (e.g., "I'll be mommy, and you be daddy"), and finding humor and interest in "potty talk."

Concerning Sexual Behaviors

- Preoccupation is one of the characteristics of concerning sexual behaviors. If a child has been spoken to, has received redirection regarding specific behaviors, and these behaviors persist, this may signal that specialized support is warranted.
  - Some examples of concerning sexual behaviors in this age-group include:
    - continuing to engage in masturbation-like behaviors in unsafe ways (using unsafe objects or engaging in these behaviors in public) after having received redirection.

- continuing to attempt to touch the genitals of others after having received redirection.
- attempting to look at and/or touch the genitals of others by following them into bathrooms or changing rooms and peering under the doors within these settings, especially after having already received redirection.
  - This also includes behaviors related to pulling down the pants of others in hopes of seeing their genitals, looking up skirts or down shirts for the purpose of seeing private parts, and doing so against the other person's will.
- preoccupation with adult sexual behavior, often seen in their play and/or in sexualized language being used.
  - Sexualized play may look like using dolls to enact sexual scenes, using toys in unintended ways like rubbing their genitals against plushies, or attempting to insert toys anally or vaginally.
  - Sexualized language is referring to the use of adult slang to describe sexual acts and knowing the details of adult sexual acts.

Problematic Sexual Behaviors

- When preoccupation turns into persistence, concerning sexual behaviors often turn into problematic sexual behaviors. If a child has had specific and repeated guidance from adults but the concerning behaviors persist, it is important that additional resources, such as a well-trained therapist, are brought into the picture.
  - Some examples of problematic sexual behaviors include:
    - persistently touching their own genitals or engaging in excessive masturbation-like behaviors that impacts their interest and engagement in other nonsexual activities. This frequent self-touch may result in physical complaints such as sores forming on the genitals.
      - It is noted that if any sexual play or behaviors are resulting in injury to the child, these behaviors should be viewed as problematic and appropriately addressed as soon as possible.
    - persistent attempts to touch the genitals of other children or adults.
    - engaging in sexual play or behaviors in public.
    - simulating sexual activities with other children.
    - engaging in sexual activities with other children, including sexual play that involves penetration with objects or body parts.
    - sexual play that involves force of any kind.
    - accessing sexually explicit material.
    - touching the private parts of an unknown adult or an animal.

Children Five to Nine Years of Age

Normative Sexual Knowledge

- Awareness around general privacy, and body privacy, increases.
- Most begin puberty around the age of ten but notice body changes as early as seven or eight years old.
- By seven to eight years old, they understand rules of society and that public sexual behaviors are not allowed. They develop better body boundaries and practices. Sexual behaviors continue, but in private.
- They have knowledge about birth, adult sexual activity, and pregnancy, which increases by the age of ten years.
  - The accuracy of the knowledge they have is dependent on their exposure to accurate information and education.

Normative Sexual Behaviors

- Within this age-group, we continue to see curiosity around sexual behaviors, body parts, and touch; however, body awareness and privacy around bodies increases, thus, touching and looking at others' genitals is no longer considered particularly normative. Curiosity around this remains, but enacting these curiosities becomes less common.
  - Normative behaviors include:
    - touching their own genitals and engaging in masturbation or masturbation-like behaviors.
    - curiosity about
      - other children's genitals,
      - relationships,
      - differences between the sexes, and
      - questions about where babies come from and how they are made.
    - using slang words when talking about private parts.
    - accidental exposure to pornography.

Concerning Sexual Behaviors

- Preoccupation, or intense interest, in sexual topics continues to be a characteristic of concerning sexual behaviors in this age-group. If behaviors persist, even with redirection or the answering of questions, this can let us know that the behaviors are becoming concerning and may become problematic if not intervened upon.
  - Some concerning behaviors include:
    - touching of their own privates or masturbating in non-private places like school, the living room, the grocery store, and the like.
    - exposing their own privates in non-private places.

- continued and persistent questions around sex and sexual activity, even after receiving age-appropriate answers to these questions.
- hypersexual themes present in art, play, or discussions with peers.
- purposefully accessing pornography.
- persistence in wanting to touch the private parts of others, even after redirection.

Problematic Sexual Behaviors

- If a child has had specific and repeated guidance from adults but the concerning behaviors persist, we deem these behaviors problematic.
  - Some examples of problematic sexual behaviors within this age range include:
    - excessive masturbation or masturbation-like behaviors leading to a decrease in normal daily activities, or physical complaints, like chafing or sores.
    - repeated masturbation or masturbation-like behaviors in front of others.
    - rubbing genitals on people or things.
    - forcing other children, especially younger children, to engage in sexual games, sexual activities, or watching pornography.
    - advanced sexual knowledge.
    - talking about sexual acts in details.
    - simulating oral or penetrative sex.
    - sexual messaging on devices (including sexual messages and/or sending sexual pictures).
      - This includes posting any sexual videos, pictures, or conversations.
    - sexual behaviors toward animals.

Children Ten to Twelve Years of Age

Normative Sexual Knowledge

- Around the age of ten, most youth understand the basics around puberty, childbirth, and procreative processes. Their vocabulary and understanding of bodies, body processes, and sexual activities increases.
  - Again, normative sexual knowledge is an important part of building a healthy understanding of appropriate sexuality; however, this knowledge is dependent upon a child's access to correct information via formal and informal education.
- Within this age range, children begin experiencing external influences, such as social media and media in general, peers, and societal gender-based expectations, as well as internal and hormonal changes that come from puberty.

xxxviii   *Some Things to Note Before We Get Started*

Normative Sexual Behaviors

- Curiosity remains present; however, we begin to see curiosity shifting more heavily toward sexual behaviors and an increased need for, and desire of, privacy.
  - Some examples of normative sexual behaviors for this age-group include:
    - masturbating in private.
    - using sexual language and engaging in "potty humor" that's sexual in nature.
    - kissing, flirting, hugging, and holding hands with peers of a similar age.
    - beginning to explore with relationships, and possibly having a first boyfriend or girlfriend who is of similar age.
    - more online access to games and social media.
      - perhaps having their own social media accounts, though it is noted that these accounts should still be heavily monitored by caregiver(s).

Concerning Sexual Behaviors

- By this time, there should be a good understanding of body boundaries and privacy. If behaviors are reflecting poor body boundaries, or a lack of concern around privacy, we begin to consider these behaviors concerning and potentially on the road to becoming problematic.
  - Some examples of concerning sexual behaviors for youth ten to twelve years old include:
    - exposing genitals to others.
    - attempting to expose the genitals of others.
    - secretive internet use.
    - being worried about the impacts of sexual activities such as pregnancy and sexually transmitted diseases and infections.
    - purposefully viewing pornographic material.
    - drastic changes in behaviors and interests.
      - This could look like a drastic shift in one's friend group, physical appearance (via clothing and/or makeup; not including gender presentation), and personality, as well as the development of friendships with individuals who are much older or younger than themselves, and so on.
    - bullying that involves elements of sexual aggression.

Problematic Sexual Behaviors

- Problematic sexual behaviors for this age range can include sexual behaviors that are compulsive and persistent, and the redirection of these behaviors has failed, or the behaviors have become chronic and habitual.

- ○ Some examples of problematic sexual behaviors for this age range include:
  - ▪ compulsive masturbation:
    - • which can lead to physical complaints like sores, rashes, friction burns, and so forth.
    - • which can impact their engagement in other activities due to the excessive amount of time spent masturbating or struggles with completing a task due to the intense urge to masturbate.
  - ▪ exposing genitals in public.
  - ▪ engaging in self-touching behaviors, or masturbating, in public.
  - ▪ sending sexual images of themselves to others.
  - ▪ harassing others for sexual images.
  - ▪ sexually explicit talk:
    - • with peers, younger children, adolescents, or adults.
    - • sexually explicit talk online, in games, or on social media.
  - ▪ forcing other peers or children to engage in sexual activities, such as oral sex or sexual intercourse, or simulating such acts.
  - ▪ extensive pornography use.
  - ▪ sexual behaviors toward animals.
  - ▪ attempting to use power (age, size, strength, popularity, knowledge, etc.) to manipulate others into engaging in sexual behaviors.

TREATMENT STEPS

Before jumping into the details of the curriculum, I want to provide a brief visual of the different treatment components covered within the curriculum. As discussed throughout this book, children who engage in problematic sexual behaviors are a diverse population with varied needs. It is important that the treatment plan considers the varying levels of support, types of treatment, and education these children and their families need. For this reason, it is not expected that every client will neatly fit into one of the four examples I've provided below; rather, these are examples of how necessary treatment components may vary from client to client. For some clients, a short intervention addressing elements like safety, boundaries, and body rights may suffice. For other clients, more intensive treatments that address each of the components present within the curriculum may be needed. Regardless of the child, there are some treatment components that will always be included.

When looking at the four different examples below, you will see that each includes building rapport, the foundation (safety planning, boundaries, body rights, types of touch, and emotional recognition and regulation), body awareness, healthy relationships, and future safety. This is because these are the elements most strongly related to education, awareness, and safety. These elements are used to teach age-appropriate sexual education, limit setting, rules around sexual behaviors, and abuse prevention, all of which decrease the risk of future problematic sexual behaviors and victimization.

Much of the education provided throughout the curriculum can be taught in a straightforward manner with cognitive behavioral therapy (CBT) and expressive therapies, utilizing interventions like puppets or a sand tray. Depending on the child, their age, developmental level, and so on, you may find that some information is best taught via CBT, and other information is better taught and internalized via expressive therapies. Personally, I've found that using both is fruitful, and that the "acting it out" piece that is often present within expressive therapies, like play therapy, can aid with retention and internalization.

I provide a brief description of the type of client, and age range, that may be best suited for the specific treatment steps used within each example. This is present at the top of each example. Again, this should be used as a guide, not a rule. Some factors that may play into changing the treatment steps, and the components included are age, developmental level, trauma history, frequency and intensity of the problematic sexual behaviors, and so on. Caregiver engagement is imperative. Their involvement in the treatment process is the single most important element associated with a reduction in problematic sexual behaviors and minimizing future risks of victimization (DeLago et al., 2019; St. Amand et al., 2008). For this reason, caregiver participation is a non-negotiable, albeit involvement can shift to meet the needs of each family.

At an outpatient level, I meet with children once, maybe twice, a week for an hour at a time. One or two hours a week is not enough time for children to learn new material and make long-term changes; this is done at home. Caregivers need to be involved in the treatment process so that they too learn and understand the information being discussed. This allows them to reinforce what is being taught in sessions and they can model healthy behaviors and boundaries at home. Practicing these behaviors throughout the week, and having consistency in doing so, is what creates meaningful and long-term change.

Full Treatment Protocol

I use this protocol when working with an older child (approximately eleven to twelve years old) who presents with normative developmental functioning. This client would be presenting with more invasive and engrained problematic sexual behaviors, and they have engaged in these behaviors with others. Typically, they have engaged in these behaviors with a younger child, perhaps a sibling, and there are clear power differences. This protocol focuses on education and accountability for the past problematic sexual behaviors. Much of the accountability work they will engage in is education based, however, given their developmental level they will also be expected to participate in perspective taking exercises. They will engage in an impact project where they will address the impacts their problematic sexual behaviors have had on the victim. They will participate in work within the following treatment modules:

(1) *building rapport*, which includes getting to know the client, getting to know the family, and building trust; (2) the *foundations of treatment*, which include safety planning, learning about boundaries and body rights, and learning about the different types of touch; (3) *body awareness*, which includes learning coping skills and interventions, working on emotional recognition and regulation, and learning the anatomical body parts; (4) *history*, which includes learning about trouble thoughts and completing a life history and sexual history timeline; (5) *ownership*, which includes taking responsibility for past problematic sexual behaviors and engaging in at least one of the accountability activities; (6) *healthy relationships* and *appropriate sexuality*, which includes the components of a healthy relationship and the components of consent, sexual safety, and psychoeducation around pornography; (7) *victim awareness*, which includes learning about the differences between empathy and sympathy, learning about the differences between intent and impact, education around the impact that problematic sexual behaviors can have, and at least one activity that addresses the direct impact their behaviors may have had on the victim; and (8) *future safety* and *finishing strong*, which includes the creation of a safe-play plan and a full treatment review.

Protocol for Younger Children Who Have Engaged in Problematic Sexual Behaviors Toward Others and/or With Themselves

I use this protocol when working with a younger child (approximately seven to ten years old) who has engaged in problematic sexual behaviors that have impacted other children. Typically, they have engaged in problematic sexual behaviors with peers who are of a similar age, but these behaviors could have also been enacted with a child younger than themselves. These clients may be experiencing self-focused problematic sexual behaviors, in addition to trying to engage in these behaviors with others. This protocol focuses on education in addition to work around understanding the consequences and impacts of problematic sexual behaviors. This looks very similar to the protocol discussed above but has been shifted to meet the developmental needs of a younger client. The main difference is that there is some focus on accountability, but less so due to developmental differences. These clients will engage in treatment work within the following treatment modules.

(1) *building rapport*, which includes getting to know the client, getting to know the family, and building trust; (2) the *foundations of treatment*, which include safety planning, learning about boundaries and body rights, and learning about the different types of touch; (3) *body awareness*, which includes learning coping skills and interventions, working on emotional recognition and regulation, and learning the anatomical body parts; (4) *history*, which includes learning about trouble thoughts and completing a life history and sexual history timeline; (5) *ownership*, which includes taking responsibility for past problematic sexual behaviors toward others, participating in the developmentally appropriate accountability activity, and then engaging in an activity that explores healthy ways to get their needs met; (6) *healthy relationships* and *appropriate sexuality*, which includes the components of a healthy relationship, the components of consent, sexual safety, and brief psychoeducation around pornography, unless more detailed education is warranted; (7) *victim awareness*, which includes learning about the differences between empathy and sympathy, as well as the differences between intent and impact, engaging in psychoeducation around the impact that problematic sexual behaviors can have and, if appropriate, engaging in a developmentally appropriate activity that addresses the ways their behaviors may have impacted the victim; (8) *future safety* and *finishing strong*, which includes the creation of a safe-play plan and a full treatment review.

Protocol for Young Children Who Have Engaged in Self-Focused Problematic Sexual Behaviors but Have Not Acted out With Others

This is the protocol I may use for a younger child (approximately seven to ten years old) who has problematic sexual behaviors but has not engaged in these behaviors with others. These behaviors tend to be self-focused; therefore, this protocol focuses on education and does not include material associated with accountability. There is, however, broad discussion and education around the impacts that problematic sexual behaviors can have. This conversation is typically present within the *healthy relationships* component of treatment. These clients will engage in work within the following treatment modules.

(1) *building rapport*, which includes getting to know the client, getting to know the family, and building trust; (2) the *foundations of treatment*, which include safety planning, learning about boundaries and body rights, and learning about the different types of touch; (3) *body awareness*, which includes learning coping skills and interventions, working on emotional recognition and regulation, and learning the anatomical body parts; (4) *history*, which includes learning about trouble thoughts and completing a life history and sexual history timeline that highlights their engagement in self-focused problematic sexual behaviors; (5) *healthy relationships* and *appropriate sexuality*, which includes the components of a healthy relationship, the components of consent, sexual safety, education around the impacts that problematic sexual behaviors can have on victims, and

brief psychoeducation around pornography, unless more detailed education is indicated; (6) *future safety* and *finishing strong*, which includes the creation of a safe-play plan and a full treatment review.

Protocol for the Little Kids

This is the protocol I use when working with little kids (approximately four to six years old) who have engaged in problematic sexual behaviors. Regardless of whether these behaviors are self-focused or if they have engaged in problematic sexual behaviors with another peer, I focus on education and safety, given their developmental capabilities. These young children will engage in treatment work within the following treatment modules.

(1) *building rapport*, which includes getting to know the client, getting to know the family, and building trust; (2) the *foundations of treatment*, which include safety planning, learning about boundaries and body rights, and learning about the different types of touch; (3) *body awareness*, which includes learning coping skills and interventions, working on emotional recognition and regulation, learning the anatomical body parts, and, within this section, also engaging in some exploration around the experiences the child has had and how they may have impacted their engagement in problematic sexual behaviors (at times, this is done alone with the caregiver); (4) *healthy relationships* and *appropriate sexuality*, which includes the components of a healthy relationship, the components of consent, discussions around body safety, including a brief discussion with caregivers about the appropriate supervision needed when their child is on technology; (5) *future safety* and *finishing strong*, which includes the creation of a safe-play plan and reviewing the treatment they have engaged in.

Part I

CURRICULUM

Chapter 1

Building Rapport

When working with children who have engaged in problematic sexual behaviors, it is imperative we address these behavioral problems through a holistic lens. We should be asking ourselves about the contributing factors that impacted our clients' choice to engage in these behaviors. Children who engage in problematic sexual behaviors have often experienced trauma and share commonalities with one another, as discussed throughout this book. Viewing their problematic sexual behaviors as a manifestation of their inner turmoil allows us to understand that these behaviors are symptoms of a larger issue. By addressing their problematic behaviors, in addition to the factors that have contributed to these behaviors, we are better able to help them make the appropriate changes needed and address internal challenges related to these factors. Clinicians working with these children must understand that before diving into the work to address sexualized behaviors, they will be working on developing an effective relationship with their client, the family unit, and any systems the family may be involved in. To do this, the crucial and necessary first step in this process is *building rapport*.

Therapy 101: the basis of every successful therapeutic relationship begins with trust. As mentioned previously, the children we are working with have experienced adversity, and often, their trust has been broken in ways they did not expect or deserve. Additionally, caregivers are likely experiencing a lapse in trust due to their child's boundary concerns and harmful or inappropriate sexual behaviors. It is crucial that the therapist works to gain the trust of their client, as well as the client's caregivers, from the very beginning of the treatment process.

BUILDING TRUST

As we know, trust is earned. A critical step in earning our client's trust is creating an environment that enables them to feel safe. Building this trust begins with rapport, something we should all be familiar with.

At the beginning of treatment, the problematic sexual behaviors will be acknowledged, but they will not be the main focus. It's important that the child understands why they are meeting with you, and that you are aware of their problematic sexual behaviors, but that this work will come later. After you demonstrate your awareness of these behaviors, you can focus on building trust.

Your first focus should be building a safe and stable foundation for the client and their family to work from. The therapist should first check in about any pressing needs, such as safety plans or concerns, and answer all questions the client and/or caregivers have. It is not uncommon for families to have many questions and concerns when beginning the treatment process, especially if there is any sort of agency involvement, like an open case with the Department of Human Services (DHS). The therapist should answer these questions and discuss what the family needs to feel comfortable moving forward in the treatment process.

Building Rapport Age Considerations

As mentioned above, building rapport should be the first order of business when starting treatment. In my experience, clients in this age range either present as open and ready to engage or avoidant. This will be assessed when completing the initial mental health assessment, and it will inform clinicians what the first steps in treatment will look like.

In my experience, this age range is unique—they tend to be more open and participatory in discussing their problematic sexual behaviors compared to their adolescent counterparts. This may be a result of their developmental level, as children between the ages of four to ten years are more likely to follow through and listen to adults when asked to participate in these discussions. Additionally, younger children are not usually involved in the juvenile justice system, thus there is less fear of punitive consequences or legal ramifications, which may enable them and their caregivers to speak more freely. That being said, this openness is not true of all children in this age range and may also be related to the response their caregivers had when the behaviors were discovered. If the caregivers' response was shame based and the child experienced significant emotional distress, they are often more hesitant to open up and acknowledge the behaviors. Though a client who is immediately open and willing to discuss their problematic sexual behaviors seems like something we'd want, we should aid the client in pumping the brakes and first create space for the client to learn and integrate the foundations of treatment before moving forward. It is important that the child has the skills to appropriately regulate and cope with any challenging feelings that may come up when discussing their problematic behaviors before getting further into treatment.

Even though I've noticed that this age range appears more open to discussing their behaviors and less likely to minimize these struggles, it does not mean that they are thrilled about the idea of discussing these behaviors. Again, avoidance is not atypical and should be expected. As the client gets more comfortable, and the therapeutic relationship grows, they will begin opening up more freely. In my experience, it has been helpful to frame the future discussions about their problematic sexual behaviors as a key to their own healing.

Building Rapport With Clients

Be warm and inviting with your verbal and nonverbal communication. Be expressive and even goofy!

Be nonjudgmental when they disclose their behaviors. Judgment can be sensed by the client and then further internalized as shame. Ensure they understand that part of your role is to have unconditional positive regard for them. When they disclose their problematic sexual behaviors, do your best to show them that you see them, hear them, and you aren't going anywhere. If at first they are hesitant to discuss why they are meeting with you, I might start the conversation by saying, "It's my job to talk about problematic sexual behaviors. I have done this for so many years, with so many clients, I promise, there is nothing you can say that will surprise me, I've heard it all! Nothing you say is going to scare me away."

Always see and appreciate the good child behind the problematic sexual behavior(s). You can help them with this by expressing that they are good kids who are having a hard time. Though they might have made mistakes that have harmed others, I assure them that they are not their mistakes, and it's important they hear this. I may normalize mistakes and unsafe choices by saying something like, "Wait, do you think you're the only one in this room who has made a mistake? No way! Do you think I'm perfect? Absolutely not, I've made plenty of mistakes!" Then, if their caregiver is in the room, I'll look at the caregiver and ask, "What about you, are you perfect?" to which they often reply, "No," and acknowledge that they have made mistakes too. This is a playful way to show the client that perfection is not expected, and that we have all made mistakes. I follow this up with a conversation around learning from mistakes and getting help when we need it.

Be patient and go at their pace. If you begin rushing them, or pushing your own agenda in sessions, they will pick up on this, shut down, and lose trust.

This age range responds well to play! Be open to getting on the floor, playing games, watching videos, and discussing topics of their choosing in a playful and appropriate manner.

Building Rapport With the Family

Like our clients, caregivers may also be hesitant to engage in the treatment process. They may feel fearful of judgment, concerned about the way their child will be viewed, and misinformed about the treatment process and protocol for helping children with problematic sexual behaviors. Many times, families come in worried and concerned for their child, as well as their family's future. It's imperative that, as their child's therapist, you are communicative and honest about what they can expect in treatment. A clear discussion about expectations should be had at the beginning of services, and caregivers should be made aware of the role they will be playing in their child's treatment. In working with this age range, caregivers are expected to be a part of the treatment process. They are crucial to the discontinuation of their child's problematic sexual behaviors, and the importance of their engagement is clearly discussed within the research. Each family is different; therefore, the level of caregiver engagement will differ. A good rule of thumb is, the younger the child is, or the lower the child's functioning, the more sessions the caregiver(s) should be involved in. Having this therapeutic contact within sessions not only supports the client in the moment but also ensures that what is being discussed and learned in session is being brought into the home. This is also important for older children, but they are better able to "teach" their caregivers what they've learned after completing activities. This may look like a quick check-in at the end of each session where the child can teach their caregiver the information they learned or present the work they completed. It's expected that caregivers will be involved in at least two sessions per month, at minimum. A child's success is linked to their caregiver(s)' engagement throughout this process, a fact that I impress upon caregivers from the beginning of our time together.

It is recommended that the clinician spend part of the mental health assessment talking with the caregivers individually, especially if the child is avoidant of discussing their problematic sexual behaviors or the impacting factors that contributed to these behaviors. Speaking with the caregiver(s) individually allows us to gain a better understanding of the issues at hand, get an adult perspective regarding the behaviors and events leading up to the problematic sexual behaviors, and allows the caregiver(s) space to speak freely without worrying about the impact their words, or feelings, about these behaviors would have on their child.

Rapport-Building Activities

The mental health assessment itself can be used to begin the rapport-building process. Many kids coming into treatment may have the idea that the only thing they will be working on, or talking about, is their problematic sexual behaviors. As we know, our clients are not the sum of their behaviors; rather, this is one small part of who they are. It is critical that we continue to remind our clients, and their families, of this throughout treatment. Helping clients understand that treatment is much more than focusing on and discussing their problematic sexual behaviors helps to create a space where they feel they can discuss past and present struggles from all areas of their life, not just related to sexualized behaviors. To discuss their struggles and challenges, our clients need to build trust, and to do this we begin by building rapport. I've provided a list of activities that help with rapport building below. Again, this time is meant to focus on the child as a whole. This is our chance to get to know them as a person, to understand their interests, to figure out what makes them unique, and to find their strengths. Do not focus on their problematic sexual behaviors, there is a time and place for that; but for now, focus on the child, not their behaviors.

Question Jenga

Purpose. This activity is engaging and tactile. For those who appear nervous, struggle with eye contact, or are conversation avoidant, this activity works well. It is a safe and nonthreatening way to start engaging in therapy, communicating thoughts and feelings, building bonds between the therapist and client, and modeling healthy play and engagement for the caregiver.

Process. This activity is easy to set up and engage in. All you need is a Jenga set and a pen. The clinician can write icebreaker questions on the Jenga blocks. You can also keep blank blocks in the room and allow your clients to come up with some of their own questions. Once you've added all the questions, you are ready to play! Set the Jenga up, and take turns with your client, pulling one block at a time, reading each question, and taking turns answering it. This activity can easily include caregivers, and they may want to come up with some questions as well.

Question Examples.

- If you could have any superpower, what would it be?
- What is your favorite/least favorite thing about your family?
- What is your favorite sport?
- What are you most afraid of?

- What was a time that you felt loved?
- If you could only eat one thing for the rest of your life, what would it be?
- What is an activity that makes you feel strong?
- What is your favorite/least favorite subject in school?
- If you could see your future, what job would you have?

Candy Land Color Game

Purpose. This activity works well for the younger clients, as there is no reading or writing required and it may be a game that they are already familiar with. It can be a great way to get them to start talking about themselves and their life while utilizing a game that is accordant to their developmental level. It takes the pressure off of making direct eye contact and avoids a rigid question-and-answer structure.

Process. Sit down with your client and determine a topic for each color. For example, Green: Tell me something about your family; Blue: What makes you happy? Yellow: What questions do you have about therapy? Red: What's something you want me to know about you? Once you've determined the topic that corresponds with each color, you can begin playing the game. Each time you move, you answer the question/topic that correlates to the color you drew from the deck.

Beach Ball Icebreaker

Purpose. This activity works well as an icebreaker at the beginning of sessions and acts as a gentle introduction to the therapeutic process. It can be played for however long the client is interested. Sometimes this activity has so much value in terms of rapport building and communication that it can be considered more than just an icebreaker and used throughout treatment. It can be used during weekly check-ins, as a session-check-out, or a way to take breaks when working on challenging content throughout the treatment process. At the very least, it is an effective way to get the conversation started, engage in playful movement and connection, and get clients into their bodies.

Process. The first step is to find a large, lightweight (inflatable) ball of some sort. Beach balls work well, as their surface area is large, easy to write on, and soft. After you have inflated the ball, you can begin writing questions on it. The client can add questions if they'd like, but they are not required to do so. After setting this up, you begin by throwing the ball back and forth and whichever question your right index finger (or any finger you and your client decide on) lands on, you read and answer it aloud. The questions on the ball should fit for the level of depth, thought, and emotion they are capable of at that time. For newer clients, innocuous questions can be used, like "What is your favorite cartoon?" or "What is your favorite food?" These are typical in the beginning of rapport building and are best used when trying to build trust, safety, and communication during the early stages of treatment. Additionally, this activity can be used further into therapy by increasing the intensity of the questions—that is, "What is a fear you have?" or "What is one thing from your life you wish you could change?"

Pro Tip. Get several beach balls and make one a "beginning treatment ball," one a "young children ball," one an "older kids ball," and so on. If you don't have the means to buy several balls, you can use a dry-erase marker or sticky notes so the questions are easily changeable.

Talking While Drawing

Purpose. This is exactly what it sounds like. You supply your client with art materials, and they can draw while talking. They can also utilize the art to communicate what they may be struggling to say with words. This is a good way to bridge communication gaps and build rapport by engaging in an activity that accesses different parts of the brain. It can be much less intimidating to focus on art than on a strange adult they do not know yet.

Process. The therapist provides paper, pens, crayons, markers, and so on, and the client can choose what materials they wish to use. The therapist can draw along with them if it helps build a sense of connection. From there you can draw and talk openly, you can come up with a theme together and then draw something related to this theme, you can work on a picture together or separately, or sit silently and color.

Pro Tips. Providing a theme can be useful to advancing therapy to deeper levels. At some points (when you are past the initial rapport-building phase), you can use art to externalize challenging feelings or thoughts the child has. An example of this would be asking them to draw their anger. Be sure to remind them that there are no rules when it comes to art. It can be abstract, big, small, colorful, messy, and so on. Also, try not to just sit and watch the child draw. This may make them feel uncomfortable, or they may feel hypercritical of their own drawings as they may feel that you are looking at and/ or judging the drawings they are creating. Draw along with them, or collaboratively if they invite you to do so. If you are a phenomenal artist, try using your nondominant hand so the child doesn't feel frustrated or self-conscious about their own art skills.

Chapter 2

The Foundation of Treatment

Safety Planning, Boundaries, and Types of Touch

Safety planning is an integral part of treatment. With older youth, there is often some sort of outside entity, such as the juvenile courts, that enforces safety plans and structure for the youth. When working with children who have no agency involvement, there is no outside enforcement of safety plans, and the therapist is placed into this position. It's uncommon for youth twelve years old and under to have any contact with the juvenile courts, but involvement with the Department of Human Services (DHS) can occur. If the client has been referred via DHS, there may be a safety plan in place, but typically we see that these cases are only open until the child is connected with appropriate therapeutic services. Once this occurs, DHS often closes the case and they are no longer involved with, or in charge of, the safety planning for the family. At other times, a family may reach out and begin services when the problematic sexual behaviors are discovered. Perhaps these behaviors were reported to the Child Abuse Hotline, and the report was closed at screening, or maybe they are still waiting for a DHS caseworker to be assigned. Regardless, it is likely that therapy will be the first place they create a safety plan for moving forward.

Since treatment is often the first step in addressing and healing the child's problematic sexual behaviors, these families are often looking for support in how to begin this journey. The first step should be to assess for safety within the home and begin coming up with a realistic safety plan to keep the client, the client's family, and the community safe. Creating a realistic safety plan that meets each family's unique needs will help ensure there is a shared language and expectations regarding safety as the families move forward in the treatment process.

BASICS OF A SAFETY PLAN

When developing a safety plan, it's essential to look at all parts of the child's life. Are they involved in sports? Where did the problematic sexual behaviors occur (home, school, sleepover, etc.)? How does the family unit function? Does the child have siblings? Has the child acted out with anyone in their home? And so on. Though we may not be privy to all of this information, it's essential to find out the following:

What behaviors have happened, or what concerns do the caregivers have regarding their child and the presenting concern?
As mentioned above, some children want to speak about this topic while others are avoidant. Regardless, it is recommended that the therapist sit down with the caregiver(s) and discuss the concerns they have and what they know about the problematic sexual behaviors their child has exhibited or engaged in.

Whether the child has engaged in problematic sexual behaviors with anyone in the home.
This is an essential detail to have when safety planning. If the child has acted out with someone in the home, there will be more extensive safety planning to ensure everyone in the home is kept safe. In some very rare instances, it may be recommended that the child be removed from the home, but this is infrequently seen with children, and chances are that if this is occurring, the child's behaviors have intensified to a degree requiring a higher level of care. There are also times where the victim may feel unsafe at home with the child who enacted the problematic sexual behaviors. If this occurs, and the victim needs the child with problematic sexual behaviors to leave home in order to feel safe or to aid in their healing process, alternative living arrangements may need to occur. That being said, out-of-home placements are much rarer with this age range. Often out-of-home placements are avoided, and ultimately, the decision should be made when considering the impact on the victim. Some children may have ongoing concerns, anxiety, or challenges living with their sibling due to fear of continued sexualized behaviors, others may find it more disruptive and traumatic to be separated from their sibling if the child with problematic sexual behaviors is taken from the home. This decision should be made after discussions with the family, the survivor, and the survivor's therapist (Swisher et al., 2008).

If there was hands-on sexual contact with another youth.
Clinicians should check to see whether these behaviors were disclosed to the other child's parents, whether these behaviors have been reported, and

whether the children continue to have contact with one another. These questions will help you determine what next step needs to be taken, such as contacting Child Protective Service (CPS), discontinuing contact, and so on.

Once you have the answers to these questions, you can begin creating a holistic safety plan. The initial safety plan usually includes the following goals:
Creating safety in the home for all members of the family. Providing a definition of what appropriate supervision is and who appropriate supervisors are. Typically, an appropriate supervisor is an adult who is aware of the problematic sexual behaviors/boundaries, they understand the child's unique needs regarding supervision, and they're willing to provide the level of supervision needed in any context, such as in the community, around other children, and so on. This supervisor will also need to be provided with a copy of the child's safety plan. This safety plan will offer guidance and rules for safety around extracurricular activities like sports, activities, camps, and so on. It will also offer a list of guidelines and rules for home, school, and the community that the child is expected to follow. Depending on the caregiver and their comfort level, the clinician may or may not be the driving force in creating this safety plan and ensuring the appropriate entities are made aware of it.

THE SAFETY PLAN

The safety plan should be created with full cooperation and input from caregivers. Depending on the family, there may be outside agencies or important individuals involved that will also need to review, agree to, and follow the safety plan. This may include school staff, teachers, additional supervisors, coaches, and so on. A written safety plan is best, as it provides clear statements of the rules and expectations and can be referred, discussed, and modified in an ongoing manner. An example of an initial safety plan is provided in the appendix of this book. *The safety plan is a living document.* It will change throughout the child's time in treatment. As the child progresses in their therapy, they will begin earning back privileges and trust, and their safety plan should reflect this growth. The last thing we want is for the child to be living in a sterile, rule-filled bubble for the duration of their treatment. We want them to understand the importance of these safety rules, while also allowing them to make some of their own choices as they earn trust. This will ensure that they've internalized these rules and can make healthy choices on their own. We would rather them mess up and make a poor choice while they still have the safety net of treatment.

It is noted that there may be times when separate safety plans are indicated. If a child is having significant struggles at school, or while riding the bus, creating an additional safety plan specific to this setting can be helpful. When creating a school-specific safety plan, it is important to involve the school, as they can provide valuable information regarding rules and supervision that may already be in place, as well as insight into what may, or may not, be realistic to implement while the child is at school and in the classroom.

BOUNDARIES

Before moving deeper into treatment, we must continue developing a strong therapeutic foundation. In addition to building rapport, the base of this foundation includes the following treatment modules: boundaries, types of touch, and emotional recognition and regulation. I often use a metaphor when discussing the importance of these three modules, that way I can create a picture of the upcoming process. One of the metaphors I often use involves building a Lego house, as many of my clients enjoy Legos and have experience playing with them. I ask my clients how they would build a house, and once they have explained it, I ask them what the bottom should look like. I ask them if it would be a good idea to build my own Lego house with one small Lego on the very bottom. Generally, my clients will say, "No" and look at me like I have three eyes. They usually tell me that there should be a bigger base with many blocks at the bottom to support the house. This is when I explain that it is the same idea when it comes to their treatment. We can't just focus on the behaviors that have brought them into treatment because this is only one part of their entire story, or, one part of the Lego house, if we are sticking with the metaphor above. After this, I discuss building the "foundation" for treatment by learning about boundaries, types of touch, and being able to recognize and regulate our emotions. If clients know how to have healthy boundaries, can avoid unhealthy touch, and can recognize and regulate emotions appropriately, it decreases the risk of further problematic sexual behaviors occurring. Once they have learned about and mastered these skills, it is time to focus on the other details of treatment. Below are the three types of boundaries, three types of touch, and the emotional recognition and regulation techniques I use.

Physical Boundaries

When discussing physical boundaries, we can break this topic into two parts: personal space and personal possessions. The younger the child, the more they engage in black-and-white thinking. For that reason, when working with this age-group, I break physical boundaries down into two different boundaries. These boundaries are "bubble space boundary" and "stuff boundary." When learning about boundaries, I encourage caregivers, the client, and any other children in the home to learn about each of these boundaries, utilize this language in the home, and keep rules around these boundaries consistent for all members of the household.

Bubble Space Boundary

Bubble space boundary boils down to bodily autonomy. It represents the boundaries we have regarding our bodies and the direct vicinity around our bodies. To facilitate understanding of this concept, I have my clients put their arms out and spin in a circle. Once they are done spinning, they are asked to reach up as high as they can and then reach all the way down to their toes. I explain that all the air their body just touched is considered their personal bubble. If your client needs a more concrete visual representation, a Hula-Hoop works well. After they understand their bubble, we begin discussing how bubbles change.

Our personal bubbles shrink, or grow, depending on who we are around, how we are feeling, and how much trust we have in that person. I start this conversation by asking them to state the name of the person they trust most in their life. Once they've chosen someone, I ask them to show me, with their arms, how big their personal bubble is when they are around this person. Typically, they will make a very small bubble to show they have great trust in this person. Occasionally they may be confused and say they have a big bubble around this person. If this happens, I gently ask them about their bubble and why they would want to keep this person far away, as that's what big bubbles are for. At this point they understand what is being asked and will correct themselves to show a small bubble for this person. The next step will be to look at the inverse. I will ask them to show me how big their bubble would be around a stranger in the grocery store. This opens a larger conversation around trust, how we learn to trust others, and how to identify the safe people in their lives.

While having conversations about protecting and respecting bubble boundaries, I bring in the topics of consent and bodily autonomy, sometimes referred to as "body rights." I explain both consent and bodily autonomy to them and use a YouTube video to highlight these topics. There are several videos readily available, however, I really like the YouTube video titled "Consent for Kids," by Blue Seat Studios. I like this video as it breaks the topic down into age-appropriate and easily accessible information for most ages. Understanding consent and bodily autonomy is imperative to helping our clients build safety for themselves and build respect for the safety of others around them.

Stuff Boundary

Material boundaries, also known as "stuff boundary" or "thing boundary," depending on the client's preference, is a subsection of physical boundaries.

It is intended to help clients understand the difference between their stuff and the stuff that belongs to other people. This boundary is like bubble space boundary in that we teach our clients to respect and protect this boundary in the same way—asking before touching someone's stuff and waiting to hear the answer. Clients should be taught that they should not touch the items of other people unless they have asked and have received consent to do so. This applies to their items as well. Often clients will present a scenario like, "Well, Mommy moves my shoes without asking." At this point you can begin discussing these scenarios with your client and their caregivers. This also opens the conversation up to discuss boundaries and their place at home. You can begin discussing new house rules that reflect the learning your client is engaging in, and caregivers can model their respect of these boundaries as well. Practicing these boundaries at home not only helps the client retain the new information but also helps increase safety among members of the home.

Emotional/Mental Boundaries

This boundary refers to the verbal and emotional limits we follow to best protect mental and emotional safety. This boundary teaches the importance of emotional safety for all. With younger kids I find myself calling this boundary the "talking-feeling boundary." This boundary is a little more difficult to teach, as it is not as concrete as the boundaries discussed above. It is easier to see when physical boundaries are being broken, as it involves physical touching; however, when it comes to our emotional and mental boundaries it can be trickier to demonstrate. Children need to have a good understanding of nonverbal social cues and empathy to fully grasp this boundary, both of which may be developmentally advanced for our younger clients. Though it can be challenging to explain this boundary, it is absolutely possible. To do so, it is recommended that the therapist use a lot of examples. I prefer to use a feelings chart when discussing the examples so that my clients have a visual tool for learning the new information.

I like to pull out a feelings chart, or any other items that list a wide variety of emotions. I've also found that using emojis can be helpful and most children are familiar with them. Once there are visual representations of different feelings in front of the client, I will go through different phrases like "I like your shoes," "Your hair looks stupid," "If you don't give me your cookie, I'm going to tell your mom you hit me," and so on. After each phrase, I will pause and ask the client to point to how they would feel if someone said this to them. Once they've gone through some examples, I ask them to discuss a time in their life when someone hurt their feelings and a time when someone said something that made them feel happy. In this conversation, I begin to help the client link feelings to the different ways that people speak to or interact with them. I explain that our feelings can impact the way we speak to others, and the way others speak to us can impact our feelings.

At this point we will also begin discussing body language, as this is the main tool we use when assessing whether we have crossed someone's emotional boundaries. Here I address common body language and engage in activities where my client will work on reading body language. A fun activity that aids with this practice is playing "feelings charades," further explained below. Teaching our clients that their words can have an impact, just like unwanted touch, will help address any inappropriate discussions or language that may accompany their problematic sexual behaviors.

Feelings Charades

This activity is exactly what it sounds like. The client, caregiver, and therapist will take turns embodying an emotion. The others will guess what emotion is being acted out based on the body language being presented. This helps kids improve their social skills as it helps them understand body language, the use of nonverbal communication, and aids them in becoming more aware of what to attend to when assessing body language.

Practicing Boundaries and Body Rights

When going through each of these boundaries, it is recommended that the clinician add an additional activity to help support their client's treatment retention and understanding. In my experience, I've found that kids have responded well to drawing each of these boundaries. An example of this activity is provided in the appendix of this book, along with a blank copy that is ready for use. Another option, if the client is more active or doesn't like drawing, is creating a dance move for each of the boundaries. Once they have engaged in the activity of their choosing, the clinician can help them practice differentiating boundaries by creating scenarios and asking the client to pick out which of the boundaries are present in the scenario, either by pointing to their drawing or doing their dance move.

For example, a scenario used to assess the child's understanding of the information could be "Sara took Ethan's pencil out of his hand because she needed an eraser." The client is then asked to respond to this scenario and state which boundary was broken. In this example, the client would point to the drawing or do the dance move to identify that Sara broke Ethan's material boundary, or "stuff boundary." They are then asked how they would correct the scenario. Practicing this several times over is recommended, as well as having the client come up with their own examples. If the caregiver is not present for this activity, I ask the client to "teach" their caregiver what they've learned the next time they are present.

TYPES OF TOUCH

When describing touch, we can generally break it down into three categories: "safe (or good)," "unsafe (or bad)," and "sexual" (or "secret," depending on the age and/or preference of the child).

Safe/Good Touch

When describing safe touch, I highlight that a key component of this type of touch is consent. Another key component is that it is safe for the person who is doing the touch, and safe for the person who is receiving the touch. After providing this information, I ask my clients if they can think of some examples of safe touch. Typically, they can come up with a few, and once it seems like they are running out of steam, I provide some other examples. Some examples of safe touch that you can use when discussing this topic with clients include high fives, fist bumps, hugs, handshakes, and pats on the back. There are plenty of others, but these are just a few to get you started. I highlight the importance of consent, even when engaging in something as innocuous as a pat on the back. In doing so, I might provide the following example: "I'm super sick and sneezing all over the place. I'm coughing and you walk up. Since you're my friend you see that I'm coughing and jokingly pat me on the back, as if my coughs are because I'm choking. Little did you know that I hurt my back from sneezing and coughing so much, and when you go and pat me on the back, it really hurts, and I yell. You didn't ask to pat me on the back, but you got in my bubble and did it anyways. This hurt me and I got upset because I'm already in a bad mood from being sick. If you would have asked me if you could pat me on the back, I would have said no and explained it's because I have a hurt back." Though this example is a bit silly, it highlights how a safe touch can turn unsafe when we neglect to ask before touching someone.

Unsafe/Bad Touch

After describing safe touch, children have a pretty easy time describing unsafe touch. When discussing this type of touch, I highlight that unsafe touch is, well, unsafe for our body or the body of the person being touched. It's touch that can hurt, as well as touch that is nonconsensual. Similarly to safe touch, I will have clients think of as many examples of unsafe touch as they can. Some examples of unsafe touch include kicking, hitting, biting, scratching, spitting, pushing, and flicking. There are other types of unsafe touch, but these tend to be the most common responses you will hear from clients. Typically, clients don't need an in-depth example that explains why unsafe touch is unsafe; it's pretty obvious. What I will provide is a brief example of how quickly safe touch can turn unsafe if they haven't received/given consent. I might say something like, "Let's say you are at the park, and you are playing basketball, and while playing basketball a person comes up to you out of nowhere, picks you up, and gives you a big ol' bear hug. How would that make you feel?" Most can identify that this would be very uncomfortable and would creep them out. If they don't, this can be diagnostic, and I will take note and come back to this and the larger topic of safety at another time. I continue on and further make my point by saying, "Well, isn't a hug a safe touch?" to which they will hopefully reply, "Not unless they have my consent!"

Sexual/Secret Touch

When describing this type of touch, I try to make it as straightforward and simple as possible. I tell my clients that this kind of touch involves body parts that are covered by a swimsuit. I ask kids to tell me what parts are covered when a boy is in swim trunks, and what parts are covered when a girl is wearing a bikini. I don't expect them to use anatomically correct names for these parts at this point in the treatment process, as we have not talked about this yet. After identifying these parts of the body, I explain that sexual touch is when another person uses any part of their body to touch someone in these areas. Sometimes children might feel uncomfortable or shy about saying the word "sexual," and in these cases I refer to this type of touch as "secret touch," explaining that when people engage in this type of touch, they sometimes ask the person they are touching to keep it a secret. This opens dialogue around the importance of telling an adult if someone asks them to keep touching, or other things, a secret, as this should be a red flag for them that the person is doing something that isn't okay.

Further Learning Related to Touch

After describing each type of touch individually, I share that these three types of touch are not mutually exclusive, for example, you can have "safe sexual touch," like when adults engage in consensual sexual touch or healthy masturbation. You can have "unsafe safe touch," like unwanted or nonconsensual hugs, and you can have "unsafe sexual touch," like sexual abuse or the problematic sexual behaviors your client has engaged in. By creating the three categories discussed above, it is easier to define different types of touch and highlight the types of touch we are trying to encourage, as well as the types of touch we are trying to discourage.

Once the different types of touch have been explained, different examples of each have been provided, and there has been a discussion regarding the ways that different types of touch can make people feel, it is time to move on to creating a "types of touch list." Before I discuss this, I'd like to highlight an important discussion that should be had with each client.

Just as there are some boundaries that appear more black-and-white and are easier to see when broken, this too can be the case with types of touch. However, not all boundaries are easy to see when broken, and the same goes for the feelings that come with different types of touch. It is easy for kids to understand that "safe" touch leads to "good" feelings, and "unsafe" touch leads to "bad" feelings, but when it comes to sexual touch, feelings can get murky and aren't as clear. It is important to normalize the possible confusion that kids may have around this, as some who have been victimized themselves did not want the touching to happen but might acknowledge that the touch made their bodies feel "good." This can be an upsetting and confusing experience for them. They may feel that their bodies have betrayed them, or that there is something wrong with them, so discussing the variety of feelings that come with different types of touch, and normalizing these feelings, can be helpful for healing the relationship our clients have with their bodies. It is also noted that everyone gets to decide what constitutes a safe touch. One client may think that being tickled is a safe touch because they enjoy it, whereas another client may place tickling into the unsafe touch category.

"Types of Touch" Activity

This activity can be modified to meet your client where they are at. As mentioned previously, some kids want to discuss their behaviors immediately, and others may take a while to feel comfortable enough to discuss the details of their actions. Regardless of where they are in this process, the activity looks similar. Have your client fold two sheets of paper into thirds or create three separate boxes on each sheet. One sheet of paper is for the types of touch they have engaged in and the other is for the types of touch others have done to them. Each paper will have section, or boxes, titled "safe touch (or good touch)," "unsafe touch (or bad touch)," and "sexual touch (or secret touch)." As the activity progresses, each of these sections will have a list of touches that correspond to each of these specific types of touch. You can help your client write these down, or the client can do this themselves, depending on their comfort level with reading and writing.

Once the papers have been set up, the client can choose which paper they would like to begin with—types of touch that have been done to them, or types of touch that they have done to others. The three different types of touch will be discussed, but avoid getting too far into the details, as their level of coping has not yet been assessed. This activity is meant to help the client become more comfortable talking about types of touch, not to have them dive into the details of their own trauma or problematic sexual behaviors. We don't want to get too far into these details because we want to ensure the client has the appropriate coping skills and emotional recognition and regulation to handle any big feelings that may come up when discussing these experiences. Though we will not be getting into the details of the touching, this activity helps us assess the client's level of awareness and comfort in discussing this topic and can give us an idea of how they feel discussing their behaviors and lived experiences. Some may have little difficulty opening up and discussing this topic, whereas others may only want to engage in the "safe touch" portion of the activity. I meet my clients where they are at and understand that, for some, this activity may take one session and, for others, it could take many. If they are really resistant or unable to discuss these types of touch, I will have them draw the types of touch and go from there. An example of this is provided in the appendix.

If the client is not ready to discuss the types of touch they have engaged in, I've found that they often have an easier time beginning with the touches done to them. Starting with this part of the exercise gets them warmed up and allows them to talk about the different types of touch, but it does not create as much pressure as they are not talking about or focusing on their own choices, and they may not feel as guilty or judged. If they are still hesitant to discuss their own behaviors after exploring the behaviors they have experienced, or after drawing the types of touch as discussed above, you can start with a more removed conversation around this topic. If they are especially hesitant to discuss unsafe or sexual touch, I ask them about unsafe or sexual touches they may have witnessed (asking about movies, music, magazines, TV shows, etc.), rather than focusing on them, their families, or the touching that has occurred. This technique can be used to discuss the other types of touch as well. This can help break the ice, while keeping it at a comfortable distance for our avoidant clients.

After this activity, the clinician should spend a period of time discussing the types of touch that are appropriate for kids and discussing ways to ensure that unhealthy and hurtful touches are minimized.

Chapter 3

Body Awareness

When working with children ages twelve or younger, I've found that they often appear avoidant or disconnected from their feelings, and they may struggle to find the language to explain their inner workings. Part of this may be developmental, but I believe that a part of this is linked to the maltreatment and trauma that a significant portion of our clients have experienced. I see clients use disconnection as a coping strategy, and though this disconnection may feel helpful in the moment, it is important that our clients begin working on reconnecting to their feelings and their bodies. This may feel scary or foreign, but it is an integral part of the treatment process. If our clients can't tell the difference between their frustration and anxiety, how can we expect them to appropriately understand and cope with these feelings and care for themselves in healthy ways?

CHECKING IN

The skill of noticing and reacting to our feelings is like exercising a muscle—the more you use it, the stronger it gets. I highlight the importance of practice by providing an example like, "If I want to get a six-pack, can I do thirty sit-ups and get a six pack?" Most will laugh or roll their eyes and say, "No." I then ask, "Well, if I do thirty sit-ups every day for one week, will I have a six-pack now?" Again, they will humor me and say, "No." Then I say, "Well, if I do thirty sit-ups every day for a year, do you think I'll have a six-pack then?" At this point they will catch on to what I'm saying, and I will highlight the importance of consistent practice. We cannot expect monumental change in one short week, whether it's building a six-pack or connecting to our bodies and feelings. This process will be lengthy, but the more our clients practice connecting to their feelings and bodies, the easier it will get for them to regulate in healthy and effective ways. To start getting kids more aware of their feelings, it is a good idea to have them practice this skill in each session, and at home whenever possible. One easy way to practice in session is via a "feelings chart."

Feelings Chart Check-in

A feelings chart is exactly what it sounds like, a chart with a list of feelings accompanied by faces. You can easily find or make one of these for your office, and regardless of whether it's homemade or store bought, it should have at least two things: feeling words and faces that depict them. The visual piece is important, as this models common nonverbal depictions of these feelings. Clients may struggle to know exactly what feeling they're experiencing, but they will likely have a much easier time picking a face that looks like what they are experiencing. At the start of every session, have your client pick out a feeling from the chart to reflect how they are currently feeling. Once they've chosen one, have them process how they know they are feeling this way. You can do this by asking questions like, "How do you know you feel happy?" "Where do you notice it in your body?" "What's another time you've noticed that same feeling in your body?" and so on. This can help them process feelings and pick up on cues they are noticing inside of their body. Typically, these check-ins start with some of the more commonly discussed feelings, like sad, happy, and angry, but as the client continues practicing this skill, they will begin growing this muscle and their answers will begin to reflect this growth. Ideally, clients will eventually recognize their current feelings, they will be able to discuss where they are feeling it in their bodies, and they will have an idea of what events may be influencing this emotion.

Occasionally, there will be clients who are so far removed from their emotions or who experience too much discomfort discussing their emotions that they are unable to partake in a feelings chart check-in. In these cases, I know it will be important to process this in treatment and unearth where this aversion comes from. I remain curious about how this avoidance has served them in their past, but I do not push them to participate. Instead, I may model a feelings check-in by picking a feeling face from the chart and talking to them about where I feel it in my body. This could look like me pointing to both the tired face and the excited face and saying, "Man, I'm excited that we are together and getting to talk today, I feel that in my chest, almost like bees buzzing around. I also notice that I'm feeling tired though. It feels like my eyelids weigh a million pounds." I gently ask them if they've ever noticed these sensations, or if they notice any other sensations in their body. If they say yes, then I ask if they will share more about a time they experienced this, or what they are currently noticing; and if they say no, I say, "That's okay, it can be hard to notice the feelings and sensations we have in our bodies," and we move on.

If a child is significantly detached from their body or feelings, a feelings chart activity may be too advanced, and it is recommended that the clinician creates space to explore this concept but in a less direct and personal way. Using puppets is a great way to model the experience of checking in with oneself and assessing our current emotional state and needs. If you use this strategy, you will need at least two puppets. I will pick up a puppet and ask the client if they want to choose a puppet. As you guessed, this can go two ways: either the client wants to engage with the puppet, or they don't. Luckily, it's easy to modify this check-in activity on the fly. I've provided an example below.

Puppet Check-in

If they choose to use a puppet, I will make sure that I'm directly speaking to their puppet or using my puppet to speak to their puppet. I almost pretend like the client isn't there at the beginning. Usually, I start by introducing myself to my puppet and asking their name. For this example, let's say the puppet is Ms. Frog. Ms. Frog will then introduce herself to my client's puppet and ask my client's puppet what their name is. I will use a fun voice to differentiate myself from Ms. Frog. Once my client's puppet has introduced themself, in this case let's say it's Scout the Shark, I introduce myself to Scout the Shark and go back to talking to Ms. Frog. Here is how the process may look:

ME. "Ms. Frog how is your day going so far?"
MS. FROG. "Oh my goodness, it's been terrible! Someone almost stepped on me when I was headed to the pond."
ME. "Oh dear, what was that like for you?
MS. FROG. "It was terrifying! I could feel my heart speed up, I thought it was about to beat out of my chest!"
ME. "Woah! That does sound scary. I remember a time when I was walking across the street and a bicycle came out of nowhere and nearly hit me! I jumped up and screamed. I could feel my heart speed up and I almost lost my breath."
MS. FROG. "It was a startling start to my day, but I'm feeling much better now. I went to the store, grabbed my favorite snack, and then took a lovely nap. What about you Scout, how has your day been?"

At this point, the hope is that your client will play as Scout the Shark and the conversation will continue. You will ask Scout open-ended questions about his day, as well as questions related to the conversation you and Ms. Frog had. You, or Ms. Frog, might ask Scout whether there has been a time when he has noticed his heart beating quickly, or a time when he has been startled or scared. If your client did not choose to use a puppet, the check-in will just be between you and Ms. Frog, and you can continue the conversation until you have covered several feeling words and identified several body sensations associated with these feelings.

The idea is that the clinician is modeling conversations about feelings, in hopes that this strategy allows their client to practice thinking about feelings, or discussing their current feelings, but in a way that feels more accessible and less direct and vulnerable.

Whether it's via play or a feelings chart, a feelings check-in should occur in each session, and as the client becomes more skilled, the clinician and client can choose whether they'd like to phase out the feelings chart, and/or puppet play, and practice sitting with themselves and deciphering how they are feeling without visual assistance.

Before beginning further work on emotional recognition and regulation, I sit down with my clients and take the time to read *Listening to My Body*, by Gabi Garcia. This short book does an incredible job of describing feelings and sensations in a straightforward and easy-to-understand way. I use much of the information in this book when teaching my clients about the "feelings chain," a topic discussed below. I find that reading this book is a great way to prepare clients for the work they will eventually be engaging in.

EMOTIONAL RECOGNITION AND REGULATION

Breaking down the process of recognizing our emotions and how we react to them allows our clients to see that they have control over their actions. During this portion of treatment, I provide psychoeducation and explain the "feelings chain." This chain, modeled on the cognitive behavioral therapy (CBT) model of emotions, breaks down into four parts: sensations/triggers, feelings, thoughts, and actions. I've provided further details about each of the "feelings chain" components below.

Feelings Chain

This portion of treatment provides clients with education around several elements associated with emotional recognition and regulation. They are taught to understand and recognize clues in their body that help decipher their current emotional response or experience. Being able to understand how they are feeling allows them to identify tools they can use to take care of themself, leading to healthy and safe choices. The ability to do so allows our clients to experience emotions or reflect on events that bring up big feelings while still experiencing a sense of control over themselves and their bodies. This is a powerful skill to possess and can be especially helpful when processing past trauma and challenging experiences.

Sensations/Triggers

A sensation is a detection of external or internal stimuli, while a trigger is an event or circumstance that can lead to sensations and feelings. These are rather abstract concepts for young kids, so when teaching this portion of the chain I use examples that clients will be familiar with. I start by discussing sensations that are easily noticed and have been experienced before. A list of examples that I often use are a growling stomach, a dry throat, goose bumps, and welling or watering eyes. Even the youngest of kids can remember a time where they were so hungry their stomach growled, or a time where they played outside for so long that their throat or mouth became dry.

I start with having them write down, or verbally list, every sensation they can think of. Then I have them describe how the sensations feel in their body and where they are felt. Once they have exhausted the list of sensations they know, I will bring up other sensations they may have missed but are familiar with. After they seem to grasp the concept of sensations and triggers, we move on to feelings.

Feelings

A feeling is an emotional state or reaction. This is something that is a bit easier to explain to clients, however, it is still more abstract than the following pieces of the feelings chain. Ideally, clients will have had some practice noticing and naming feelings via their feelings check-ins discussed above.

I start by having my client write down, or discuss, as many feelings as they can think of. If they struggle with this, I come up with scenarios that would generally evoke emotions, such as, "How would you feel if your friend threw a ball at your head?" or, "When your mom gives you a hug while you are crying, how do you feel?" This helps the client think of specific scenarios rather than the more nebulous experience of noticing their feelings out of the blue. After they demonstrate a good understanding of feelings, we move on to the next step in the feelings chain: thoughts.

Thoughts

A thought is an idea that involves the processing of information. In my experience, this step, as well as the next, seems easier for clients to understand. They have had a lot of experience with thoughts, as they often have to choose whether or not to react to thoughts throughout their day.

While looking at, or discussing, the list of feelings and sensations they've come up with, the client will pick two that go together appropriately, like "goose bumps" and "cold," and then they will be asked what kind of thoughts come to their mind when they realize they are cold. Often, they say something like, "I need to go inside," or, "I should put my coat on." Beginning with this type of example will help clients practice the feelings chain without bringing up big or overwhelming feelings. The hope is that, eventually, as they learn interventions and coping tools, they will be able to explore some of the more difficult examples, like the feelings chain that was present during their engagement in problematic sexual behaviors. The last piece of the feelings chain is actions.

Actions

An action is the process of doing something. This action can reflect the thoughts that came before it.

At this point in the chain, it should be fairly clear to the client that the action is likely going to reflect the thoughts they provided one step earlier. If we stick with the same example from above, the client has already put together that the sensation of goosebumps tells them they are cold. They have the thought, "I should put a jacket on," and we follow up and ask them what they think their action would be. Generally, they will say something along the lines of, "Well, I put the jacket on." At this point, I congratulate them and let them know that they have just completed the feelings chain.

This step is also where you can begin discussing the concept of intent versus impact, and the consequences that come from our actions, both negative and positive.

Locus of Control

After going through each of the steps within the feelings chain, I teach clients about the concept "locus of control." I do this by going through each of the four steps discussed above and asking the client, at each step, "Do you think you have control of this step?" At the end, I reveal that the only two steps they can actually control are the final two: thoughts and actions. I further explain that we are not able to control sensations, triggers, or our feelings. Clients are often surprised to hear this; however, they seem to understand after being provided a few examples. Some examples I use, in question form, to highlight their inability to control their feelings are, "Do you like feeling angry?" or, "If you could, would you ever choose to feel nauseous?" "No" is often the response to both questions. At this point, they recognize that if they could control their feelings, they would never choose to feel challenging emotions such as grief, guilt, embarrassment, anxiety, and so on.

I use the feelings chain, and their understanding of locus of control, to break down the process of making choices and engaging in actions. This breakdown helps demonstrate that behaviors don't just come out of thin air. Kids, like adolescent clients, will often state that their behaviors "just happened." However, clinicians understand that these types of behaviors are often rooted in a multitude of issues and do not just show up overnight. Both concepts can also be used to show clients that they do have control in their lives, while also normalizing their lack of control over triggers, sensations, and feelings.

Now that they have received the appropriate education and have a good understanding of this material, it's time to practice! Examples of the feelings chain process are provided in the appendix. One focuses on a more general feelings chain, and one focuses on a feelings chain connected to problematic sexual behaviors. A blank copy is also provided.

BUILDING COPING SKILLS AND INTERVENTIONS

Feelings can be overwhelming and exhausting, especially for clients in high-stress households or who have previously endured abusive situations. These clients may learn to disconnect from their bodies and emotions because they recognize that experiencing all of their feelings isn't sustainable, doesn't feel safe, or is overwhelming. Instead, they may learn to ignore their feelings and bodies to detach from their pain, fear, stress, and so on. Rather than acknowledging and sharing their feelings, they may act out in other ways to demonstrate how they are feeling. This can come out a number of different ways—shutting down, engaging in angry outbursts, or participating in self-harming behaviors. Children do not engage in these behaviors for fun or enjoyment, they act out in these ways because they have learned, and likely believe, that they are the best way to get their needs met. Clinicians should never shame clients for the coping skills they've developed, even if they are maladaptive. Instead, it's our job to acknowledge the purpose these behaviors have served in the past, while also helping clients build healthier and more adaptive coping skills for the future.

Teaching our clients to acknowledge and sit with feelings is an important part of helping them build healthy and appropriate coping skills. This is especially helpful for our clients as they move through treatment, as it is likely that they may feel guilt, embarrassment, confusion, and other challenging emotions related to their problematic sexual behaviors. To sit with feelings, we must first learn how to tolerate these feelings. Once we can sit with challenging emotions, and see that they do not last forever, it becomes easier to allow them in. A piece of learning to sit with these feelings is learning to sit with our body. This can be a challenge for adults, let alone children. One way that I begin practicing these skills with clients is by using mindful movement and breath. I've provided a few ideas below to get this ball rolling.

Mindfulness Cards for Deep Breathing

I have a set of cards that I've created over the years. These cards include short breathing exercises, calming movement, and brief mindfulness exercises. Typically, I will have a client look through the deck and pick one of the cards, and once they have made their selection, I will read the card aloud and we will do the exercise together. Depending on the child, we may start with a card at the beginning of our time together to set the tone for our session, or we may end our time together with a card to prepare them for their transition out of the therapy room and back into their daily life. Occasionally, clients will ask to start and finish with one of the cards, but this is pretty rare. More often than not, my clients don't like engaging in these exercises and may put up a fuss, stating that "it's boring" or they "don't do breathing." I validate their feelings but reiterate the importance of checking in with our brain and body and the practice this requires. Their disinterest in mindful exercises is understandable, especially if they are still trying to avoid feelings. That's why I try and use fun materials to supplement these exercises. I've provided an example of how I do this below.

Bubble Breathing

One of the cards in my deck explains the mindful breathing skill deemed "bubble breathing." There are many iterations of this breathing activity, and there is no right or wrong way to practice this skill. I've found success using supplemental materials while teaching it.

When a client picks this card, I read it aloud, sharing the activity instructions. The card goes something like, "Close your eyes and imagine it's summer. You feel the sun on your face, smell the grass in the air, and hear other kids at the park. I want you to imagine that you have a tube of bubbles. You twirl your bubble wand in the tube, pull it out slowly, and look at the way the liquid catches the sun. After slowly pulling your bubble wand out, you bring it up to your mouth. You take a big breath in through your nose, and then slowly and softly blow onto your bubble wand. You begin to see bubbles floating into the sky and popping over your head. You do it again, dipping your bubble wand into the tube, pulling it out, taking a big deep breath in through your nose and slowly blowing out through your mouth. You keep doing this until the sky is filled with bubbles." After allowing them time to finish the activity and open their eyes, I will pull out a tube of bubbles and have the client practice this activity in real life.

I ask them to play around with their breathing and see what it does to the bubble-blowing process. If they breathe out fast and hard, they quickly learn that they can't create bubbles. I ask them to see what happens if they take a really short and quick breath in and out. After trying several different strategies, we come back to the long, deep breath in through the nose and the long, slow breath out through the mouth. By the time they are done with this activity, they have engaged in quite a bit of breathing, they have practiced mindfulness, and they are able to tangibly understand the ways that different types of breathing can create different outcomes. I tie this back to feelings by modeling the different types of breathing that help with different types of emotions. I might say, "When I'm mad, I'm already energized by the anger, so to cool off and slow down I will take a few big bubble breaths like you just did. Other times I might need to build up some energy. I know that when I get ready to jump off a tall rock into the water, I feel nervous, so I energize myself with a few quick breaths in through my mouth and out through my mouth. Other times when I'm feeling nervous, I like to use, 'lions' breath' because it helps me get all of the nervous butterflies out of my stomach. What I do is I take a big breath in through my nose and then I stick my tongue out and breathe all the air out of my lungs as fast and as hard as I can. A lot of times a funny sound will come out of my mouth too." I model these different breathing strategies as I describe them.

This big of an activity won't happen every time you practice breathing in sessions, but I've found that starting with an activity like this will help with buy-in and clients are more likely to practice different types of breathing in the future.

Another resource that I've found incredibly helpful for teaching young children about mindfulness is the book *Breathe Like a Bear*, by Kira Willey. This book has many great mindfulness exercises, and if a child prefers to use this book over the deck of cards, I have them pick a page each session and we read the page and practice the exercise together. I also have clients teach their caregivers the different breathing techniques they learn and ask that these be practiced at home each week.

LET'S TALK ABOUT BODY PARTS

An essential part of treatment is not only providing psychoeducation around body awareness and coping strategies but also educating our clients about their bodies and different body parts. Many prominent organizations, and much of the pertinent research regarding prevention, safety, and age-appropriate developmental knowledge, report that by kindergarten age, children should be able to identify the anatomical names of body parts. This may be shocking for many adults, as discussing penises, vulvas, and vaginas seems taboo. However, this is an integral part of keeping our clients safe. Knowing their body parts helps them talk about their bodies, is essential to processing past victimization they may have endured, and helps establish a shared language. The main reasons for teaching our clients the appropriate and anatomical names for body parts are discussed below.

Normalizing Body Parts

We want to normalize body parts and take away any shame associated with them. We don't create nicknames for our hands or our legs, and this is because society has deemed these parts "appropriate" and, therefore, there is no need for silly nicknames. Unfortunately, private parts have been wrongly deemed "inappropriate" by society; thus, there are many nicknames for these body parts, and we are often taught that we shouldn't discuss them. While we can acknowledge that there is a right time and place to discuss this topic, we want to address this larger dynamic and reject the idea that private parts are inherently "bad," "sexual," or "inappropriate." We want to normalize these parts of our body as being instrumental to our lives, because without them, we couldn't survive. There is no need to feel shy or tiptoe around these body parts, but we should highlight the importance of keeping these body parts private, hence the frequently used phrase "private parts."

I often provide information through a framework that views these body parts as functional rather than sexual. I discuss the important roles they play in excreting waste from our bodies and how this is essential to our survival. In this conversation I discuss the importance of being clothed and covering these body parts to keep them private, not because they are bad, but because they are so important, and we need to keep them safe.

Private parts are not inherently sexual, and they should not be seen as such. It is important to make a distinction between having a body part and how one uses that body part. Normalizing genitals as having an important function, such as urinating, helps kids see that their privates are used for normal daily functions and should not be avoided. There is a big difference between urinating and touching someone with the body part they urinate out of, so making this distinction is important. In addition to normalizing body parts and providing a framework for why we keep them private, engaging in education related to our bodies serves as a protective measure and increases safety.

Safety!

If children do not know the names of their different body parts, we cannot expect them to tell us how they have been hurt or how they have possibly hurt others. When a child falls off a bike and says, "I skinned my knee," we know exactly where they injured themselves. This helps us assess the injury, ensure it is appropriately treated, and keep an eye on the healing progress. You can see the importance of understanding where and how the child was injured. We need to ensure that children can do this when it comes to their private parts as well.

If a child says, "She hurt my privates," this can mean many different things. Providing children with the different names of their private parts and helping them understand that no one should be asking to see or touch these parts provides them with the language and understanding they need to help keep themselves safe. It ensures that they can describe the ways that someone has crossed these boundaries or provide details if someone attempts to do so.

How to Teach Kids About Body Parts

An easy way to begin this conversation with kids is to have them label a body. You can draw your own stick figures or find body outlines online. First, I explain what "anatomical" means, since this is a foreign word to most young clients. Once they understand this word, I ask them to look at the figure in front of them and label as many body parts as they can think of. Kids will usually label the head, hands, legs, feet, arms, and stomach. At this point, I ask them to think hard about other body parts. They may label the nose, eyes, mouth, fingers, and so on. After giving them time, I assess whether they have labeled the private parts. If they have, but haven't used the anatomical names, we will go through them together. If the child has avoided labeling the private parts entirely, I will explore this with them. After doing so, we will go through the different body parts together. I don't go into extreme detail when discussing private parts, but I do discuss the following parts, provide an age appropriate description about the function of these parts, and I expect clients to know each of these parts and where they are on the body:

Male: anus, buttocks, penis, testicles, scrotum, nipples
Female: anus, buttocks, vulva, vagina, breasts, nipples

Though I have listed the body parts above as "male" and "female" it is important to note that gendering them in this way is not recommended when working with gender diverse youth. It is important that we provide education about body parts with gender inclusive language, and can do so by focusing on body parts without assigning them to a specific gender. When referring to these anatomical body parts and providing education we can use inclusive language, such as "a person with a vagina" rather than "a girl with a vagina." Once they have participated in the education and conversations discussed above, and they can correctly name and label where these body parts are located, we can move forward.

The Puberty Talk

If the child is young and still several years from entering puberty, the discussion on this topic will be more general. I still provide psychoeducation around puberty and body changes, but this conversation does not have the same level of detail as it does for someone who is nearing puberty. With younger children, I tend to provide them the following information: the age in which puberty generally begins, the general body changes that happen during puberty, and who they can talk to if they have questions about these topics in the future.

If the client is inching closer to the age of puberty, or is especially curious or concerned about this process, I will provide more information. We discuss body changes in more detail, and I also provide information regarding healthy masturbation, further discussed below. Prior to having this conversation, I check in individually with the caregiver(s) and discuss the information I'd like to share regarding puberty, body changes, and masturbation. I explain the importance of providing factual and candid information around these topics and ask if they would like to be a part of this conversation with their child. If not, then I inform them that their child will be presenting their learnings during a check-in at some point. I provide them with the details of what I will be discussing so they have the information and opportunity to address any concerns they may have. This can also prepare them for potential questions their child may have in the future.

Occasionally, caregivers are uncomfortable with me providing sexual education. If this is the case, I ask to meet with them individually and we further discuss their concerns and viewpoints. I validate their feelings while also providing facts related to the importance of children receiving age-appropriate sexual education. I tend to focus on the safety piece, as parents feel particularly aligned with the goal of improving safety for their child. I assure them that the information I'm providing is age-appropriate and discuss the likelihood of their child seeking this information elsewhere should we neglect to discuss it with them. I explain that though these conversations can be awkward and uncomfortable, it's much better than the alternative—the internet. Children will absolutely turn to the internet, and to peers, to access this information. As we know, the internet is full of misinformation and can be horrendously inaccurate. Should their child turn to the internet to answer their questions, it is likely that they will stumble across information that's not age-appropriate, find themselves looking at inappropriate images or websites, and end up having more questions than when they started their search. Helping caregivers understand this typically helps them shift their views and allow their child to participate in this part of the treatment process.

Healthy Masturbation

Clients should not be shamed for having sexual needs and should be taught that masturbation is a healthy, normal, and appropriate way to have their sexual needs met. This conversation will look different depending on the age and understanding of the client. With older clients, clinicians should discuss healthy habits regarding these behaviors, such as always masturbating alone—only doing so at home, in their room, with the door closed and locked—cleaning up after themselves, and not using pornography but, rather, healthy thoughts. For our younger clients, this may be too much information, as many of them may not even know what masturbation is. To meet them where they are at, we can translate this information into age-appropriate language, such as, "If you feel like you want to touch your privates, the only place you can do that in a safe way is in your room at home. The door should be closed, and you should always be alone." If the child does not have a bedroom, then the same information can be provided for the bathroom. Again, some parents may be uncomfortable with this topic. If so, the clinician should discuss the therapeutic purpose for this treatment conversation and provide psychoeducation, if necessary.

Chapter 4

Client History

Once you have created the foundation for problematic sexual behavior–specific treatment (education around safety planning, boundaries, types of touch), you've adequately prepared and provided your client with strategies to recognize and cope with overwhelming feelings (education around the feelings chain, increasing mindfulness, and utilizing interventions and self-regulation exercises), and you've provided your client with the language to sufficiently speak about their actions and experiences (education around anatomical body parts and body awareness), it is time to move into the next phase of treatment: information gathering.

This chapter is named "Client History" because, at this point within the treatment process, you will be learning about and gathering the details of what brought your client into treatment. In this portion of treatment, we will begin learning about and addressing common patterns of thinking that can prove to be problematic, gain a full understanding of the behaviors that brought our client into treatment, and, last, get a full look at the client's life history and sexual history to better understand the factors that may have preceded their problematic sexual behaviors.

The time it takes to get through this section of treatment will vary. A client who is more open to discussing the details of their behaviors and life experiences will move through this area of treatment quickly, whereas a client who struggles to acknowledge their behaviors and life history will move through this section slowly. Some clients seem to share information freely, whereas others experience significant struggles. There are several variables that may make this work more challenging for some, such as unprocessed trauma, denial, or shame. Understandably, it will take time to sift through these challenges. When working with a variety of clients, we should also have a variety of ways we can access and work on information. Below I've provided several methods I use to gather and process information related to my clients' lived experiences and problematic sexual behaviors.

GATHERING CLIENT HISTORY

Before gathering the details of our clients' problematic sexual behaviors, it's helpful to understand the events that led up to these behaviors. This can help provide structure for the next portion of treatment and eases our clients into this work rather than pushing them to discuss the details of their problematic sexual behaviors right away. We do not want to fast-forward through this portion of treatment as it is incredibly valuable. It allows us to better understand our clients—how they present and what behaviors they have engaged in. This portion of treatment can also identify potential victims that we were previously unaware of. This is important because it not only enables us to identify victims but also allows us to take the steps needed to get them support and services.

If the client is struggling to discuss details related to their life or their problematic sexual behaviors, it can be a good idea to request the caregiver's engagement in these sessions. The caregiver will serve as an active participant in these sessions, demonstrating to their child that the information is okay to share and that they are safe and supported. Normalizing any difficulties the child is having, and explaining why discussing this information is important, are also steps that can help the child open up. Oftentimes, children who struggle to discuss the details of their problematic sexual behaviors are fearful of possible consequences—judgment, getting taken out of their homes, and so much more. Understanding why the child is having a difficult time discussing their behaviors can help the clinician and caregiver reassure them that they are not in treatment because they are in trouble or because they are a bad person but, rather, because it can help. Therapy should be framed as a tool to help the child ensure that their future choices are healthy and that they have the skills to move forward with a healthy understanding of themselves, their bodies, and relationships. Frame the therapy room as a judgment-free zone.

Having the caregiver in the room can help address any fears the child may have of being abandoned, punished, or so forth. It can be helpful to remind the child that, in most cases, the caregiver is already aware of the behaviors and that's why they are meeting with me. At the beginning of this process, it's okay to have the caregiver provide a few of the details that they know. This can break the ice and gives the child permission to begin discussing their behaviors. By the end of this process, whether it takes half of a session or many, the child will be able to discuss their own behaviors using their own words. I've provided several activities below that can help clients get to this place. Prior to sharing these, however, I will offer a few tips for helping shy children open up.

Ways to Help a Shy Client Open Up

Use play! Puppets are a tool I use frequently as they can help a child open up in less direct ways. The therapist can use puppets to ask pertinent questions, model that discussing a topic is okay and gives the child some tools to process difficult questions in a less direct manner.

Discuss the events like a story or movie. Use questions like, "If your life was a movie, who would play you? What would we see?" and so on. As they begin talking, encourage them to share details by saying something along the lines of "people in movies don't just get from the bottom of the stairs to the top of the stairs, they take it step by step. The movie shows their shoes, the stairs they are on, their hand on the rail, and so on. I want it to be like you are explaining what happened, but you are the director, and this is your movie. Give me all the details."

Use fidgets, art, and movement. Engaging in activities, rather than sitting across from the client and expecting eye contact, can be much less intimidating. Stimulating both sides of the brain may make it easier for the client to access and discuss challenging content.

Now that we have a few tricks up our sleeve, we are ready to discuss the different ways that clients can share details from their lived experiences, potential impacting factors, and problematic sexual behaviors.

Life History and Sexual History Timeline

This activity is often done with adolescents; however, children who are older or higher functioning can also engage in this activity. This activity allows clients to discuss pertinent details and events in a linear way. When completing this activity with younger clients, it is likely that their timelines will have fewer details in certain areas. This is due, in part, to their age, but also due to the developmental differences between this age-group and their older adolescent counterparts. This activity is focused on the details regarding their lives, the events leading up to the problematic sexual behaviors, and the problematic sexual behaviors themselves. Laying these details out in a linear fashion can help clients better see and understand the precursors to their choices, helping them better understand that the roots of these behaviors are much more complex than simply waking up one day and deciding to engage in inappropriate touching. This activity can also highlight possible triggers and experiences that may have impacted their curiosity around, or learning of, sexualized behaviors.

Children are sexual beings in the sense that they experience natural curiosities about their own bodies and the bodies of others and engage in exploratory touch with themselves. They are not, however, sexual beings in the sense that they are physically or emotionally ready to engage in sexual behaviors with others. We know from the literature that children with problematic sexual behaviors have often experienced maltreatment such as witnessing domestic violence, experiencing abuse, being exposed to inappropriate boundaries or sexual material and so on. Some of these experiences may be direct, like being shown pornographic material or being sexually abused, and some of these experiences may be indirect, like walking in on their caregivers having sex or watching a movie with sexual scenes in it. These direct and indirect exposures have impacts, and often these experiences have direct impacts on the problematic sexual behaviors they've engaged in.

When discussing this with clients, I often use the metaphor of a light switch. The light switch represents sexual thoughts and behaviors. Typically, this light switch is turned on when individuals begin going through puberty; however, when young kids are exposed to experiences like those discussed above, this light switch is turned on prematurely and can lead to problematic boundaries, thoughts, interests, and behaviors. Once this light switch is turned on, it is difficult to turn off. Thus, the work is not necessarily about turning the light switch off, it's about supporting our clients and teaching them how to appropriately manage these feelings and thoughts and how to get their needs met in healthy and safe ways moving forward. Figuring out where and when this light switch was "flipped on" can be helpful in conceptualizing the problematic sexual behaviors.

This timeline can be completed in several ways, and the child should be given the opportunity to engage in this activity in any way they want. In my experience, the older the client is, the more traditional their timeline is. The younger the client is, the more art based it is. Regardless of how they'd like to create their timeline, I often start the activity by saying something along the lines of, "This activity is going to look at what makes you, you! We are going to look at all the events and experiences you've had in your life, and we want to pay special attention to anything that made you feel big emotions." The client should be allowed to add anything they'd like to their timeline, and if their caregiver is not present during its creation, they should be invited into the session to review it with their child once it is completed. It is important for caregivers to have an idea of the way their child makes sense of the experiences they've had, what impacted their child's engagement in problematic sexual behaviors, and any possible triggers or events that they should be aware of.

Traditional Timeline

For this activity you will need paper and a writing utensil. Take a sheet of paper and create a horizontal line through the middle of it. Assign one side for "positive" events, memories, and experiences and the other for "negative" events, memories, and experiences. How they perceive these memories, events, and experiences will dictate which side of the timeline they place it on. On the far left of the page, you can put the client's birthday, as this is when their timeline starts. Have them recall the earliest memory they have and carry on from there until they reach the end of their timeline, which will represent current day. The timeline should have all major events, any impactful experiences, and their history of touching behaviors.

If the caregiver is not present while the client is creating their timeline, you will need to verify that there are no major events, behaviors, or experiences missing. Once this is verified, the client will invite their caregiver into a session and present their timeline.

Pro Tip. It can be helpful to write the sexual history portion of the timeline in a different color to help differentiate and highlight some of the areas that may have impacted the child's problematic sexual behaviors.

String of Plates Timeline

For this activity you will need paper plates to write on, a writing utensil, a hole puncher, and string. In this activity, each plate will represent an event or experience that the child would like to put on their timeline. Like the timeline discussed above, they will write out all events and experiences that have impacted them. The clinician can take on the role of scribe if the child doesn't want to write or needs support writing. Children can also choose to draw pictures or cut out pictures from magazines and place these on plates if this feels better to them. You will want to ask them about the pictures they've drawn or placed on the plate and how it relates to an experience, behavior, or event in their life. You can then write their explanation on the bottom of the plate.

Once they have filled out a plate for all of the details they want included in the timeline, the plates will be strung together on a piece of yarn. This creates a hanging timeline and makes it easier for the child, and the caregiver, to see where and when specific events happened. Having the details written down on plates and displayed in this manner can also help the child externalize these events and experiences and show them that their sexualized behaviors didn't happen because they are "bad," they happened because of a variety of impacting factors. Helping them understand this can decrease shame and help them reframe the way they view their behaviors. This can provide the client, and their caregiver, with a deeper understanding of these behaviors.

TROUBLE THOUGHTS

Trouble thoughts are ways of thinking that allow for avoidance of responsibility. I call them "trouble thoughts" because we often see this type of thinking when a child is in trouble or thinks that they are going to be in trouble. I also call them "trouble thoughts" because this type of thinking usually gets us into more trouble. In the context of problematic sexual behavior–specific treatment, we want to address these ways of thinking to help our clients make healthier choices and to develop a healthy sense of responsibility and accountability over their choices.

Trouble thoughts tend to get worse the more the child uses them, potentially developing into a habit and becoming so engrained they don't even realize they are using them. Luckily, children are in the best position to identify and fix these problems as they have high levels of neural plasticity. The ins and outs of neural plasticity are much too advanced for children; however, an age-appropriate example explaining this process may work well. Children seem to be more familiar with "muscle memory," so I often use this phrase when talking about this topic. An example you can use to help explain this concept might sounds like, "Imagine it's winter and everyone has been inside for the past few days because of a snowstorm. The snow has piled up and no one has played in it yet. Finally, it stops snowing and your caregiver lets you go outside. You want to go sledding, so you find a big hill, set your sled up, and take off. This first ride goes pretty slow, because there is so much snow piled up and no one has made a path for the sled to follow. You eventually get to the bottom, and now the snow has been patted down by your sled and there is a path to take. You head to the top of the hill and start again. This time the sled goes quicker because you've already created a path. The snow is still pretty thick, since you've only sledded down it once. Now, imagine you've been down this path fifty times! The snow has been packed down so much that the sides of the path have turned into walls. What would happen if you tried to turn the sled off the path?"

Typically, the client says you can't because you will run into the snow walls. If they don't, you can help them get to this conclusion. Once they understand the story, I explain that this is the same way our brains work. When we have a new thought or start to practice a new skill, it's very difficult. Our brain isn't used to it, so it takes more concerted effort. Now I ask them, "If we continue practicing this thought or skill what happens?" They typically say that it gets easier. If they don't, then again, you can help them to this conclusion. Finally, I ask, "What happens if you practice this for years and years?" They usually understand that at this point the new skill or thought would come easily, almost like autopilot or muscle memory. Then I explain that this new skill is like the sledding path. It is very easy to navigate once there is a defined path. Now, this is great if the thought/skill/path was a good one, but if it is a negative/unhealthy/unsafe one, then we need to change it. This can be very difficult if we are used to using it, just like the difficulty we would have if we tried to turn off the well-defined sledding path with big snow walls.

I explain that if someone is used to lying all day every day, they are going to have a tough time changing that behavior. When we use trouble thoughts, our brain gets used to this way of thinking. I inform clients that trouble thoughts do not help us and only hurt us in the long run, so we need to challenge and change them. This takes time, but if practiced over and over, it gets easier until eventually the trouble thoughts are gone and replaced with healthy thoughts. This portion of treatment is preventative and proactive for young children as they have not created long-lasting, engrained thought patterns in the same way older folks have.

Trouble Thoughts Activity

I have a list of common trouble thoughts, and the first part of this activity is providing clients with the different trouble thoughts and a definition for each. During this time, I provide examples, share about times I've used the specific trouble thought we are reviewing, and ask about times that they've used that trouble thought. We work our way through the list, and once it appears that they have a good understanding of the different trouble thoughts, I have them engage in a mix-and-match activity. This activity is used to assess their understanding of the content, and their ability to notice these types of thinking in real-life scenarios.

I recommend that caregivers participate in this activity if they were not present when their child was learning the different types of trouble thoughts. It allows them to develop a shared language around unwanted thought patterns, provides them the tools to implement this same practice at home, and enables them to therapeutically challenge their child when they are engaging in these ways of thinking. If the child is old enough, and it makes sense given the details of their situation, they may be asked to identify any trouble thoughts that occurred during their problematic sexual behaviors.

Trouble Thoughts Mix-and-Match

For this activity, you will need scissors and the worksheet provided in the appendix. In this activity, you will create a set of cards by cutting out the different trouble thoughts from the worksheet provided in the appendix. There are examples of each trouble thought on the worksheet, and you will need to cut these out as well. Have your client lay the trouble thoughts out on the floor or on a table. Then take the examples that you cut out, mix them up, and read them aloud. After reading the example, give it to your client and they will take the example and place it under the appropriate trouble thought. If this activity appears to be too easy, there is a blank copy of this worksheet available in the appendix. Have your client create their own examples that correspond to each trouble thought. Once they have finished, they can facilitate the activity and have you match their examples to the appropriate trouble thought.

Chapter 5

Ownership

When we think about accountability, we think about someone owning their choices and taking responsibility for the impact these choices have had. This may be in reference to the impact these choices have had on their own life, or the impact these choices have had on the lives of others. When a child has engaged in problematic sexual behaviors, it is appropriate to expect a level of accountability. How this accountability looks will depend on several factors like age, developmental level, and whether other children were involved in the problematic sexual behaviors. The accountability expected from a twelve-year-old who has engaged in problematic sexual behaviors with a sibling will look drastically different from the accountability expected from an eight-year-old child who pulled her pants down at a sleepover and showed her friend her vulva. Regardless of how this process looks, there is a level of accountability expected for every client who has engaged in problematic sexual behaviors with another child.

Ideally, this portion of treatment should not be too challenging for clients, as they have been working up to this section for some time now. Treatment work related to accountability involves components from each section of treatment that they've completed thus far. Clients have already discussed the types of touch they have engaged in, they have explored the details regarding the events leading up to their problematic sexual behaviors, and they have taken ownership for their behaviors rather than engaging in thought patterns that allow them to avoid responsibility. This section of treatment works to glue all these pieces together so that the child can demonstrate appropriate accountability for their past problematic sexual behaviors. This portion of the curriculum also addresses the initial feelings and triggers that impacted their engagement in problematic sexual behaviors and explores healthy and appropriate thoughts and actions that can be used in the future, should these feelings or triggers resurface.

ACCOUNTABILITY

This portion of treatment reflects on the problematic sexualized behaviors from beginning to end. Historically, interventions and techniques used to treat adults with sexual offending behaviors informed the treatment of adolescents with harmful sexual behaviors (Adler & Pruitt, 2012). Interventions used with adults, such as exploring their sexual abuse "cycle," were later used when treating adolescents. As I've noted throughout this book, adolescents who have engaged in illegal sexual behaviors should not be treated like "mini adults," just as children who've engaged in problematic sexual behaviors should not be treated like "mini adolescents." Using a one-size-fits-all paradigm will inevitably lead to faulty treatment conceptualizations, such as the idea that children have a sexual abuse "cycle." Children do not present with the same level of insight and planning as adolescents or adults. Often, a child's problematic sexual behaviors are actions of opportunity. Though the child may know that these behaviors are wrong, they do not have the same understanding as adolescents or adults, and they do not have the same level of understanding when it comes to recognizing the impact that their behaviors can have on others. This sets problematic sexual behaviors apart from the sexually abusive behaviors of adolescent or adult clients.

To help our clients see that these behaviors are an escalation of feelings, poor choices, and problematic thinking, I recommend that they engage in a visual activity to help lay these pieces out in one place. Doing so aids our clients in recognizing that their behaviors were a piece of a larger process, something that's missed when the behaviors are the only focus. Prior to doing this work, it's important to consider our client's developmental level. For older clients, or clients who are higher functioning, I often use the "staircase activity." This activity highlights the steps in which these hurtful behaviors came into fruition. If the client is younger, has trouble engaging in detailed processing, or tends to struggle with written work and prefers creative activities, I often use something called the "weed activity." This activity, like the staircase activity, is meant to help our clients understand their behaviors as a series of choices, feelings, and events, not just as behaviors that came out of nowhere. The weed activity can be viewed as a simpler version of the steps activity and is aimed at helping younger clients connect the dots between their feelings, their thoughts, and their actions.

Last, after our clients have participated in one of these two accountability activities, it is time for them to engage in a corrective process that looks at more appropriate ways to handle the feelings and thoughts that are associated with their problematic sexual behaviors. It is likely that similar thoughts or feelings will come up in the future, so it is important for them to identify where their thoughts and choices went awry and determine how they can correct them when they come up in the future. The activity I use to highlight this process is called the "flower activity." It is very similar to the "weed activity," however, there are some shifts that enable the client to make appropriate choices that end in healthy behaviors. The healthy behaviors are represented by "the flower," whereas the unhealthy behaviors are represented by "the weed." These activities are discussed in further detail below.

The Staircase

This activity involves five steps and is very similar to the feelings chain activity that the client completed in chapter 3, but it is more detailed given the knowledge they've gained over their time in treatment. This activity is generally used with the older and/or higher functioning children who have engaged in problematic sexual behaviors with another child. Start by having them draw a staircase with five steps or use the blank staircase activity provided in the appendix. Next, have the child label each of the steps: (1) "sensations and triggers," (2) "feelings," (3) "thoughts," (4) "plans," and (5) "actions." Once the staircase has been set up, the client starts to explore and list the pertinent information within each step. They label the sensations and triggers that were present, the feelings that they experienced, which then led to the thoughts of wanting to engage in problematic behaviors. Then, if applicable, they explore the plan they created to engage in these actions. As mentioned previously, children do not necessarily have a plan to engage in these behaviors as they are often actions of opportunity. That being said, older clients, or clients who have a long pattern of problematic sexual behaviors, may create plans that allow them to engage in these behaviors. If this is the case, they will explore this step. If this does not fit for the client, then they will skip this step and move on to the last step: actions. This is where they list the problematic sexual behaviors they engaged in. A breakdown of these steps is provided below.

1. Sensations/Triggers

This is the step where clients discuss the discoveries they've made in their timeline, or other areas of treatment, that point to where their behaviors may stem from. Triggers may include inappropriate material they were exposed to, their own victimization, and so on. Examples of sensations and triggers that could be listed in this step are "Feeling a tingly sensation in my genitals" or "My brother showing me pornography." This step serves to list initial impacting factors that triggered the occurrence of the following steps.

2. Feelings

This is the step where clients identify and list the feelings that stem from the triggers and sensations identified in step one. These feelings also influence the following steps. Some common feelings include curiosity, confusion, arousal, excitement, and boredom. Clients should list all of the feelings that they believe were present. Some clients may struggle with this portion of the staircase, as they are still working on connecting to their body. If this happens, I have the client move on to the next step—thoughts—and then they can come back to the feelings. The thoughts they have often stem from their feelings, therefore, they can work their way backward. For example, they may not know how they were feeling, but a thought they had was "I want to know what a vulva looks like." If they can identify this thought, the clinician can help them identify the feeling behind this as curiosity.

3. Thoughts

In this step, the client identifies the thoughts that are/have been present prior to their engagement in problematic sexual behaviors. These thoughts typically mirror the behaviors that they go on to engage in, but they can also include thoughts that they don't act on.

4. Plans

This step is one that becomes much more detailed as the client ages. Younger kids may not have a cohesive, well-thought-out plan. Again, children often engage in problematic sexual behaviors when the opportunity arises but do not often construct these opportunities. For example, a boy has been having thoughts about what it would feel like to touch another boy's penis and he finds himself outside at daycare and notices that he and another boy are under the slide together. He may take this moment to ask the boy to show him his penis, or ask the boy if he can touch it. The boy did not create this opportunity via planning; it was an opportunity that presented itself.

5. Actions

This is the final step on the staircase, and this is where the client lists the types of problematic sexual behaviors they've engaged in.

Follow-up Discussion

Once the client is done filling in the staircase, the clinician helps the child understand which steps they have control over and which steps provide opportunities to discontinue inappropriate behaviors. In doing this, the client explores alternative choices they can make should similar sensations, triggers, feelings, or thoughts come up in the future. This highlights that the child can easily "walk back down the staircase" if they have the right tools, helping them see that they have a lot of control over their choices in the future. The quicker they can turn around when they notice they are on the staircase, the safer it is. As previously noted, a blank copy of this activity and a completed example are available in the appendix.

The Weed Activity

This activity is generally used with younger children who have engaged in self-focused problematic sexual behaviors, or with young children who have acted out with another child. You can start this activity by getting a blank sheet of paper and drawing a horizontal line one-third of the way down. This line represents the ground. Under this line, your client will draw the "dirt," "seeds," and "roots," and above the line your client will eventually draw the "weed." As mentioned, this activity is like the staircase activity but geared for younger children. There may not be as much detail present in this activity, but it still provides a visual of the ways that these components are connected and how they led to the problematic sexual behaviors. The different components of this activity are explained in detail below. There is also a blank copy of this activity, along with an example, in the appendix. In the descriptions discussed below, I present the information as if I'm helping the child write the specifics with the drawing. This isn't necessary if the client wants to write it out, but I've found that younger children often ask for my help with this.

The Dirt

The dirt represents the experiences, sensations, and/or triggers that led to the feelings the client had when they engaged in their problematic sexual behaviors. Write the different triggers, sensations, and experiences in this portion of the paper.

The Seeds

The seeds represent the feelings that were present for the client when they engaged in their problematic sexual behaviors. The feelings are the element from which everything grows. Each feeling should be represented by a seed. You can write the feeling inside the seed or somewhere near the seed.

The Roots

The roots represent the thoughts that ultimately led to the problematic sexual behaviors. Typically, these thoughts closely mirror the behaviors the child engaged in. The thoughts that stem from a specific feeling should be attached to that feeling. This will look like drawing a root that comes from that seed.

The Weed

The weed represents the problematic sexual behaviors. You can have the whole weed itself represent the problematic sexual behaviors, or you can have each leaf represent a specific different behavior that the client engaged in. List their behaviors there.

Follow-up Discussion

Not only does this activity help our clients view their behaviors as a series of feelings and choices but it also depicts these behaviors as having grown over time. Our clients, just like everyone else in the world, will continue to grow, and this activity shows that they have power and control over how they choose to grow, and this is demonstrated in their future actions. If they choose to disregard everything they have learned in treatment, and continue on the path of hurtful behaviors, they will grow, but in ways that are harmful to themselves and others. This is why the activity portrays their harmful actions as a weed. Weeds are often unwanted, and we pluck them from gardens. We, as clinicians, can provide our clients with the tools to eradicate the weeds from their gardens, but they must make the choice to uproot and kill these weeds, meaning they must make the choice to discontinue problematic sexual behaviors. After choosing to discontinue these behaviors we can help them replace these weeds with beautiful, healthy new flowers. These flowers are the appropriate and healthy behaviors they can choose to engage in. Treatment is meant to help children grow in positive ways and support them in making healthier and safer choices in the future. The following activity is meant to represent just that.

The Flower Activity

This activity is like the weed activity, as there is dirt, seeds, and roots; however, instead of a weed, it has been replaced by a flower. The purpose of this activity is to explore how our clients can avoid any future problematic or harmful sexual behaviors by replacing unhealthy thoughts with thoughts that will produce positive and healthy behaviors and choices. This activity allows them to explore other ways to handle their feelings, and how they can handle challenging triggers or experiences in the future. The different components of this activity are explained below.

The Dirt

The dirt represents the experiences, sensations, and/or triggers that led to the feelings the client had at the time they engaged in their problematic sexual behaviors. This will be exactly as it was in the weed activity, with no changes.

The Seeds

The seeds represent the feelings that were present for the client when they engaged in their problematic sexual behaviors. Again, this will be exactly the same as the weed activity with no changes.

The Roots

This is where the activity begins to change. In the weed activity, the roots represented the unhealthy thoughts that ultimately led to the problematic sexual behaviors. In this activity, the client is going to come up with healthy thoughts and ways to manage the feelings that were present when they sexually acted out. This is important because no one can control their feelings, and it is likely that these feelings will resurface in the future. Though we can't control our feelings, we can control our behaviors and how we react to feelings, and these behaviors start with thoughts. In this exercise, clients can be proactive and come up with some healthy and appropriate ways to deal with these feelings when they appear again in the future. Caregivers can also act as supports here and help their child come up with ideas for a healthy plan of action.

The Flower

The flower represents the positive behaviors that we want to see flourish. These behaviors can be different interventions our clients have learned, such as reaching out to a trusted adult for support, engaging in healthy masturbation, distracting themself with a fun activity, and so on. The client should list as many healthy behaviors as they can think of, and the clinician and caregiver can provide additional interventions and behaviors once the child is done.

Follow-up Discussion

After this activity is completed, it is important that it's shared with the client's caregiver(s) if they were not present during the activity. The caregiver(s) should be aware of the client's triggers and feelings at the time of the acting-out behaviors, as this allows them to better support their child in the future. Reflecting on this activity with their child will also give them insight into the type of thinking that led to the acting-out behaviors and how they can better check in with and support their child in the future. This helps them better understand the role they have in supporting their child's healthy choices, encouraging new healthy behaviors, and helping their child avoid unhealthy patterns.

Chapter 6

Healthy Relationships and Appropriate Sexuality

When working with young children who have engaged in problematic sexual behaviors, I believe that one of the most important pieces of treatment is building their knowledge of healthy relationships and appropriate sexuality. Developmentally, empathy work and accountability work will look different when working with younger kids; however, the healthy relationships portion of treatment remains relatively similar to the work I do with adolescents. Regardless of age, healthy relationships contain similar components. Whether someone is nine years old or ninety years old, they deserve to be respected in their relationships and to feel safe and comfortable. One way to promote this is to teach our clients the different components of a healthy relationship and ensure that each component is present within their important relationships. If they notice that some of these components are missing within an important relationship, we can explore the changes that would need to be made to improve the relationship.

Obviously, our clients are at an age where deeply romantic relationships are not appropriate; however, platonic friendships are always appropriate, and these relationships can be equally fulfilling and meaningful. When children grow up with healthy friendships, they have a better framework for what healthy romantic relationships should look and feel like in the future. Giving our clients the tools to ensure healthy friendships is setting them up for successful and healthy relationships in the future, platonic and romantic. When addressing this treatment module, the three biggest features I focus on are the components of a healthy relationship, consent, and how to stay safe and keep others safe in relationships. These topics are discussed in detail below.

COMPONENTS OF A HEALTHY RELATIONSHIP

When we stop and think about the different parts of a healthy relationship, we may struggle to isolate the most important pieces, get bogged down in details, or feel rather uncertain about the true definition of a healthy relationship. Fear not, understanding the most important elements that make up a healthy relationship can be boiled down into one simple acronym: CERTS.

CERTS

CERTS is an acronym used to easily remember the different components of a healthy relationship. CERTS stands for consent, equality, respect, trust, and safety. Our clients should have a good understanding of each of these components, and they should be discussed in detail. Regardless of age, I always teach this piece of treatment. This information is a fundamental part of preventing further unsafe behaviors and unsafe relationships, both for our clients and those around our clients.

Consent

Consent, when we boil it down, is permission. Consent is the permission we need to move forward with doing something. Consent occurs when one person voluntarily agrees to the proposal of another person. When explaining consent to younger clients, it's recommended that the definition be as simple and straightforward as possible. When working with young clients, I usually break consent down into two main parts: asking and listening. The younger the client is, the more black-and-white I try and make this concept. At the beginning of treatment, they are taught that before entering anyone's "bubble space" or touching anyone's things, they need to get consent. This means they need to *ask* and then *listen* to the answer they are given. They are taught that if the person says, "Yes," they have received consent, but if the person says, "No," does not answer, or appears uncertain of what is being asked, then they have not received consent and should not move forward with what they were asking to do. For young children, "Yes," is the golden word when we are talking about consent. Though we as adults know that consent is not this black-and-white, I present it this way when I'm first teaching this concept to young children. Once they have a firm understanding of the basics regarding consent, I start to discuss more of the nuance. An example of this nuance would be discussing the legal age of consent for activities. I teach clients that children cannot legally consent to certain things, such as signing legal documents, marriage, joining the military, voting, or consenting to sexual behaviors. This highlights the gray areas of consent, where yes doesn't always mean yes.

With some of the older children I work with, I provide psychoeducation and discuss the different types of consent, like implicit versus explicit consent. This conversation is only appropriate for those who have a good understanding of consent and do well with abstract thinking, otherwise this can be confusing. Ultimately, each of our clients should understand consent at its core and feel confident in their ability to ask for consent and understand when it is being given.

Equality

When discussing equality within a relationship, I break it down and describe it as *shared power, knowledge,* and *age.* Obviously, there are additional factors when it comes to equality in relationships, but for the sake of teaching this to those under the age of twelve, we focus on these three elements. An important component of consent is being informed and understanding what is being asked of you, and this too is something that is required to have equality within a relationship. If there are different levels of knowledge between two people, this can lead to power imbalances. If there are large knowledge differences, like the differences in knowledge between a seven-year-old and a twelve-year-old, this creates inequality, whereas having shared knowledge fosters equality. If one person is making all of the choices this leads to inequality within the relationship. An example I use to display this is, "If your sibling always got to choose the movie, would that be fair?" which is generally met with a resounding, "No!" and then we explore how we could make it fairer.

Last, age is an important piece of equality, and tends to be more important the younger someone is. A five-year difference between a forty- and forty-five-year-old does not create vast power differences, whereas that same five-year difference between a five- and ten-year-old, or a ten- and fifteen-year-old, creates very big power imbalances. Age gaps have the potential to be much more problematic for younger individuals, as the developmental periods between ages are much larger. The bigger the age gap, the more unequal the knowledge, thus the more unequal the power is between the two individuals. A rule of thumb is that if an individual is more, or less, than two years younger than a client there needs to be additional conversations to address and create equality within the relationship.

Respect

Typically, this component of CERTS is the easiest to teach, as most clients have already had some sort of education regarding respect. This is often seen in the form of the Golden Rule: treat others as you would like to be treated. When talking about respect and its role in healthy relationships, I believe that it is intrinsically linked to boundaries. If a boundary is set and the other person ignores it, it can be seen as disrespectful or unhealthy, but at its worst, it can be unsafe. People can show respect through their words, as well as actions, and it is imperative that our clients understand how to engage in relationships in a healthy and respectful way, verbally and nonverbally.

Trust

Once again, many of our clients have a pretty good idea of what trust is, as it's talked about in everyday life. I teach clients that trust is built over time and needs consistent tending to. I explain that once you have built trust, this does not mean that it will automatically remain. Trust is something that is ever evolving and based on interactions between people. Teaching kids that trust is built over time helps them understand that a trusting relationship requires knowing the person. This helps with safety, as they learn that getting to know someone takes time and they cannot trust someone until they have witnessed how this person behaves in a multitude of situations.

In this section, I also teach my clients about how quickly trust can be broken. Unlike building trust, losing trust can happen in a matter of seconds. Typically, each client you meet can provide a personal example of how they have lost trust by lying or sneaking and can provide examples of how others have broken their trust. In some cases, breaking someone's trust might involve many small choices over a period of time. In other cases, breaking someone's trust can involve one big event, such as engaging in problematic sexual behaviors. Behaviors like stealing someone's cookie or touching someone's buttocks can be quick, but they can have a long-lasting impact on trust. For this reason, it's important that we teach clients about ways to maintain and build trust, as well as ways to avoid breaking trust.

Safety

When discussing safety with clients, I often have them imagine a time when they felt safe, and then I have them describe it to me. We further explore the scenario they imagined, and process what about it made them feel safe. In doing this, they realize that safety is not just a physical quality, but it is an emotional one as well. Within this section, clients explore what it is that makes them feel safe and how to ensure these needs are being met within their relationships. We discuss holistic safety, which includes the body, mind, and feelings, and what to do should they feel that their safety is being compromised. They may come up with a variety of ideas, but one that is always emphasized is seeking out a safe adult when they feel that their safety has been broken, or if they are feeling uncomfortable about a situation or person.

With older clients, this section can be broken down further into two types of safety: holistic safety and sexual safety. Holistic safety is discussed above. With clients who are nearing the age of puberty, it can be helpful to provide education around sexual safety. Though this may seem counterintuitive, it's important. The reality is that many children in today's world are exposed to sexual material at an early age, and providing them with tools to keep themselves safe as they grow up and navigate society is important. Delaying information about safe sex, how to keep their bodies healthy, and sexually transmitted disease (STD) prevention does not delay sexual activity, but it does encourage sexually transmitted infection (STI) prevention, testing, and treatment. Not only does a lack of high-quality and age-appropriate information about developmentally appropriate sexuality lead to an increase in STIs, unwanted pregnancies, and so on, but it also leaves children vulnerable to sexual harm and exploitation. A lack of education ultimately leads to unsafe behaviors and choices. This information should be presented in a developmentally appropriate way, and it should not be skipped over just because the clients we are working with are "young."

Follow-up Discussion

Once clients have learned the different components of a healthy relationship, we will use this information and walk through a few of their important relationships. I typically use a relationship with a caregiver, a relationship with a best friend, and, if applicable, the relationship they had/have with the child they engaged in problematic sexual behaviors with. Each of these relationships have distinct differences that we can explore.

When it comes to a relationship with a caregiver, there are definite differences in equality, as there should be. It is not expected that a caregiver and a child have the same level of power in their relationship, but this does not mean that the relationship is inherently unhealthy. I ask the client to explore other ways that their caregiver gives them power, even if the caregiver is the one who makes many of the decisions, like the house rules. Shared power can be seen in the bodily autonomy caregivers afford their kids. A client may discuss their ability to choose what they wear to school, decide what cartoons they watch, or have control over their body and choose when and whether they want to give caregivers a hug. This demonstrates to the child that though their caregivers have more power in the relationship, there are pieces of equality present, and this power imbalance does not mean it's unhealthy.

The relationship they have with a best friend is often explored in detail, as this relationship, unlike the relationship with their caregiver, should be a more straightforward example of a relationship that contains each component of CERTS. We will discuss the different ways they practice consent with their friend, and the ways their friend practices consent with them. After providing a few examples, we will also explore ways they keep their relationship feeling equal, the different ways they show respect for one another, how they have built trust with each other, and ways that they are safe with one another. We will also talk about what they can do should one of these components become damaged, like getting into a fight and calling their friend a mean name. This action will surely upset their friend, leading to a small rupture in trust and their friend feeling disrespected. These ruptures are a normal part of relationships, but the important piece is that there is repair. We will explore this together, discuss ways that they can repair the relationship, and what they can do to avoid similar situations in the future. This will highlight the importance of tending to relationships and building an understanding that relationships are fluid and that sometimes components of CERTS will be stronger than others.

Last, looking at the relationship with the person they engaged in problematic sexual behaviors with can help highlight the components of CERTS that were missing, or the components of CERTS that were broken when they engaged in these behaviors. This helps highlight the interconnected nature of these components and demonstrates that when one component is ignored or broken, it has a domino effect—all other components are often impacted. Each client will be different, but one broad example of this would be to start by looking at trust. Let's say the client engaged in problematic sexual behaviors with their younger sibling. Engaging in these behaviors clearly broke their sibling's trust, and in fact, the child may have used their sibling's trust to engage in the behaviors in the first place. If the child has misused their sibling's trust, this demonstrates that the child was not being respectful as they acted in unsafe ways and hurt their sibling's body. Safety was missing, as the younger child could not give consent. Though the younger sibling may have agreed to engage in the behaviors, they did not have an equal understanding of what it was they were consenting to, as the older sibling had more power and knowledge. The child may have tricked their younger sibling into these behaviors, demonstrating the power imbalances present.

COMPONENTS OF CONSENT

Though my conversation about consent starts with teaching children the basics of consent, asking and listening, it typically evolves into a more nuanced conversation that includes the acronym created by Planned Parenthood: FRIES. This five-letter acronym helps break down the components that must be present to receive, or give, healthy and true consent. FRIES stands for freely given, reversible, informed, enthusiastic, and specific.

Depending on the age and developmental level of our clients, this portion of treatment may be condensed and discussed along with CERTS. I, however, like to make FRIES its own section to bolster a deeper understanding and richer conversation around consent. Consent, as mentioned above, is often taught in absolutes, like, "Yes means yes, and no means no." Though this can be a helpful framework for young children, this conversation must evolve, as this interpretation fails to look at the details important to consent. If someone says, "Yes," but they have no idea what they are agreeing to, then this is not, in fact, consent. I teach clients that consent is a mutual understanding and agreement, and each of the components below are required to reach this mutual understanding and agreement.

Freely Given

Consent needs to be freely given. This means that if anyone is bribed, tricked, threatened, guilted, or coerced into saying, "Yes," then they have not given consent. Consent is when they are saying yes, because they want to say yes! I provide examples to highlight the importance of consent being freely given, and how it may feel if this component of consent is ignored. An example I may use to highlight this feature of consent is:

> Imagine you are sitting down to eat lunch. You are starving and you know that your caregiver packed you your favorite dessert, a big chocolate chip cookie. As you are about to take a bite of your cookie, your friend walks up and plops down next to you. They look at you, they look at your cookie, and then, with the best puppy dog eyes they can muster they say, "I'm so hungry, I forgot my lunch today. Can I *please* have your cookie?" Now, you've been looking forward to this cookie all day, and you really want the cookie yourself. You hesitate and your friend goes, "Please, please, pleeeeease." You don't want to give them the cookie, but you feel guilty and don't want them to think you're a bad friend, so you reluctantly give them your cookie.

After going through this example I ask, "So, is this consent?" This highlights the ways that people can guilt us into doing things we don't want to do. Even though the example may look like consent, consent does not occur unless both people are wanting and agreeing to the behavior/choice/arrangement, and it's clear that if given their way, the child from the example would not have freely given up their chocolate chip cookie.

Reversible

It's important to clarify that consent can be given and then taken away. Just because someone says, "Yes," does not mean that this decision has been set in stone. Once someone says, "No," clients are taught that this needs to be accepted and whatever the person originally consented to needs to stop immediately. An example I may use to highlight this is:

> My friends, Mica and Erica, ask if I want to go to the mall after work. I tell them I'd love to since I need a new pair of shoes and I haven't seen them in a while. I'm super excited to join them, but as the day continues, I develop a massive headache. By the end of the workday, my head is pounding, and I no longer feel like going to the mall. I reach out to Mica and Erica and tell them I have a headache and I won't be able to meet up with them. They are bummed but say that they understand and that we can go to the mall when I'm feeling better.

After finishing my example, I ask my clients, "So, what do you think, did Erica and Mica respect my decision of reversing my consent?" In this example, they followed this component of consent and allowed me to reverse my initial consent. This highlights the reality that someone can say yes to something and then change their mind, and that's okay! We might think that we want to do something, but then when we are doing it, we change our mind. If someone forces us to continue doing something once we've changed our mind, this is not consent.

Informed

To give consent, one must know what they are agreeing to. If someone agrees to something that they don't understand, they can't actually be a consenting participant due to their lack of knowledge on the subject. We can't agree to something if we don't know what it is we are agreeing to. This component of consent is closely linked to the "s" in FRIES: specific. I may mention this briefly but tend to hold off until we are talking about that component, so I don't confuse clients. A silly example I use to highlight the importance of being informed is: "I tell my friend Josh that I'm going to lunch and ask if he wants to join. I tell him I'm going to [insert gibberish that makes no sense]."

Now, in this example, Josh can technically say, "Yes"; however, I ask my clients if this would be true consent. The answer is no. Josh has no idea what he is consenting to. I would have to provide him information, like [the gibberish place] is a hole-in-the-wall restaurant five hours away. If Josh knew this, he'd probably say no; I mean, who wants to drive five hours for lunch? Since Josh doesn't have this information, even if he said yes, he doesn't have enough information to know what he is agreeing to, and this is not consent.

Enthusiastic

Enthusiastic consent is exactly what it sounds like—enthusiastic! Agreeing to do something should come from a place of wanting to do it. If someone is saying, "Yes," to please others, is fearful of the consequences of saying, "No," or they hesitate in giving their consent, this means that there needs to be a more in-depth conversation and boundaries need to be respected until everyone is giving enthusiastic consent. For younger children, I might change the word "enthusiastic" to "excited," but the concept remains the same. An example of consent being enthusiastic is:

> Let's say I'm walking down the street with Chad, and he sees an ice cream shop. He stops and says, "Hey, do you want to grab an ice cream?" I say, "Yes! I've been craving ice cream all week!"

I then provide an alternative to this scenario:

> Now, let's say I'm walking down the street with Chad, and he sees an ice cream shop and says, "Hey, do you want to grab an ice cream?" I think about it, but I'm still super full from the dinner I just ate. I love ice cream, but I feel like it might be too much. I don't want to disappoint Chad, so I say, "Uh, yeah, um I guess," knowing I'm not feeling like eating ice cream.

After providing both examples, I'll have clients compare them. In the first example, it's clear I'm excited about getting an ice cream, thus this highlights enthusiastic consent. In the second example, I definitely seem more unsure, and might be saying yes to please Chad. In this scenario, I ask them what they think Chad should do. I follow up on whatever it is they shared, and explain that even though I said yes, Chad should pause and check in with me. I seemed unsure, so he could have said something like, "Are you sure? It seems like you aren't that excited to get ice cream. I know we just had a big dinner so we can always pass." This check-in allows me to either say something like, "Yeah, you're right, I don't think I actually want ice cream," or, if I think about it and ice cream does sound good it gives me the opportunity to say, "Yeah, I'm sure! I'm still pretty full but I'll get some, I can always put it in the freezer if I change my mind." This also highlights consent being reversible, as I can say yes to ice cream in the moment but can change my mind mid-treat. I teach my clients that it's always a good idea to double-check if someone seems uncertain.

Specific

I teach my clients that at this point in their lives, giving consent, or asking for consent, needs to be explicit and detailed. With older clients, we may have explored the differences between implicit and explicit consent while learning about CERTS; however, I explain that explicit, or specific, consent is the safest type of consent. Since they are seeing me due to past unsafe behaviors that have typically broken someone's consent, I explain that they need to practice and use explicit consent. I use the following example to highlight the concept of specificity, as this is often an abstract concept for clients:

> When you go to a restaurant and the waiter asks, "What would you like to eat?" do you say, "Food, please"? Usually, this gets a chuckle, and then I'll explain that we are being specific when we ask for a certain food item that's on the menu. To follow up on our restaurant example, this might sound like, "I would like the chicken salad sandwich with fries, please." This tells the waiter exactly what it is I am asking for, and there is no room for confusion.

I also explain that saying yes to one thing does not mean that I'm saying yes to multiple things. I highlight this feature of being specific with consent by using the following example:

> If I ask to borrow Anna's pen, and she say, "Yes," does that mean I can also borrow her calculator, markers, and paper that are also on her desk? Or, if I ask to borrow Anna's pen today and she say, "Yes," does that automatically mean that I can borrow her pen the next time I see her and I don't have to ask?

Clients will typically laugh, roll their eyes, or a mixture of the two. Then we return to the examples and I explain that just because Anna said yes to me borrowing her pen once does not give me permission to use her pen all the time. I need to ask each time I want to borrow her pen. The same is true of the other items on her desk. Just because she let me borrow her pen does not mean that she is consenting to my use of her markers, calculator, or other items. If I want to use those items, I need to be specific and ask.

HELPFUL TOOLS TO TEACH CERTS AND FRIES

Some supplemental materials I use when teaching clients about healthy relationships and consent include games and videos. There are several videos available on the internet if you type in words related to these topics, like "consent," "consent for kids," "teaching kids about consent," and so on. You can look through the different videos available and see which ones you prefer. I find that there are some videos that are better suited for my young clients, whereas others may be too advanced and are better suited for my older clients. Sometimes I'll use these videos before teaching kids about these topics.

Other times I may follow up with these videos or use them in tandem with their learning. It just depends on the client, their style of learning, and what is going to be most helpful in aiding them with understanding and retention of the material.

In addition to videos, I will also use games to teach the components detailed above. An example of a game I frequently use is called the "flower game." This game is another version of the game, "hangman," but one that I find more appropriate and less problematic. I find that if I present information in a game format my clients are more interested in the topic and willing to learn each of the components. I often play the "flower game" to help them guess the different letters while allowing them to come up with the word on their own. I've found that their investment in figuring out the word has a positive impact on their retention. Once they have figured out the word by guessing the different letters, the information discussed above can be taught, and any questions they have regarding the material can be answered.

Setting up the Flower Game

With an appropriate word in mind, the clinician will draw horizontal lines, one for each letter of the selected word. The client will guess different letters. If they guess a correct letter, the clinician will write it in the appropriate spot. If the client guesses an incorrect letter, one part of the flower will be filled in. This process repeats until the child has either guessed the word or the flower is completely colored in, and they have run out of guesses. The great part about using a flower is that you can add as many or as few petals as you like. For younger children I will add many petals so that they have a lot of guesses and do not get discouraged or feel like they "lost" the game. For my older clients, I might not provide as many petals, as I want to challenge them, and they like the competitive aspect of the game.

SAFETY IN RELATIONSHIPS

Along with discussing healthy relationships with others close to them, it is important to discuss healthy and safe relationships with oneself, and safety in the community or around others the client may not be familiar with. It's especially important that we discuss community safety with our younger clients. When children are engaging in sexual acting-out behaviors, it is apparent that they lack healthy boundaries, and this can sometimes translate into a lack of awareness of "stranger danger." This puts them at risk of being hurt and taken advantage of, thus, it is important to discuss safety protocol when they are in the community.

I often assess their level of comfort around strangers by creating a scenario and then asking them questions. You can tailor your scenario to the client and highlight the important pieces you are assessing. Here is an example that can be used universally:

> You are at the park playing, and your mom had to go to the car to get something. While she is gone a woman comes up to you crying and telling you she's lost her puppy on the other side of the park. She asks if you will help her look for it. What do you say to her? What do you do?

This type of question allows the clinician to gauge the client's awareness and understanding of ways to stay safe around strangers, and while in the community. If the client is quick to join the woman, then it is clear they need education about safety. We should be teaching our clients the importance of being cautious around people they don't know, how to uphold safe and appropriate boundaries, and what to do should they feel uncomfortable. I remind them that they have control over their body and their choices, and if someone is trying to get them to do something they don't like, they can say no and leave the situation, and should immediately seek out a safe and trusted adult.

As for personal safety, this is where clinicians can provide psychoeducation around appropriate sexuality, avoidance of self-harming behaviors, and revisit healthy masturbation. By this time, clients should have a good understanding of the elements required for masturbation (or self-touch) to be healthy. I continue to normalize feelings such as arousal, and the tools clients can use to get their needs met. I revisit the basics of healthy masturbation, reviewing the need for privacy, hygiene practices, and avoiding pornography. After reviewing the components of healthy masturbation (i.e., only engaging in these behaviors at home, only engaging in these behaviors in their bedroom with the door closed and locked, only engaging in these behaviors when they are alone, not watching pornography, listening to their body and not engaging in these behaviors to the point of self-injury, and cleaning up after themselves), I typically begin treatment work that addresses pornography consumption.

PSYCHOEDUCATION RELATED TO PORNOGRAPHY

This piece of treatment can vary drastically depending on the needs of the client. If the client has no history of pornography use, then this portion of treatment may be short and succinct. If the client has a history of extensive pornography use, then this portion of treatment will be lengthier. Clinicians will need to assess the impact that pornography has had on their clients, the level of exposure their clients have had to this material, and then engage their clients in treatment that addresses their specific needs. I've provided a brief summary of the way I work with clients who have minimal exposure to pornography, as well as the way I work with clients who have had extensive exposure and pornography use. I will always speak with the caregiver(s) prior to engaging in this work. Similarly to the sexual education discussion talked about above, I explain the importance of providing accurate and age-appropriate education. I acknowledge any concerns or discomfort they may have, while also discussing the ever-present nature of pornography and preparing their child with education to better prevent any future struggles with pornography use.

For Those With Minimal Pornography Exposure

First, I assess whether the client has ever heard of the word, "pornography." If not, I provide an age-appropriate definition like, "Pornography is a fancy word that people use when they are talking about pictures or videos that have naked people who are usually engaging in sexual touch." This provides them with an understanding of the topic and uses language that they've used throughout their treatment. Providing them with an honest definition is important. If we gloss over the definition of pornography, or avoid answering the questions they have, they may grow curious and seek this information out on their own. After explaining what pornography is in an age-appropriate way, I ask them if they have any questions. If not, we move on, but if they do, I do my best to answer them. After addressing any questions, I ask my clients if they have ever seen, looked up, or been shown pictures or videos of naked people who were engaging in sexual touch. This helps me determine whether they have been exposed to pornography. Typically, our youngest clients present as the most unaware when it comes to pornography, but this is not always the case, which is why it's important to assess.

With clients who have had brief, minimal, or no exposure to pornography, there is less of a need to go into details regarding the ways that pornography can impact the brain and relationships. I provide some psychoeducation around how unrealistic pornography is, and how this content can be confusing for kids. Though some of our clients have never seen or heard of pornography, it is important that we still address the topic. As clients grow up, they are certain to come across this content. Whether it is purposeful, accidental, or via peers engaging in conversations or viewing pornography around them, they need to be prepared.

Once clients understand what it is we are discussing, I provide an appropriate level of information. It is important to prepare them and inform them of the unrealistic dynamics and expectations that are often seen in pornography (because, again, they will eventually encounter this material). This can be as simple as comparing pornography to the movies. Often kids, even when they are young, know that movies involve actors, lighting, makeup, and so on. They understand that movies aren't real stories but scripts. The same can be said of pornography, and I share that these scripts are often unhealthy and do not involve the components of consent, or the components of a healthy relationship. Simply sharing the unrealistic nature of pornography and comparing it to movies can help create a framework for children when they do come across this content.

After this conversation, and providing education, I facilitate an activity where I ask the client to describe their favorite movie. I ask them to discuss all the really cool parts, and then ask them how they think the directors and actors were able to make those parts happen. They might discuss special effects, makeup, green screens, and so on. I then explain that the inappropriate videos of naked people engaging in sexual touch is similar. I explain the shared elements, like makeup, directors, actors, pretending and acting, tricks with the camera that makes things look different, and so on. Then I go back to their favorite movie and say something like, "That movie sounds so cool! Do you think that it's real? Do you think that would happen in real life?" Most of the time clients will acknowledge that it's unrealistic, and if they don't, I will help them to this conclusion. Then I state that it's the same thing with pornography. People may think it looks fun and exciting, but it's not real, and it doesn't depict real-life sexual relationships.

For Those With Problematic Pornography Use

For clients who have been using pornography regularly, have a history of using pornography, or perhaps pornography played a distinct role in their problematic sexual behaviors, this portion of treatment will look different. Though some of the conversations around this topic will be similar to what was discussed above, these clients will engage in more extensive psychoeducation regarding the impacts of pornography, how it can impact their brains, and what they may have "learned" about sex from pornography.

The work done with these clients is more like the work done with adolescents. I will provide information about the addictive qualities of pornography, and why it can be challenging to give this material up. I provide information about the "feel-good chemicals" that are released in the brain while watching pornography, and how bodies can grow to crave these chemicals, thus encouraging us to engage in activities that our brains know will provide these chemicals. I also discuss the novelty that pornography provides, and how this can be a slippery slope into unhealthy views on sexuality, and escalating pornography use.

I highlight this aspect by using an example involving food. I ask them what their favorite dessert is. For this example, let's say the answer is a brownie. I might say something like, "Let's pretend you've never had a brownie before. What do you think it will be like the first time you try a brownie?" Knowing that brownies are their favorite, they might say something like, "It would be incredible! I'd probably think it's the best thing I've ever eaten." Then I say, "All right, now imagine that all you can eat is brownie. That might be great for the first week, but what do you think will happen eventually?" At first, they may share that they'd never get sick of eating brownies, but eventually they will conclude that they would get sick of brownies. I explain that the same thing can happen with pornography. Now I'll ask the client what their second-favorite dessert is, and let's say it's taffy. I go through this example again, but this time I say, "Okay, so you've been eating nothing but brownies for two weeks when suddenly you are offered some taffy. What do you think you'd do, keep eating the brownies, or take the taffy?" Almost always, they state that they'd switch over to the taffy. I explain that this process continues, and each time a new dessert is added, they are likely to choose the new dessert because they are sick of the old dessert, eating it no longer excites them the way it used to, and the novelty has worn off. I point out that this is exactly like watching pornography, however, unlike desserts, there is a never-ending supply of new and novel pornography.

This highlights how pornography use can escalate, and how people can find themselves watching things that they would have never watched or been interested in when they first started watching pornography. We will collaboratively explore the issues that this could bring up. I also discuss the unrealistic nature of pornography and use a similar exercise to the one discussed in the "minimal pornography exposure" section above. After describing the unhealthy and unrealistic dynamics of pornography, we explore the role that CERTS and FRIES plays in pornography. Spoiler alert, these components rarely make an appearance in pornography. This is explored via the context of consent, healthy relationships, and what kids may be learning when these important safety components are missing. Last, we explore the ways that pornography impacted their engagement in problematic sexual behaviors. We look at the curiosities it created, unhealthy thoughts or thought patterns that were created, the unrealistic information they "learned," and any other ways it may have contributed to the problematic sexual behaviors.

Can We Stop Them?

This is a tricky question. Can we stop children from accessing pornography? The short answer is no. Given the deep-rooted place that internet has in our daily lives, it would be nearly impossible to completely stop someone from accessing pornographic material. For this reason, I view treatment work around pornography as a form of prevention. Though it may not prevent clients from accessing pornography later in their lives, it does provide clients with the skills needed to be smart consumers. Others may disagree with this approach and view this work through an abstinence-only lens. Though I can understand reasons for wanting to take this approach, I believe it is rooted in fear and prevents sufficient education. Educating our clients about the various issues present in pornography, ranging from unhealthy power dynamics to unrealistic expectations around sex, provides them with the information needed to reject the unhealthy myths that are often scripted and pushed in pornography.

Though there is no foolproof way to completely stop a child from accessing pornography, there are tools that can make this access much more challenging. I often speak with caregivers, and clients, about different tools that can limit the child's accessibility to pornographic content via technology. We discuss a variety of tools that include parent controls on devices that access the internet (such as phones, tablets, gaming devices, and smart televisions), appropriate supervision while their child is using the internet or devices that can access the internet, discouraging the use of technology devices in private places like the child's bedroom or bathroom, and having frank conversations around internet safety. We also discuss ways that the child can handle situations if they are feeling tempted to access pornography, or if someone has shown them pornography. Some caregiver(s) may check their child's search history in addition to the ideas discussed above, and though this may seem like a breach of privacy, children are children and it's part of a caregiver(s) job to protect their child from inappropriate and unhealthy materials the best they can.

Chapter 7

Empathy and Awareness

Developmentally, young children may struggle to grasp the concept and skills of empathy, as their view of the world is still very egocentric. However, we see that empathy skills grow as the child becomes more versed in assessing and sharing their feelings, and through the encouraging and empathetic responses modeled by caregivers. Empathy correlates with emotional recognition and the ability to recognize one's impact on others. Aiding clients in building stronger empathetic abilities will also enable them to have a better understanding of the impacts and consequences their actions can have on both themself and others.

Helping our clients develop a deeper understanding of the impact that their words and behaviors have on others provides another protective layer against future harmful behaviors, like bullying or problematic sexual behaviors. Most children, like most people in this world, do not want to be perceived as malicious, mean, or callous, therefore, they would not purposefully engage in behaviors that would lead others to see them in this way. Helping clients understand the difference between intent versus impact is an important part of the empathy-building process. If they can take the time to pause and think about how the other person may perceive or be impacted by their actions, they can assess whether this is the type of impact they'd like to have on the person.

Describing intent versus impact is one of the first steps in helping our clients recognize that all behaviors will have an impact. I explain that impacts can be negative or positive, and this is dependent on how their action is perceived by the other person. Helping them understand that their intentions behind an action are not as important as the impacts behind an action helps expand the lens in which they view their actions. Looking at behaviors from this perspective allows them to take a step and view their future actions or conversations through the eyes of the person they are speaking to or acting toward. These skills strengthen with time and age but also with practice. We should not expect our clients to be adept at these skills right away, but what we can expect is practice. If our clients continue to practice these skills in the treatment room, community, and at home, they will leave treatment with a stronger understanding of the inherent power their behaviors and words hold.

INTENT VERSUS IMPACT AND EMPATHY VERSUS SYMPATHY

This section will discuss the ways that you can broach this topic with your clients and provides examples of activities and ideas you can use to help your clients solidify their understanding of these concepts and skills.

Intent Versus Impact

The intent of our actions is not as important as the impact. What does the intent of our actions matter if our actions have hurtful impacts on those around us? Helping kids understand that their intentions may have been pure but the impacts were hurtful is another step toward building an empathetic worldview and caring for others outside of themselves. Teaching them that their needs are important, but that their needs should not come at the expense of others, is imperative to creating healthy and safe behaviors and choices in the future. Having an empathetic worldview where they take the experiences of others into consideration will lead to healthier relationships, increase their compassion, and increase prosocial choices. Explaining this concept to children can be challenging but providing real-world examples can be helpful. Clinicians can use the following activity to further this conversation.

Intent Versus Impact Activity

To cement the concept of intent versus impact, I have my clients participate in an activity where they take a piece of paper and fold it in half. One half is labeled "intent" and the other "impact." Once this is done, I have my client tell me about a time they got into trouble at school or at home for something they "accidentally" did. If they can't come up with an example, you can also ask about a time when they got in trouble for something that they felt was unfair. After picking an example of a time they got into trouble, we discuss the intentions behind their actions on the "intentions" side of the paper and, on the "impact" half, we write the facts of what happened in the chosen situation. For younger clients, or for clients who would benefit, we do the same activity, but intentions are labeled "what I wanted to happen" and the impacts are labeled "what actually happened."

The activity starts with your client choosing their example and writing it at the top of the sheet of paper: "One time I was outside playing with my truck and my little sister came over and sat down. She started touching my truck and trying to play with me and I told her to leave me alone. I grabbed my truck back from her, and then she started crying." When asked about the intention of these actions, my client responds, "I just wanted to be by myself, so I told my sister that." At first glance, the child might think that they've done what any sibling would do, and they feel justified in the way they handled the situation. They may say their intention was not to be mean or to hurt their sibling's feelings; rather, they told their sibling that they didn't want to play. After writing this under intent, we move to the impact portion of the paper.

Here the clinician can help the client come up with the outcome of the situation based on the facts that the client shares. They may say something like, "My sister started crying, then she went inside and told Mom, and then I got into trouble." They still may not understand why they got into trouble, and this is where breaking down intent versus impact comes into play. I summarize my client's intentions while also acknowledging the impact. I might say something like, "Your intention was to play alone, but when you made the choice to speak with your sister that way and grab your truck, the impact of your behaviors was hurtful, as seen by her tears." I explain that even though their intention was not to hurt their sister's feelings, this was in fact the impact. We then explore how and why their sister may have seen these behaviors as hurtful. This allows us to take the perspective of the client's sister, broadening their view of the situation. If they struggle with this, have them participate in a perspective-taking exercise.

You can create a similar scenario, but in this case, your client will be the person who was hurt. As an example, you can say, "You are at recess, and you see your friend playing basketball, you go over and grab the ball when it bounces your way because you want to play with him. He grabs the ball back and says, 'Leave me alone.' How does that make you feel?" This scenario can be explored, and the client can discuss the impact their friend's behaviors had on them. Next, they can explore the ways in which they'd like their friend to behave/speak with them in the future should their friend want space.

Empathy Versus Sympathy

Helping our clients understand the difference between empathy and sympathy can help them increase their awareness around the ways they respond to different scenarios in their lives. These two concepts are slightly more abstract than intent versus impact, as they are based on the experience of feelings, rather than observable facts. Empathy is vicariously experiencing the emotions of another person. You experience these emotions as if they were your own. Sympathy is the act of feeling for someone. With sympathy, you do not experience this person's emotions, you stay in your own emotions while acknowledging theirs. Empathy can be described as feeling *with* someone, and sympathy can be described as feeling *for* someone. Sympathy allows you to keep a comfortable distance from someone else's pain, whereas empathy puts you in someone else's pain, therefore, you experience their pain with them.

After providing information on both topics, I ask my client to share a time when they experienced empathy and a time when they experienced sympathy, and then we will compare and contrast these experiences. I also find that, along with this brief activity, utilizing their caregiver can help model empathy, further discussed below.

PSYCHOEDUCATION FOR CAREGIVERS REGARDING EMPATHY

Empathy typically progresses with age, but caregivers can help tend to this process and help their child grow this skill. Caregivers can utilize modeling behaviors and discuss these concepts, as well as model feelings and impacts with their kids. I have gone into each of these tools in more detail below. These are just a few of the ways that caregivers can encourage the growth of empathy within their child. This process is ever evolving and different for each child and family unit. The following points can be used as a guide, but caregivers should be flexible and use tools that they believe are best for this topic.

Listen

Caregivers can practice modeling empathy through listening rather than fixing. Caregivers care deeply about their child and do not like seeing them in pain or distress. Often, their first instinct is to step in and fix whatever may be causing their child distress. Caregivers should be encouraged to avoid this impulse and allow their child to sit in distress, or deal with the consequences of their actions without attempting to "fix it" right away. This does not mean that they should leave their child to deal with it on their own. Rather, caregivers can sit with their child while the child is experiencing this distress, acknowledge how uncomfortable their child must feel, and name feelings the child may have, while also showing their child that they are not in it alone.

The caregiver can reflect what their child is feeling while also avoiding any "quick fixes." Remind the caregiver that they are there to support and listen, not to fix.

Modeling

Caregivers should regularly talk about and express their feelings, as this models to the child that having feelings is okay. This is particularly important for challenging or distressing feelings. The caregiver's ability to identify these feelings rather than taking actions to "fix them" right away or avoiding them entirely shows the child that all feelings are safe to have, even if they feel hard. When caregivers can identify and verbalize their experience of emotions, they are actively helping their child notice and name their feelings, while simultaneously teaching them that they have permission to experience any and all feelings.

Patience and Practice

Building empathy skills takes a lot of practice, so caregivers should be patient with their child and help them practice these skills. Helping them in a consistent manner, free from perceivable frustration (as much as humanly possible), shows them that they have a safe place to practice these skills. Caregivers can help their child practice by modeling empathic responses, as discussed above, and by using extracurricular materials such as books and shows that encourage their child to practice reading body language, nonverbal cues, and learning what emotional states may look like in others.

VICTIM AWARENESS

For this age-group, victim awareness will likely look a lot different than the work done with adolescents. Again, children are not mini adolescents, therefore their treatment will differ. Though it is important for children to have awareness of the impacts that problematic sexual behaviors and sexually abusive behaviors can have on others, we want to provide this education in age-appropriate and developmentally appropriate ways. This module is meant to help our young clients build empathy and understand some of the short- and long-term impacts of problematic sexual behaviors. This not only increases their awareness around impact but also allows them to practice responsibility and use the information they've been learning throughout the treatment process.

Depending on the child, their problematic sexual behaviors, and their age and/or developmental level, this section may be condensed and activities altered. I've provided information and activities that fit for our older clients, but after assessing the individual client and their specific needs, clinicians can decide how to move forward with the content presented below. At minimum, I encourage clinicians to have a conversation with clients about the impacts that problematic sexual behaviors can have. This provides pertinent information that can help clients conceptualize the ways that experiences can impact people, even after the experience is over. This may be an important topic to address if the client has their own history of victimization or abuse. They may encounter symptoms from these previous experiences, and it can be helpful to have a framework for these experiences.

Psychoeducation Around Impacts

When discussing the impacts that problematic sexual behaviors can have, I provide one list, but discuss the difference between short-term and long-term impacts. This highlights the shifting nature of trauma symptoms, and helps children understand that these symptoms can fade and reappear at different times. The information regarding impacts can be provided in a variety of ways, so this is something I explore with each client. Some clients want to create bullet point lists, some want to create a poster that reflects the information, and others just want to talk about it. If a client wants to talk, I ask if I can write down some of what they are saying so we can look back at it later. There is no right or wrong way to present this information as long as the client comes away with the understanding that harmful sexual behaviors are impactful.

Typically, I will assess the level of understanding and awareness clients have by asking them to name/list all the potential impacts they can think of. Again, perhaps they create a list, begin working on their poster, or start discussing their thoughts. Once it appears that they are done, I ask them to shift their focus from their own thoughts to their own experiences. I ask them to put themselves into the position of the peer that they engaged in problematic sexual behaviors with. Then I ask them to reengage in the activity, writing down any new thoughts or feelings that come up for them. Once they have completed this part of the activity, we will sit down and look at what they have. The next step in this process is providing education regarding the impacts victims may experience.

I start this conversation by acknowledging that each person in this world is different, therefore the way they experience things will be different. This means that no two people will experience the same exact impacts, even if they have experienced the same exact trauma. I share that sometimes people may not look or act impacted but I assure clients that everyone who experiences unwanted sexual touching is impacted. Some of the impacts I'll discuss with clients are loss of trust, anger, nightmares, fear that the touching will happen again, confusion, victims may blame themselves for the touching behaviors, victims may feel like their body has betrayed them, victims may want to engage in sexual behaviors with others, anxiety, poor self-worth, feeling numb, becoming triggered, and withdrawing from others. Though there are many more impacts than the ones listed above, I find that providing too many can overwhelm clients. The point of providing this information and discussing impacts is not to have children memorize each and every impact. The point is to show them that these behaviors are hurtful, and this pain can last for a long time. Understanding some of the different impacts gives context to the experience victims may have and highlights the importance of discontinuing any and all harmful sexual behaviors.

To further highlight the learning in this section, I have clients engage in the activities below. The first activity focuses on the different people that have been impacted by the client's problematic sexual behaviors. The second activity is specific to the person the client has engaged in the problematic sexual behaviors with. Again, it is the clinician's role to assess each client and determine whether these activities are appropriate or needed. What is expected of a six-year-old who has engaged in problematic sexual behaviors is drastically different from what is expected of a twelve-year-old who has engaged in problematic sexual behaviors. I encourage the use of clinical judgment when deciding how to move forward.

Ripple and Rock Activity

This activity is meant to show the "ripples" that a single behavior can have and demonstrate the many people who can be impacted by it. This addresses the concept of residual impacts by highlighting that someone can be hurt, even if the behavior did not happen directly to them. In this activity I use the metaphor of a rock being dropped into the water. When a rock is dropped into a pond it does not just create one splash and sink to the bottom, it creates a disturbance across the entire surface of the pond, creating many ripples that emanate from this single rock being dropped.

In this activity, the rock represents the problematic sexual behaviors. At this point in treatment, the inappropriate behaviors have already been identified and this step should be fairly straightforward and quick. I will have the client take a sheet of paper and write down all their problematic sexual behaviors in the "rock," or near the rock. After completing this step it is time for them to reflect on the people that have been impacted by these behaviors. The ripples should go from most impacted to least impacted. This means that the first ripple they draw should represent the victim, as they are the one who was most directly impacted by the behaviors. Ideally, the client will know this right away; however, if they do not, the clinician should spend some time exploring the client's thinking around this. The clinician can support the client in getting to the place where they can recognize that the victim is the individual who has been most impacted. From here, each ripple will be different. The order of ripples, and who is included, may differ greatly depending on the family dynamics and the people involved in the youth's life. Often, caregivers and siblings are included. A completed example of this activity is provided in the appendix, as well as a blank worksheet for you to use.

Once the ripple activity is complete, the client will spend time explaining how each of the people, represented by the ripples, have been impacted. The amount of detail used will vary based on age and developmental factors, but again, the client should be drawing from the information they learned regarding impacts. Once they have done this, and discussed the impacts, the client presents this project to their caregiver—if the caregiver was not present throughout the process. The caregiver can provide feedback regarding the ways they have been impacted, further helping the client understand the impacts of their behaviors. If the victim of our client's problematic sexual behaviors is involved in services, it is helpful to reach out to the victim's therapist to discuss any impacts that the survivor is presenting with. This information can then be incorporated into the activity and discussed accordingly.

Letter of Growth

This activity is geared toward older children. A letter of growth is not necessary for all clients to complete, but some clients may benefit from this process. Additionally, there are clients who will be engaging in clarification or reunification processes with the victim. In these cases, it may be expected that some sort of letter is created. If this is the case, a letter of growth is a developmentally appropriate alternative to a clarification letter. The process of creating this letter is laid out below.

Once the client has completed their "ripple and rock activity," they have completed all treatment necessary to create an empathetic and well-thought-out letter of growth. As with the modules above, this part of treatment will look different depending on the client. Older and higher functioning clients will complete a more substantial letter, whereas younger, or lower functioning, clients may engage in a modified letter that meets their needs.

This letter should be about the growth this client has engaged in to help them become healthier and safer. It should highlight the treatment they have engaged in, shifts in their attitudes and understandings, as well as acknowledge and apologize for their problematic sexual behaviors. Depending on the child, or what the victim is requesting, this letter can be a few sentences, a series of bullet points, a paragraph, or an entire page. If there is a victim therapist involved, clinicians should work with them closely to identify the elements that would be most helpful for the victim, or specific elements the victim is requesting. Collaborating with a victim therapist will help structure this process and identify the elements that are most helpful to the victim and their healing. If there is not a victim therapist, the client can still complete a letter of growth, and explore the elements they think should be in their letter. If they are uncertain about this process, an example of how to structure a letter of growth has been provided in the appendix.

Chapter 8

Future Safety and Finishing Strong

The final step in treatment is supporting our clients in creating a "safe-play plan." A safe-play plan has the same function as the safety plans created throughout this process. It is used to identify potential safety risks, address these safety risk, and ensure that our clients and their families have the tools needed to make healthy and safe choices in the future. Prior to creating this plan, it can be helpful to engage in a full treatment review.

This review is encouraged if caregivers have not been present for sessions apart from the times their child is presenting an activity or sharing new knowledge. This review can also be helpful for the children, as their caregivers can review this information and ensure retention so they can continue implementing and modeling this information at home. If there is a treatment module that the client and/or caregiver is struggling to recall, the clinician can take time to go through this section and highlight the pertinent information. Caregivers should always be a part of this process, as it's imperative that they remember this information so that they can help their child in the future. For example, if their child is demonstrating poor boundaries, caregivers need to be aware of what the child has learned in regard to boundaries. If the caregiver knows the language used throughout treatment and has a grasp of the information that was addressed, they have what they need to support their child and hold them accountable.

SAFE-PLAY PLAN

As mentioned above, this plan is intended to help set our clients up for success. This plan is not based on our clients' past struggles but should reflect awareness of these struggles and the factors that impacted their engagement in these struggles. The plan should be focused on their future, and how to best assist them in making safe and healthy choices and having safe and healthy relationships moving forward.

I typically set this plan up by looking at the main domains of a child's life. I often have a section for home, school, community, and for older children, I might add a section for health. These plans should be created collaboratively between the child and caregiver with support from the therapist. The child and caregiver can identify boundaries, establish practices, and highlight skills and interventions that can be used to promote healthy choices and behaviors. I help facilitate this activity, but the client and caregiver are the ones responsible for the creation of this plan. This activity facilitates important discussions regarding the future, helps identify potential challenges the client might face, and different ways their caregiver can support them. It highlights the important role that caregivers have in promoting their child's safety and the safety of those around their child. It also provides a chance to reflect on past interventions and skills learned throughout treatment, and how these skills can be practiced moving forward.

An example of a safe-play plan is provided in the appendix. This specific plan is more representative of what an older child and their caregiver might create. It is pretty detailed and rule oriented, but not all safe-play plans will look this way. The younger the child is, the shorter this plan will be, as the caregiver and adults in the young child's life are more responsible for supervision and safety. As the child gets older, they begin to have more responsibilities, and this includes the responsibilities they have over their own choices and actions.

TREATMENT REVIEW

As mentioned above, the treatment review is just that, a review of treatment. This review incorporates a summary from each of the curriculum chapters and a review of each of the activities completed within these treatment areas. A copy of the information that should be present in the treatment review is provided in the appendix. While going through this review it is important that the kids and caregivers discuss the past learning, as well as ways that this learning is being internalized and used in their everyday lives. They can share examples of the different ways they are doing this. An example of this could be facilitating a review of the different boundaries and having the client and caregiver discuss boundaries that they have respected over the past week, or boundaries that have been broken over the week and the ways they are working to fix this.

The client and caregiver should complete this review in its entirety. The therapist should act as a mere facilitator, in the hopes that the client can present most of this information to the caregiver. If the client gets stuck, the therapist can encourage the caregiver to help. If the caregiver is also struggling to recall the information, the clinician can step in and review this specific material. It is not uncommon for a thorough and complete treatment review to take a few sessions. In some cases, like for young children, a condensed version of this review will take place. For older clients, a more extensive review will take place. The clinician can help structure this review by discussing the main treatment topics the child engaged in, and this will provide the clients with an outline of what they will need to review.

Part II

ADDITIONAL CONSIDERATIONS

Chapter 9

Multisystem Involvement

When working with children who are engaging in problematic sexual behaviors, it's not a question of if you will be working with a variety of systems, the question is how many systems will you be working with?

When working with adjudicated youth, therapists are working closely with the legal system, providing probation officers with pertinent information regarding treatment, producing court reports, and on occasion, being subpoenaed to testify in court. Therapists who are working with young children may not experience some of the work that's often involved with having a client who is on probation, but this doesn't mean there is no system involvement, it just means there is no juvenile justice system involvement. I have experience working with young children who have problematic sexual behaviors, as well as youth who have been adjudicated on sexual offenses. One of the biggest differences, in my opinion, is the level of case management required when working with young kids. As discussed in the research presented at the beginning of this book, children who are engaging in problematic sexual behaviors have often experienced a multitude of traumas early in their lives. Their functioning is often impacted in several ways, and it is common that these children already have multisystem involvement, and if they don't, they will likely need referrals to become multisystem involved. The already present stressors in the families we meet with are often heightened when they discover their child's engagement in problematic sexual behaviors, and they often request additional supports and resources. Each family is different, and, on rare occasions, I've had families who are not in need of additional support; however, this is something I'm regularly assessing for.

When assessing the level of support a family may need, and whether additional services or system involvement are indicated, I'll start by looking at the child and how they are functioning within a variety of settings. I'll often look at settings such as home, the community, school, and extracurricular activities. If they are having significant struggles in any of these areas, it is a sign that the treatment team may need to grow. Adults from the settings in which the child is struggling may need to be a part of treatment; whether that involvement is superficial or more elaborate differs from case to case. Below, I've discussed what systems I often make referrals to, and the ways I work with these systems.

LET'S TALK ABOUT SCHOOL

Aside from home, school is likely the environment where children spend most of their time. The development and engagement in problematic sexual behaviors stem from a variety of factors— most are based outside of the educational environment; however, these behaviors are absolutely seen within this environment. In a study done by Ey and McInnes (2017), they found that within their sample of 107 educators, 40 percent had observed children within these educational settings engaging in problematic sexual behaviors. An investigative report completed by the Associated Press's McDowell et al. (2017) highlights that children are most vulnerable to victimization by other children in their home; however, the second most prevalent location to be victimized is at school. By reviewing the federal crime data, they were able to find incidents of sexual violence involving students as young as five years old. They also found that incidents of sexual violence increase significantly around the beginning of middle school, when children are around ten to eleven years old and continue to increase until the age of fourteen. These findings demonstrate the pervasiveness of problematic sexual behaviors occurring at school and point to the need for educator training.

Schools play an important role in the prevention of problematic sexual behaviors, and educators are at the forefront. Their roles as mandatory reporters can ensure that these behaviors are reported, and their responsibility of supervising and monitoring children can lessen the risk of problematic sexual behaviors occurring in the educational setting (Briggs, 2014). Incidents involving harmful sexual behaviors often occur where adult supervision is minimal, such as on the bus, in the bathroom, and in the locker room (McDowell et al., 2017), thus providing educators with the training needed to identify problematic sexual behaviors is a crucial element of prevention measures (Kaeser et al., 2000). McKibbin and Humphreys (2023) engaged in an exhaustive review of the literature, looking at the ways that frontline professionals can be trained to identify harmful sexual behaviors, and how they can be better supported in managing these behaviors. They identify five themes that can help: "process of identification and response, knowledge required to identify and respond, skills needed to identify and respond, organization-level supports, and system-level supports." Though there is increasing awareness around the issue of problematic sexual behaviors occurring in schools, and ways to better support and respond to these behaviors, intervening on these behaviors continues to prove challenging.

Kor et al. (2023) reviewed the literature to better understand what the barriers were in responding to these problematic sexual behaviors. They found that the three biggest barriers to effectively responding to these behaviors were minimization of these behaviors, working in silos, and harmful social norms. They found that harmful sexual behaviors were minimized and normalized by both students and teachers, and widespread lack of training prevented educators from identifying these behaviors as harmful and appropriately intervening. Problematic social norms were also found to impact appropriate response to the harmful sexual behaviors occurring in schools. The most prominent of the harmful social norms were "gender norms associated with hegemonic masculinity" and the "unspoken code of silence" (Kor et al., 2023, "Harmful Social Norms section," para. 1). Both social norms created environments that promoted the perpetuation of harmful sexual behaviors and stoked reluctance to report such behaviors. Last, a siloed response within educational settings pointed to a lack of support for teachers and inadequate collaboration from outside agencies.

Understanding these barriers can help educators, and school systems in general, better understand blind spots when it comes to prevention and protection within schools. It can also help clinicians understand the role they may need to play when involving school systems. Clinicians may find themselves in different roles when it comes to the level of engagement they have with schools. For some clients, there may be minimal interactions between the clinician and school, and for others, regular communication may be indicated. Clinicians may find it helpful to provide the school with pertinent education and resources about topics that fall under the umbrella of sexual development. Clinicians may also be asked by the school to take a larger role in safety planning. Regardless of the roles in which we find ourselves as clinicians, understanding the ways we can best support educators benefits the overall goal of prevention.

Where to Start Regarding School Engagement

When starting with clients, I always make sure to ask about school while completing my initial mental health assessment. I want to know whether they have an Individualized Education Program (IEP), a 504 plan, any safety plans in place, and how they function academically. I also ask about peer connections and whether they are involved in school-based extracurricular activities.

Depending on your client and their level of needs, it may be important to have conversations with the family and determine whether discussing their child's problematic sexual behaviors with pertinent professionals within the school setting is appropriate. Often children engaging in problematic sexual behaviors have already been identified within the school setting as having challenges, and, in my experience, the school often reaches out to me once the client is engaged in services and the caregiver has signed a release of information (ROI). On other occasions, the school may be unaware that the child is involved in services and I'm the one who initiates contact. As a best practice, at the beginning of services, I will typically have caregivers sign a ROI that allows me to have contact with the school.

Children engaging in behaviors that fall within the "problematic sexual behaviors" category vary, therefore, the protocol for informing and working with schools varies. There may be times, albeit relatively few, when speaking to the school isn't necessary, times when a simple conversation regarding boundaries and how to best support the child suffices, or times when discussing the details of the problematic sexual behaviors is imperative to the safety of others at the school. To determine the level of information the school needs regarding the problematic sexual behaviors your client has engaged in, or is currently engaging in, ask yourself the following questions.

Did the problematic sexual behaviors involve another person? If the problematic sexual behaviors involved another person, it is important to have contact with the school. We want to ensure that there is appropriate supervision in high-risk settings such as the bathrooms, recess, and passing periods. Even if the problematic sexual behaviors don't involve another person, they still may warrant a discussion with the school. An example of this may be a child who is engaging in masturbation in the school bathroom, or a child who has been putting things into their anus. Yes, there is a low risk that the child is going to act out with others, but there is still a present risk of them harming themselves.

When did the problematic sexual behaviors occur? If the problematic sexual behaviors occurred relatively recently, it is likely that talking with the school is important. If the problematic sexual behaviors happened in the past and the client has a good handle on regulation skills and has been engaged in services with no additional problematic sexual behaviors, speaking with the school may not be as necessary. Instead, it may be more appropriate to inform the school that you are the child's therapist and ask them to reach out if there are any behavioral issues that begin to arise.

Are there triggers that increase the child's likelihood of engaging in problematic sexual behaviors? Some children may engage in problematic sexual behaviors for self-soothing purposes, for example, touching their penis when overwhelmed. If the child is likely to engage in problematic sexual behaviors for self-soothing or grounding purposes, it is likely that speaking with the school is important. School can be an overwhelming place for children, and this can increase the likelihood of the child engaging in behaviors to soothe themselves. Speaking with the appropriate adults at school can help them understand environments that may be challenging, and they can help the child avoid or be better prepared to handle these environments or situations. This can initiate conversations regarding other measures that can be taken to help the child feel settled and grounded in triggering situations, such as allowing the child to take breaks when frustrated, giving the child fidgets when involved in quiet reading time, providing alternative activities for the child during a school-wide assembly, and so on.

How pervasive and unsafe are the problematic sexual behaviors? If the problematic sexual behaviors are pervasive in any way and/or affect the safety of the child or others at school, the problematic sexual behaviors should absolutely be discussed with the appropriate school personnel and suitable plans should be put into place.

Individualized Education Programs and 504 Plans

Individualized Education Programs (IEP) and 504 plans are designed to support students who are experiencing challenges in school. An IEP is a tool that is accessed via special education, whereas a 504 plan does not require involvement in special education. Though they are covered by different laws, they work to achieve the same goal, helping youth be successful in their education. Determining whether a child has an IEP or 504 plan helps me understand whether they have engaged in a variety of evaluations to assess for autism, specific learning disabilities, developmental delays, and so on. I've provided a brief overview explaining each of the plans below.

Individualized Education Program

According to the department of education, a child qualifies for an IEP if they are between the ages of three and twenty-one years, attend public school, and have been evaluated as having a need in the form of at least one of the thirteen disabilities identified in the Individuals With Disabilities Education Act. These disabilities include specific learning disability, autism spectrum disorder, emotional disturbance, other health impairment, visual impairment including blindness, hearing impairment, deafness, deaf-blindness, speech or language impairment, orthopedic impairment, traumatic brain injury, intellectual disability, and multiple disabilities (Lee, n.d.).

The IEP provides resources, such as specific learning environment accommodations or modifications, and access to related services to best help the child have success within the school setting. Looking through the child's IEP, or talking with the child's IEP team, is incredibly helpful, as the plan describes how the child learns best, discusses the ways that the child can best demonstrate their learning, and shares how adults in the child's life can best support them effectively and efficiently in their learning journey.

504 Plans

Qualifications for a 504 plan are much broader than those of an IEP. A child qualifies for a 504 plan if they have "a physical or mental impairment which substantially limits one or more major life activities, has a record of such an impairment, or is regarded as having such an impairment," as well as kids with thinking or learning differences (US Department of Education, 2023, "Who Is Entitled to FAPE" section, para. 1). Those who qualify are provided accommodations to remove any potential barriers to better access learning and education.

If your client has an IEP or 504 plan, it's important for you, as the clinician, to understand what accommodations or modifications your client needs to be successful in an educational setting and translate these modifications or accommodations into their treatment work as well. We can't expect a child with dyslexia to sit and write a letter of growth in the same way we expect a child without this learning disorder to. We need to make sure that we meet our clients where they are at if we want treatment to be impactful and effective. If your client does not have an IEP or 504 plan but you think that they would benefit from one, speaking with the caregiver or the school counselor can be an important step in advocating for your client. If my client is struggling academically, and/or behaviorally, securing accommodations can not only improve their experience at school but may also help alleviate some stressors at home, decrease negative self-thoughts, and minimize struggles that may lead to suspensions or other school-based consequences.

Safety Plans for School

When starting with clients, I ask about any safety plans that may already be in place at school. Perhaps the child already has a bus safety plan due to impulsive or unsafe behaviors on the bus. Maybe the child is not allowed to walk the halls alone due to past incidents when using a bathroom pass. Regardless of whether these safety plans are related to their problematic sexual behaviors or not, it's good to understand what plans are in place and why. Understanding our clients' struggles at school helps to paint a more holistic picture of where and how they struggle. Having this on our radar can inform potential treatment goals and better guide us in moving forward in the treatment process.

If the child does not have a safety plan, I will speak with the caregiver and assess whether they have concerns regarding their child's safety, toward themselves or others, and whether there have been incidents at school that have caused concern. If they acknowledge that a safety plan could be helpful, we explore what their child may need in terms of additional support. Once a safety plan is created, either the caregiver reaches out and speaks with the school or, if they don't feel confident or comfortable in doing so, I do. I reach out to the school counselor or principal and ask to have a brief meeting where we can discuss the caregiver's concerns regarding safety and whether the safety plan we've created can be implemented at school. If the safety plan is not school compatible, we can discuss the appropriate tweaks needed to make it so, and once the plan is finalized, the caregiver and I sit down with the child and discuss implementation. Ensuring your client understands what is expected of them is a necessary step in setting them up for success.

INVOLVEMENT IN EXTRACURRICULARS

As seen throughout the research, positive activities with prosocial peers serve as a protective factor for youth who have been adjudicated for sexual offending behaviors (Zeng et al., 2015). Protective factors act as mitigators when it comes to high-risk behaviors within families or communities. We have already established that children are not just mini-adolescents in the same way that adolescents are not just mini-adults. That being said, the way that extracurricular activities serve as a protective factor for adolescents would appear similar for children. Unfortunately, when a child engages in problematic sexual behaviors, caregivers often become concerned that these behaviors may continue to occur. They may pull their child from extracurricular activities to avoid safety concerns and minimize the risk of their child acting out with or around their peers. Though the caregiver's concern is warranted and understandable, I often encourage families to keep their child involved in activities, as these activities can help with social skills and building prosocial relationships. Rather than pulling them out of the extracurricular, we can come together and create a safety plan that enables the child to continue their activities while also ensuring the appropriate level of supervision and safety to keep everyone safe. Certain extracurricular activities will require an increase in safety planning and discussions with the supervising adults, whereas others may require little to no safety planning. Each client has different needs; therefore, each family and how extracurricular activities are managed differ. I've broken extracurriculars down into two overarching categories: movement-based activities and non-movement-based activities.

Movement-Based Activities

Movement-based activities are going to require a higher level of planning and supervision due to the physical nature of these activities and the potential for increased contact with others. These activities may involve physical touching, varied boundaries, and using locker rooms, each of which needs to be appropriately addressed and planned for. The level of safety planning and communication that goes into movement-based activities is going to vary based on the client's individual needs and the extracurricular they are participating in. In setting up plans, it's important to reflect on their history of problematic sexual behaviors and boundaries. Below, I've outlined some of the elements to consider when clients are engaging in movement-based activities. Thinking about these factors can help set our clients up for success.

Locker Rooms

When feasible, I recommend that clients use locker rooms as little as possible. If they can dress for their activity at home, and avoid changing in locker rooms, this is always recommended—at least at the beginning of treatment. Locker rooms can be challenging to supervise, and they can create tricky situations for kids who are trying to work on healthy boundaries. If they are unable to avoid changing in the locker room, I ask about the level of supervision provided while children are in there. If there are no adults supervising, it is recommended that a caregiver or coach accompany the child, thus ensuring supervision and avoiding the risk of any problematic sexual behaviors occurring. If available, I also recommend the use of single-stall restrooms while changing for activities. The same recommendations are provided for times that the child may need to use the bathroom.

Communicating With Coaches/Instructors

Understandably, caregivers are anxious about their child engaging in hands-on activities with others after problematic sexual behaviors have been discovered. Not only does the physicality often bring up anxiety and trepidation but also the idea of telling another adult about the behaviors their child has engaged in. Though this discussion can be nerve-racking, it is important for caregivers to discuss their child's need for supervision and their expectations regarding rules they need to follow—to ensure their safety and the safety of other kids engaged in the activity. Caregivers do not need to go into the exact details of their child's problematic sexual behaviors, but they do need to provide some context regarding the need for heightened supervision and the safety plan that will be put into place, if warranted. Often parents will ask for support in how to go about this discussion, as they are uncertain of how to be honest while also respecting their child's privacy. When advising them on this conversation, I recommend that they stick with the "who-what-where-when-why" of the situation: *who* needs the increased supervision; *what* kind of supervision is needed; *where* supervision is needed; *when* supervision needs to happen; and *why* there is an increased need for supervision. I've created an example of what this may look like, or sound like, below.

Some caregivers may want to provide more details, and others may want to avoid going into details as much as possible. Either option can be fine, as long as a conversation around supervision and safety is happening. When caregivers are deciding how much information to provide, I encourage them to look at a few details such as how well they know the coach/instructor, how much they trust the coach/instructor's supervision, what problematic sexual behaviors their child has engaged in, and how impulsive/at risk they are for attempting these behaviors again. I often encourage a middle-of-the-road approach when it comes to deciding how much detail to share. If adequate details aren't provided, the coach/instructor may not understand the true importance of the supervision being requested or what they should be on the lookout for. If the family provides too many details, there is a risk that their child could be "othered," or treated poorly, due to the abundance of misinformation regarding kids who engage in problematic sexual behaviors. There is also the risk that this sensitive information could be leaked and then passed around to other kids and families who participate in the activity. Ultimately, the level of detail shared is decided on by the caregivers, but I frequently ask for a release of information (ROI) to speak with the coach/instructor if there are concerns regarding the sharing of information.

Example of the "Who-What-Where-When-Why" Conversation

- *Who*. My son John is excited about the upcoming basketball season; however, due to a recent incident at school, I want to talk with you about supervision for this season.
- *What*. John had some boundary struggles recently, so we want to talk with you about the need for increased supervision to keep him and the rest of the team safe.
- *Where*. We need to make sure that John is being supervised closely. There was an incident in the bathroom at school, so we request that John uses the single-stall restroom when he needs to use the bathroom. We will also make

sure that John shows up to practice ready to start so there is no reason for him to go into the locker room.

- *When.* John needs supervision at all times. He should not be left alone. Will there be an adult present throughout his practices? If not, I need to be present throughout practice.
- *Why.* As a family, we've come up with some rules that we expect John to follow. He is aware of this plan, but I think it's important you know about it too, that way you can redirect him if you see that he is slipping or engaging in behaviors that he shouldn't be. John is to use single-stall restrooms, he should not change or undress in the locker room, he knows he needs to always stay in eyesight of an adult, and he will keep his hands and body to himself at all times, unless actively involved in the game or drills.

Some families I've worked with have already discussed concerns regarding safety and already have a plan in place for sports and movement-based extracurricular activities. If they do, I ask if I can review the plan with them, that way I can be familiar with the expectations and ensure there aren't any holes or missing information that might impact the adequacy of the plan.

Non-Movement-Based Activities

Non-movement-based extracurricular activities, such as orchestra, arts and crafts, or learning a language, tend to be much easier to navigate. The lack of changing and touching required for these activities lends itself to a less anxiety-provoking environment for caregivers, as boundaries are much clearer, and the activities are easier to supervise. Though there are generally less scenarios that would involve touch or getting into others' boundaries when engaging in these activities, it is still important that the caregivers have a conversation with the instructor about safety and supervision. They can utilize the "who-what-where-when-why" format discussed above, and a safety plan specific to this activity can be created in session. The safety plan may just discuss boundaries the child should follow, or bathroom protocol, and the details shared with the instructor may be minimal. The important thing is that a conversation with the instructor, or supervising adult, happens. It's important that they understand the specific needs of our client, and what to look out for and redirect. A silly but inappropriate drawing from a child could easily be overlooked with a giggle or roll of the eyes, but if our client is engaging in these behaviors, it needs to be handled in a more direct manner and reported to the parents. Helping the instructor understand this helps us to ensure our clients are getting consistent messages and have the same expectations across settings with all adults that they regularly interact with.

FUNCTIONING WITHIN THE HOME

Throughout my time working with clients, I regularly check in on how the child is functioning in the home, what additional supports they may need, and how the caregivers are coping with the shifts that have occurred after the problematic sexual behaviors were discovered. While engaging in the mental health assessment at the beginning of services, I assess for the level of support caregivers have outside of their household. Do they have family members or friends close by? Do they get support within a faith-based setting? Do they have trusted friends that understand what is happening and can watch the client to provide some respite? Understanding the natural supports that families already have can help lay the foundation for future plans, should caregivers become overwhelmed and need some breaks.

If a client is demonstrating significant struggles at home, and the caregivers are beginning to feel burnt out, I will begin looking into these natural supports and we will collaborate and create a plan that will help the caregivers get a break. This could look like having the client spend the weekend at Grandma and Grandpa's house once a month, or creating a specific plan that allows the caregivers some space to decompress and get their needs met. If a client is experiencing significant struggles at home, it is likely that they can benefit from a break just as much as their caregivers. Unfortunately, some families have relatively few natural supports or external resources outside of the home. In these scenarios, I often look into the ways that community-based services can support these families. We will take a closer look at some of the community partners I regularly work with when it comes to families in need, and what resources they can provide to help support our clients and their families.

COMMUNITY PARTNERS

We've all heard the phrase, "It takes a village," often in reference to raising a child. This phrase comes from an African proverb communicating the message that for a child to flourish and grow, an entire community must be behind them. This community is responsible for creating a healthy and safe environment that allows them the experiences they need to develop and grow in positive ways. Though this proverb is specific to raising children, it's one I often reflect on when thinking about treating problematic sexual behaviors. As discussed throughout this book, the reasons that a child may engage in problematic sexual behaviors are diverse and the roots of these behaviors complex. The likelihood that a single mental health therapist can take on all aspects needed to treat a child exhibiting problematic sexual behaviors is almost absurd. Problematic sexual behaviors are a complicated issue, often made more convoluted by dynamics present in the child's life. I've found that the complexity of these issues almost always requires a multitude of professionals to successfully and ethically treat these behaviors. Within this section, I highlight the community partners that I often find myself working with and what kind of role they may play in supporting problematic sexual behaviors–specific treatment.

Department of Human Services

When working with this population, one of the systems that I am in contact with most is the Department of Human Service (DHS). This contact may be because the family I'm meeting with has an open case with DHS, because DHS is the legal guardian of my client, or the family needs resources and support via DHS and their various programs and resources.

DHS can support families in several ways. They provide family support services (FSS) via six avenues including voluntary placement agreements, voluntary custody agreements, independent living programs, post–legal adoption and post–assisted guardianship assistance to families, in-home family support services, and services for pre-adjudicated delinquents when ordered by the court (DHS, n.d.). In my role, the avenues through which DHS is most involved are either through a voluntary placement or due to an open case with the family.

Voluntary placements may occur when a family feels that they cannot adequately support their child and their child's needs, so they request a substitute care placement. The family still retains custody of the child; however, the child will be placed in a temporary placement outside of the home so that they can better access services for the child's emotional, mental, or behavioral health, or services for a mental disorder or developmental or physical disability (Oregon Laws, 2021).

Regardless of the avenue, if a family is involved with DHS, or if DHS is the child's guardian, clinicians need to have a working relationship with the child's caseworker. The role the caseworker plays in the client's treatment varies depending on the capacity in which DHS is involved in their life. This could range from monthly check-ins to having the caseworker present in some sessions.

Wraparound Services

Wraparound is a nationwide resource that provides families with a process to plan and implement services for their child. Wraparound is family centered— meaning, that the perspectives, ideas, and needs that the family identifies are what drives all the work in Wraparound (National Wraparound Initiative, 2024). I find that if a family already has multiple systems involved, but they are not yet involved in Wraparound, it can be a great resource to add to the mix, as it serves as a hub for the family, their providers, and any other adults who are relevant to the child's care (such as skills trainers, school counselors, teachers, etc.). Families are supported by their Wraparound team as the Wraparound facilitator pulls together professionals, natural supports, and people from the larger community to help build a team to support the child and their family. The next step is creating goals and a vision, which are created by the family with the support of their Wraparound facilitator, and then this plan is put into action. Wraparound is specifically meant to support high-needs children and their families so they can maintain placement in their homes and communities, rather than needing referrals to higher-level care or alternative placement.

When families are involved in multiple systems, or with multiple providers, it can create challenges, as each entity may create a specific plan with specific goals and communication between these entities may be lacking. This can be overwhelming for clients and their families, as it may feel like they are being asked to work on too many differing goals, which can further lead to burnout. Rather than ask more from these families, Wraparound aids families in bringing the entities together so the team can work on creating an individualized plan of care that is shared across services. This ensures that the many different providers/services/professionals working with the family are on the same page when it comes to the family's goals and their vision for success.

Though Wraparound services are available throughout the country, the information regarding these services varies from county to county. Qualifying factors in one county may differ from another, so you may need to do some research to determine whether a client you'd like to refer would meet criteria. I've provided criteria for two different counties in Oregon to highlight the differences you may see between counties when assessing a client and whether they are eligible for Wraparound services. Below, I have listed the criteria for Washington County Wraparound Services, as well as the criteria for Multnomah County. It is also noted that once you refer a client to Wraparound services, they may require a brief eligibility meeting to discuss the specific client, whether they meet criteria to be accepted into Wraparound services, and why they would benefit from these services.

Washington County Wraparound Eligibility Criteria (Health Share of Oregon, 2024):

- Must have the following: The youth being referred is under the age of eighteen years, the youth has coverage through Health Share Washington County Medicaid, the youth lives within Washington County, Multnomah

County, or Clackamas County, and the youth must be involved in at least one other system (i.e., qualifies and is involved in one of the following: special education, developmental disabilities, Juvenile Justice, mental health services, Department of Human Services).

- Children ages five years and under must have at least two qualifying criteria. Though I have not listed all the criteria, I've provided several of the criteria that children I'm meeting with may be experiencing: current significant household stressors like poverty; their parent is struggling with their own mental health or substance-use issues; they are at risk of losing placement in school or day care due to increasing problematic behaviors; and they are being exposed to domestic violence.
- Youth ages six years and older must have at least two qualifying criteria. Again, I have not listed all the criteria but rather focused on the criteria most common for the youth I meet with: they are at risk of being taken out of the home due to escalating behaviors; they are at risk of being taken out of school due to escalating behaviors; increasing risk of harm to others or themselves is increasing; they need a higher level of care than outpatient services can provide.
- Or, if a client doesn't meet the criteria above, but has current enrollment in one of the following services and has Health Share Washington County, they are eligible to access Wraparound services, Secure Child or Secure Adolescent Inpatient Programs, Psychiatric Residential Treatment Services, or the SAGE Residential Program.

Multnomah County Wraparound Eligibility Criteria (Multnomah County, 2024):

- The youth has or is eligible for an Oregon Health Plan.
- The youth has a qualifying mental health diagnosis.
- The youth is under eighteen years of age.
- The youth has multisystem involvement—meaning, they are involved in services within at least one of the following categories: special education, DHS, Juvenile Justice, mental health, substance abuse and addictions, developmental disabilities, or medical involvement (due to pervasive or complex conditions).

Wraparound services are family driven and youth guided, so it is imperative that the family and youth be active participants in the team. On occasion, I have youth who refuse services and avoid all participation in their Wraparound teams. In my experience, this is rare, but when this has happened, I have referred the family to Intensive Care Coordination (ICC). If the family continues to need support, but they are unable to engage in Wraparound services to fidelity due to lack of child engagement, this is another option and one that is discussed later in this chapter.

In my experience, Wraparound teams vary in size, and this is often related to the level of support and resources the family needs. I typically refer a family to Wraparound services for two reasons. First, the family needs increased support and resources to support their child. Second, the family already has many entities involved but are struggling to juggle the different resources and providers—having a coordinator to act as the hub for all these services can be incredibly helpful.

When I refer a family for the first reason—that is, they need increased support and connecting to resources—the team starts out small. Typically, this includes the Wraparound coordinator, the family, and you (the clinician who made the referral). From here, the Wraparound coordinator collaborates with the family to better understand what they are hoping to achieve through Wraparound services, the goals they have as a family, and what additional supports or resources are needed to achieve these goals. From here, teams grow, as the Wraparound coordinator reaches out and attempts to engage the various entities that can help the family achieve their Wraparound goals. To give an idea of this process, and how this may look, I've provided an example of this progression below. It is noted that this is example is based on real experiences I've had on different teams; however, it does not represent a specific team I've been a part of. The details are fabricated and/or altered to ensure confidentiality.

Initially, I started seeing Conner for problematic sexual behaviors, as he had been referred by his mental health counselor. This other therapist had been working with Connor on impulsivity and trauma, but when the problematic sexual behaviors were uncovered, Connor was referred. As Connor engaged in services, and I got to know him and his family unit better, it became apparent that Connor was struggling in several settings, including school and home. Additionally, there were significant stressors in his relationship with his caregiver. Connor's caregiver was honest about the struggles they were experiencing and their need for more support, stating that their current situation was not sustainable. At this point I made a referral to their county's Wraparound services, and they were accepted after a brief eligibility meeting. Their initial Wraparound team included Connor and his caregiver, the Wraparound coordinator, Connor's other therapist, and me. As time progressed and the team honed in on the needs of Connor and his family, the Wraparound team grew, first adding in a parent support specialist for the caregiver, then Connor's teacher, his school counselor, the medical social worker, Connor's coach, and a close family friend who was able to provide respite.

When I refer a family that is already involved in a number of services, but the caregivers are struggling to manage the various entities and resources present on their child's care team, the team will likely start out as much more robust. In this case, I refer the family to Wraparound services and express their need for support with the intensive planning they are involved in. This allows the family to step back and focus on their child, their child's needs, and their family's needs, while allowing a Wraparound coordinator to take on the intensive planning and coordination that's needed to help the family. Once accepted into Wraparound services, the coordinator reaches out to the family and collaborates on goals. They also discuss the current services and resources the family is already a part of so that the coordinator can reach out and include them on the Wraparound team. Once this has taken place, the coordinator reaches out to the different entities and professionals that the family wants on their team and creates the team. To give an idea of this process, and how it may look different from the example above, I've provided an example. Again, this example is based on real experiences I've had on different teams; however, it does not represent a specific team I've been a part of. The details are fabricated and/or altered to ensure confidentiality.

I started working with a family who'd been involved in services for many years. Marcy, the child, was referred for services due to the discovery of problematic sexual behaviors occurring with her sibling. Marcy had an extensive history of trauma and had already been involved in several services, including mental health therapy, family therapy, and occupational therapy. Additionally, the family had taken classes through DHS, were a part of a faith-based support group, had a supportive extended family; yet, the family was still experiencing significant struggles. The caregivers were juggling therapy appointments, appointments related to the child's mental and medical health, safety planning for extracurricular activities and trips, upholding strict safety plans at home, and the list went on. This level of coordination was clearly creating a significant amount of stress for the family, and they acknowledged a foreboding sense of burnout. After gaining a better understanding of just how many services, professionals, and appointments Marcy had, it became clear that a referral to Wraparound services would help lessen the load on the caregivers. I made the referral, Marcy and her family were accepted, and the Wraparound coordinator reached out to collaborate with the family on goals to better understand what professionals and supports were already in place. They also explored ways that the family could feel better supported, and after this, the Wraparound team was created. The initial Wraparound team included Marcy and her caregivers, the Wraparound coordinator, Marcy's teacher, Marcy's soccer coach, her school counselor, her developmental disabilities (DD) case manager, Marcy's other mental health therapist, her occupational therapist, and me. Through this process, resources were provided to help ease some of the stress on the family, while creating a forum where all supports could touch base and ensure they were working toward the same family goals.

When comparing these two examples, it is clear that Wraparound team sizes can vary; however, regardless of team size, the goal remains the same: helping families with complex needs strengthen their support network so their children can remain in their homes and communities, while also helping families connect to services and resources to best meet their individual needs.

Intensive Care Coordination

Intensive Care Coordination (ICC) is like Wraparound services in that it is a nationwide program, present within states and communities across the country. It is a voluntary service for individuals with complex mental health needs, and similarly to Wraparound services, provides a hub for the many professionals that may be on a client's treatment team. ICC utilizes a collaborative team-based approach, like Wraparound, however, it does not require participation from the youth in the same way that Wraparound does. Obviously, buy-in from the youth is preferred, however, ICC allows for support, even when the client is at a place where they are unable or refuse to participate. This is important for families, as it allows them access to resources and the ability to receive support while navigating systems even if their child cannot see the level of support required to help them be successful in their community. It is noted that ICC is a tool available to children, youth, and adults, however, for our purposes I will be speaking about ICC as a service to support the children and youth we work with.

Intensive Care Coordination teams vary based on the level of care a child needs, and they can drastically differ in size. Teams generally involve the identified client, though in the case of children and youth, as mentioned above, their engagement in the team is not a necessity. Teams also include the family, the ICC coordinator, and any current community partners, providers, and supports that are already in place. This means that teams can start small but typically grow to include supports that ICC is helping connect the family with. Teams may also start off rather large if the client and their family already have connections with multiple providers and supports prior to starting with ICC.

To give an idea of who may be present on an ICC team, I've provided an example below. This example is based on different experiences I've had on ICC teams but does not reflect or represent a specific team I've been a part of. Again, the details are fabricated and/or altered to ensure confidentiality but represent a high-needs child who has many significant challenges, in addition to problematic sexual behaviors.

In this particular case, Jordan and her family started in Wraparound services; however, Jordan became very unhappy with her involvement on this team and refused to be an active participant. At this point, the family was referred to ICC so that they and the team could continue receiving the high level of support and resources needed for Jordan, while also respecting her desire to discontinue her engagement. Jordan no longer attended monthly meetings, but all other service providers maintained their engagement in this case and participated on the ICC team. The members present within this team included the ICC coordinator, Jordan's resource parents, her DHS caseworker, her lawyer, Jordan's school teacher and school counselor, her developmental disabilities (DD) case manager, her skills trainer, her medical social worker, her psychiatrist, and me.

As you can see by this example, teams can involve many different professionals. In my experience, a team of this size is not common, but it does happen. Having a team of this size can present many challenges if there isn't regular communication and shared goals. Having a structured monthly meeting can ensure that professionals are not inadvertently undermining the work another professional is doing, or duplicating work that is already being done. It ensures that each professional works on their specific piece of the larger goal and creates accountability and communication across the team.

Respite Services

Respite services are generally offered nationwide and can be utilized as a resource regardless of age. Individuals may utilize respite services when caring for aging parents, when a spouse has a chronic illness or disability, or when caring for a high-needs child. In my work, I generally refer a family to respite services when the child and their caregiver(s) need a break. Respite care can be planned or emergency; however, for our purposes I will only be discussing planned respite for children, as this is typically the type of respite that I make referrals for.

Respite programs are intended to provide short-term respite for families who can utilize this support to maintain a healthy and positive relationship with their child (ARCH National Respite Network & Resource Center, 2013). Respite provides a break for the person receiving care, as well as the caregiver, and as we've discussed, children who have engaged in problematic sexual behaviors generally require a lot of support in the form of supervision, redirection, and so on. It's no wonder that caregivers can become overwhelmed and exhausted when supporting their child and their various needs. The child may also be experiencing distress at home for several reasons, such as a strained relationship with their caregiver or frustrations involving a sibling. Helping our clients, and their families, get a break from one another can be very important to sustainability, as this break may be the difference between keeping their child in the home or requesting an alternative placement.

When it comes to accessing respite, I often refer my clients to a respite program through one of our local nonprofit organizations. They have certified resource homes that provided a safe, structured, and stable environment for youth. If you are unsure of how to access respite services for a client you can often access this information through local mental health agencies, or, if your client is involved in Wraparound services or Intensive Care Coordination, the facilitator can point you in the right direction.

When it comes to respite care for children who have engaged in problematic sexual behaviors, it is important that these behavioral concerns are shared prior to placement. Some of the things I look at when considering what an appropriate respite setting might look like for my clients with problematic sexual behaviors include:

- Does the child need to be separated from other children? If not, what age range is appropriate for the child to be around? If there are other children in the home, it is important that they do not have their own history of problematic or illegal sexual behaviors.
- Will the child be sharing a room with another child? If so, this is not a safe setting for them. They should have their own bed and their own bedroom.
- What level of supervision does the child need, and can it be adequately provided in the respite home?
- What does access to technology look like in the respite home? Can they be sure that the child is not accessing inappropriate content, and if not, what can be put into place to avoid this?
- Ensuring there is open and honest communication between the respite home and caregivers.
- Providing the respite caregiver(s) with any pertinent information and safety plans needed to help the client maintain appropriate and safe boundaries in the home and in the community.
- Talking about, and agreeing to, recreational activities and plans that may occur while the child is staying there.

Ultimately, respite care should provide the child with a consistent and safe environment away from their home. It's important that the respite caregiver understand the client's history of problematic sexual behaviors so that they can fully understand the needs of the child. This allows the provider to arrange whatever may be needed to provide safety and support, not only for the child but also anyone else who may be in the home.

Child Advocacy Centers

Child advocacy centers (CACs) may or may not play a role in the work you are doing with a child who has engaged in problematic sexual behaviors. CACs are responsible for coordinating the investigation, treatment, and prosecution of child abuse cases. In 2022, more than 380,000 children were served by more than 950 CACs nationwide (Office of Juvenile Justice and Delinquency Prevention, 2024). As of early 2024, there are nearly one thousand CACs that provide support and services in all fifty states within the United States (National Children's Alliance, 2024a). As discussed in the literature at the beginning of this book, 92 percent of children who engage in problematic sexual behaviors have experienced neglect, witnessed domestic violence, or have experienced one or more forms of abuse (physical, emotional, or sexual) (Vizard et al., 2017). Knowing that this population has experienced abuse at rates higher than the general population suggests that asking clients and their caregiver(s) about prior contact with a CAC, or referring them to a CAC if needed, may be an important step in the treatment process.

If referring a family to a child advocacy center, I recommend ensuring the center is accredited through the National Children's Alliance's National Standards of Accreditation. Determining the accreditation status of the CAC you refer to will help ensure that the care your client, and their family, receives is high quality, consistent, and evidenced based.

CACs play a vital role in helping children who may have experienced abuse. The multidisciplinary team (MDT) model used by CACs limits duplicative interviews, promotes collaboration across disciplines, and allows for the child and family to access a number of resources within one space. Accredited CACs have teams comprised of several disciplines including medical professionals, victim advocates, forensic interviewers, law enforcement officers, mental health providers, prosecutors, Child Protective Services, and case managers. The CAC is also responsible for conducting forensic medical exams and interviews. Detectives and child welfare workers are often present for these evaluations and collaboratively address complex situations to determine next steps in an investigation, ensure child safety, and connect families to necessary resources.

During the beginning of services, I determine if the child has been interviewed at a CAC. If they have, I ask the caregiver to sign an ROI so that I'm able to contact the assessment team and obtain a copy of their evaluation report. This can provide the clinician with important details regarding past abuse and paint a fuller picture of the experiences their client has had without requiring an additional interview of the child regarding these experiences. If the client wants to discuss their experience at the CAC, or details from the past abuse, they can, but having access to the evaluation report enables the client to disclose as few, or as many, details as they want. The information you gather from child abuse evaluations at CACs may impact case conceptualization and treatment goals, so having this information early in the process is helpful.

Survivor Therapist

When working with children who have engaged in problematic sexual behaviors, the involvement of another child or youth is something that is bound to come up. When another child or youth is disclosed as being involved in the touching behaviors, we will need to gather pertinent information before moving forward. Another child or youth being added into the mix can raise questions around mandatory reporting, victimization, connecting survivors to appropriate services, and so on.

So, what do we do if we are working with our client and they disclose that another child or youth was engaged in the problematic sexual behaviors? We begin gathering the information needed to respond in a timely and appropriate manner. If the other child, or youth, is much older than your client, this may be a red flag that your client is the identified victim. If there are power differentials present, like your client is lower functioning or differently abled and the other child or youth is not, this is another red flag that your client may be the identified victim. When discussing problematic sexual behaviors that involve another child or youth, I recommend assessing for the following details: power differentials, significant age gaps, coercion or force, aggression, and painful or scary sexual behaviors. If these characteristics are present, sexually harmful behaviors have occurred and need to be addressed. When this type of information is shared in session, I determine whether it has been previously disclosed. If not, I call the child abuse hotline to report this new information. This information is then shared with the client's caregiver, and we determine if a plan is needed for moving forward.

If my client is the identified victim, I speak with the caregiver about getting their child evaluated at a CAC. Then we work on implementing any additional safety measures that are needed, such as discontinuing contact with the other child, implementing stricter safety measures in the home, and so on. Once the problematic sexual behaviors have been reported, a referral to a CAC is made, a forensic medical exam and interview occur (if the CAC deems it appropriate), and safety measures are put in place to protect the child from further victimization, we continue problematic sexual behaviors–specific treatment. At times, discontinuing problematic sexual behaviors–specific treatment and focusing on their own victimization may take precedence. Processing their own experience of abuse may highlight the impact that this experience plays in their own problematic sexual behaviors.

If my client discloses problematic sexual behaviors toward another child or youth, and these behaviors have not been previously reported, I call the child abuse hotline and make this report. Once these behaviors have been reported, my hope is that the other child or youth will be connected with victim-specific services. In a perfect world, the series of events would look like this: problematic sexual behaviors are reported to the child abuse hotline, the behaviors are investigated, and the identified victim is referred to a CAC, the CAC determines whether a forensic interview and exam is needed, the CAC provides therapy to the identified survivor or provides referrals to a survivor therapists, and then the child engages in survivor specific treatment. When the identified survivor is engaged in services, it creates the opportunity for their healing, and the chance for collaboration between the victim therapist and problematic sexual behaviors therapist.

Engagement and collaboration with a survivor therapist look different from client to client. There may be times when the survivor therapist is hesitant to work with the problematic sexual behavior–specific therapist, or times where there is no survivor therapist to work with. Ideally, there will be a collaborative relationship between the problematic sexual behavior–specific therapist and a survivor therapist. This collaboration enables the survivor to access anything they may need to heal. An example of this might look like the survivor therapist sending the problematic sexual behavior–specific therapist a series of questions that the survivor has. The problematic sexual behavior–specific therapist goes through these questions with their client and the client provides appropriate answers, which are given to the survivor therapist. Then the survivor therapist reviews these answers with the survivor and sees if they have more questions. This collaboration provides the survivor with whatever they may need from the individual who hurt them. At times, the survivor may want nothing to do with the child who hurt them, other times they may want something specific, like a meeting to share their feelings about what happened. This meeting may look similar to a clarification meeting.

For context, a clarification meeting is a restorative justice process where the offending youth is asked to take full accountability for their sexually abusive behaviors, often by reading the survivor a letter. The letter is used to take accountability for their abusive behaviors and provide details about the sex offense–specific treatment they've engaged in, and how they are becoming a safer member of society. In my experience, these meetings are more frequent when the youth has been adjudicated for sexual offending behaviors, also known as illegal sexual behaviors (ISBs), but absolutely occur with non-adjudicated youth and children as well. For more information on this process, I recommend the book *Clarification and Reunification: Guidebook for Working With Youth and Families Impacted by Sexual Abuse*, by Keith Ovelmen (2021).

When working with younger kids, it is likely that this process will look different. Rather than writing a clarification letter, the child who engaged in problematic sexual behaviors may write a "letter of growth," discussed earlier in the curriculum. At times, the identified victim may not want a letter, and they would rather have questions answered, a meeting where safety is discussed, an apology from the child who hurt them, or a plan on how to move forward with spending time together. These meetings are flexible and fluid and can include whatever the survivor may need. The survivor is the one who gets to decide how things move forward, and it's the job of the child who engaged in the problematic sexual behaviors to respect their wishes.

Chapter 10

Common Characteristics, Barriers, and Challenges When Working With Children Exhibiting Problematic Sexual Behaviors Who Are Twelve Years of Age and Younger

As with any population, there are common challenges and barriers that we experience when working with problematic sexual behaviors. These challenges and barriers exist on a spectrum, ranging from struggles with the individual client, to challenges within family units, all the way to barriers present within societal systems. As a clinician, it can be helpful to understand what challenges, issues, patterns, or barriers may arise in your work within this population. Being better prepared for these challenges can aid in early detection of these issues and a quicker response of therapeutic intervention can occur.

The years I've spent working with children who are engaging in problematic sexual behaviors has given me a unique perspective. I've gained a greater understanding of the common challenges and barriers that come up for this population, and I've developed skills to deal with these issues. Not only have I noticed common patterns and characteristics present in children engaging in these behaviors, but I've also ascertained some underlying dynamics within systems that can challenge meaningful therapeutic progress. Below, I've outlined common characteristics, barriers, challenges, and issues experienced when working with children who engage in problematic sexual behaviors.

COMMON CHARACTERISTICS, BARRIERS, AND ISSUES SEEN IN CHILDREN WITH PROBLEMATIC SEXUAL BEHAVIORS

When working with children who have engaged in problematic sexual behaviors, you may or may not experience a level of resistance when starting services. Children might think that they are in trouble and that's why they are in your office. They may have experienced shaming and judgment from others when their behaviors were discovered, further causing them to withdraw or avoid this topic. Clients may feel the need to guard information related to their own behaviors, such as their own experience of abuse. Uncertainty, anxiety, and resistance is to be expected. As I laid out in chapter 1 of the curriculum, building rapport and creating a safe environment for your client is imperative for building trust. The more trust they have, the more information they are willing to share. Initial struggles with engagement can be expected; however, this current chapter is less about the obvious challenges that can arise, and more about the distinct challenges experienced when engaging in problematic sexual behavior–specific treatment. We will look at some of the common struggles that children I'm working with endorse, and elements that can impact therapeutic progress. We will also look at these challenges from a broader lens by exploring the ways that caregivers and systems can impact treatment.

Attachment Challenges

As discussed in the literature review at the beginning of this book, children who struggle with problematic sexual behaviors have a high rate of early childhood trauma. These lived experiences can create significant attachment wounds, and these wounds can impact a variety of elements associated with treatment. These challenges will likely impact the treatment process, making progress on the problematic sexual behaviors challenging. Disruptions in attachment are therapeutically challenging, and this trauma can show up in the therapy room in a variety of ways.

Clinicians may experience increased opposition and defiance from their client, the client may present with extreme people-pleasing tendencies, the client may be overly dependent on the engagement of their caregiver in sessions or may present with challenges linked to emotional volatility. These struggles can be addressed in sessions, but it is possible that children with severe attachment struggles will need additional support outside of the services they are receiving to address their problematic sexual behaviors. This may look like referring the family to a family therapist who specializes in treating early childhood trauma and attachment. We can also provide caregivers with attachment-specific resources and help them build skills to assist their child when the child is experiencing behavioral dysregulation. Providing caregivers with information about attachment can help them better understand their child's behaviors, but there is a chance that more therapeutic support will be needed. If this is the case, problematic sexual behavior–specific treatment may be paused, and the family will be referred to the appropriate resources. If the child needs a higher level of care, this is something we can support the family with. Once these challenges are addressed appropriately, the child can reengage in problematic sexual behavior work, if indicated.

Neurodivergence

If you work with children who have problematic sexual behaviors, you have likely worked with children who are neurodivergent. Not every child who has engaged in problematic sexual behaviors is neurodivergent, and not every child who is neurodivergent will engage in problematic sexual behaviors. That being said, children who are neurodivergent are overrepresented in the population of children who engage in problematic sexual behaviors, and empirical research indicates that this is a distinct subgroup within the larger group of children with problematic sexual behaviors (Hackett, 2014; Evertsz & Kirsner, 2003).

The term "neurodivergence" is used to describe people who fall under the neurodivergent "umbrella." This umbrella term describes people who have variations in their mental functions, and these variations impact how their brain works. This can include a wide array of differences, including medical disorders, learning differences, and neurological or developmental disorders. There are many disorders, disabilities, and conditions that fall within the category of neurodivergence; however, the types of neurodivergence I see most often include developmental disabilities, autism spectrum disorder, fetal alcohol spectrum disorder, and attention deficit hyperactivity disorder.

Children who are neurodivergent experience a distinct set of challenges that neurotypical children may not struggle with. Struggles with impulse control or challenges with learning, for example, may increase the difficulties our clients experience when working on goals related to decreasing problematic sexual behaviors, such as controlling impulses and integrating learned skills. Better understanding the ways that neurodivergence can impact a child and their functioning can highlight additional treatment areas to explore. Knowing that a client has been diagnosed with autism spectrum disorder may allude to a treatment plan that includes goals related to improving social skills and the ability to read social cues, in addition to their problematic sexual behavior–specific treatment goals. If a client with problematic sexual behaviors also has a diagnosis of fetal alcohol spectrum disorder (FASD), the clinician needs to know about the specific strengths, challenges, and level of impairment the child experiences with their diagnosis. Better understanding the neurodevelopmental domains impacted by the FASD will productively inform the treatment plan and highlight areas where the client can use more support. Additional support in this case could look like providing the family with local FASD-specific resources or referring them to an additional service, such as neurofeedback, while engaged in problematic sexual behavior–specific treatment.

Ultimately, treating neurodivergent children with problematic sexual behaviors requires clinicians to understand their clients' distinct needs, levels of functioning, and the strengths and challenges related to diagnoses of neurodivergence. Better educating oneself in the ways that developmental disabilities, autism spectrum disorder, fetal alcohol spectrum disorder, and attention deficit hyperactivity disorder are addressed and treated therapeutically will help clients experience treatment success. If clinicians are aware of how these neurodevelopmental differences may be influencing the problematic sexual behaviors, they can be more effective in their treatment planning.

Mental Health Challenges

As discussed throughout this book, working with children who have problematic sexual behaviors requires us to use a holistic lens. The behaviors they are exhibiting did not develop in a vacuum. They stem from a multitude of factors, including experiences of neglect, difficulties within the family environment, witnessing domestic violence, and experiencing abuse (Vizard et al., 2007). Given that most clients presenting with problematic sexual behaviors have endured at least one form of maltreatment, it should come as no surprise that comorbid mental health disorders within this population are common.

Findings within the literature highlight that many children presenting with problematic sexual behaviors also qualify as having dual diagnoses, with most having at least one mental health diagnosis in addition to their problematic sexual behaviors (Gray et al., 1997; 1999; Chaffin et al., 2008). Two of the most common comorbid diagnoses seen in this population include conduct disorder and attention deficit hyperactivity disorder (Gray et al., 1999). Additionally, posttraumatic stress disorder and other internalizing diagnoses such as depression and anxiety are not uncommon. Given the high prevalence of comorbid mental health diagnoses, the Association of Treatment of Sexual Abuse Task Force on Children With Sexual Behavior Problems has identified that, at times, the problematic sexual behaviors may become the secondary priority in treatment, as addressing mental health concerns like suicidality, self-harm, and intense or intrusive trauma symptoms may be the primary priority (Chaffin et al., 2008). Once the child is stabilized and has addressed these concerns, they can engage in work around their problematic sexual behaviors.

Children engaging in problematic sexual behaviors are also at an increased risk of engaging in other high-risk behaviors (Szanto et al., 2012). For this reason, initial assessment should look at a variety of factors like trauma history, behavior across settings, and general functioning, in addition to assessing the problematic sexual behaviors. This will provide clinicians a clearer understanding of what factors are impacting these behaviors, how to intervene appropriately, and what additional care the child may need. If a clinician is treating problematic sexual behaviors, they also need to be proficient in the treatment of trauma. Understanding how to work with comorbid mental illnesses and the way these illnesses present is a must when working with this population.

Arousal in the Treatment Room

Clinicians working with clients who have engaged in problematic or illegal sexual behaviors have plenty of experience talking about sexual behaviors, thoughts, and arousal, but what happens when arousal shows up in the treatment room? When working on problematic sexual behaviors, it's clear that there will be discussions about sexual content, and this can create a variety of responses in our clients. Some may feel embarrassed and become withdrawn, others may be uncomfortable and become loud and goofy, alternatively, some may become aroused. Rather than ignoring the reality that discussing sexual content can be arousing, I'm direct about this from the beginning.

Before discussing sexual content or going into the details of a client's problematic sexual behaviors, I have a discussion with my client about the possibility of body responses related to these conversations. I normalize that our bodies respond to stimuli and highlight this by discussing our senses. I lead my client through psychoeducation around the different senses, and the ways our senses provide our bodies and brains with information and feedback. This won't be a completely foreign concept to them, as we will have already discussed the ways that sensations and/or triggers lead to feelings, which then lead to thoughts, and then actions. A deeper dive into this information, and body awareness, is available in chapter 3 of the curriculum. While having this conversation, I provide a nonsexual example and have them identify some of the body responses they may experience, such as, "Think about when you put a sour candy in your mouth —What happens?" Most of the time they can identify that sour candy will make their mouth water. Then I ask them to imagine eating a sour piece of candy in that moment. I follow up with a question like, "Do you notice any changes in your body when you think about putting a piece of sour candy in your mouth?" This generally elicits one of three answers: "Yes! My mouth is watering," "No, I don't notice anything that feels different," or "I don't know." Their response can be indicative of how connected or disconnected they are from their body and may highlight some areas they will need to work on in treatment. Take note of this, and then, regardless of their response, use this opportunity to point out the connection between talking or thinking about something and the ways that our bodies can respond. Once this has been explored, I transition into a conversation around the upcoming discussions we will be having.

I am straightforward when acknowledging that we will be discussing sexual touching, and I normalize that some kids may begin to feel aroused by this. Together we will explore what "clues" their body may give them when they start to feel aroused. This helps me assess the level of understanding they have regarding their own body sensations, and more broadly, their concept of arousal. After exploring this, we will create a plan for what they can do if they start to feel aroused in session. The plan can be created in several ways, but I've found that kids seem to like "code words," and they work well. After exploring the different clues that their body gives them to let them know that they are starting to feel aroused, they will come up with a code word. A code word can be any word a client chooses and is used as a cue to indicate arousal. Once a client uses their code word, you can provide them with positive feedback on their ability to listen to their body and notice these clues. When a client uses their code word, it is time to switch the topic to something that isn't treatment related such as, sports, TV shows, an upcoming birthday party, and so on. After several minutes of engaging in alternative discussions, you can come back and revisit how they are feeling in their body. Typically, this distraction will extinguish the arousal they were experiencing, and they can carry on with the treatment-related discussions or activities they were working on before. If they are still feeling aroused, or this experience was dysregulating for them, then you can collaboratively make the decision to pause whatever it was they were working on and transition into a different activity.

Pornography Use

When looking at the etiology of problematic sexual behaviors, there is no singular experience, event, or factor that is responsible for these issues. That being said, there are absolutely factors that can impact children who are already vulnerable to engaging in these behaviors, and pornography is one such factor (DeLago et al., 2019). In the juvenile world, sex offense–specific treatment includes work specific to past pornography use and how this may have impacted their engagement in sexual offending behaviors. When it comes to treating children with problematic sexual behaviors, pornography use is sometimes overlooked since we don't typically associate pornography use with young kids. Whether we like it or not, children are accessing pornography, and we must assess for current and/or past pornography use when treating our clients.

DeLago and colleagues (2019) examined multiple factors, including exposure to sexually explicit material, that impact the different types of problematic sexual behaviors children may engage in. The mean age of their sample was ten years old, which fits nicely with the contents of this book since we are focusing on children twelve years old and younger. They found that children who had viewed pornography had a higher likelihood of engaging in more invasive problematic sexual behaviors, compared to those who had no exposure to pornography. When we are meeting with children who have enacted sexual behaviors on another, and these behaviors are invasive, such as placing their finger into another child's vagina, it indicates a strong likelihood of exposure to sexually explicit material and should be assessed.

There are several forms of sexually explicit content within a variety of medias, such as hypersexualized cartoon characters and sexually explicit songs; however, *Flood* (2009) points out that these other forms of sexual media do not have the same effects on sexuality as pornography does. This is due to the explicitness, and the violence and hostility, specifically toward women, that is portrayed in this content. He provides an overview on the impacts that pornography can have on adolescents and young people, highlighting concerns related to healthy sexual development and potentially problematic outcomes that may perpetuate troublesome behaviors and beliefs. Given the concerns regarding the negative impact that pornography use can have on sexual development, it has been identified in research as a "child protection issue" (Ey & McInnes, 2017, p. 14).

When it comes to the ways that pornography use is addressed in treatment, I stand by the idea that knowledge is protection. Speaking with clients about the pornography they have consumed helps provide a framework to better understand what kind of education and exploration will need to occur in treatment. Understanding key factors, such as frequency of use, the type of pornographic content being consumed, and what the client has "learned" from the pornography, can aid clinicians in creating a treatment response specific to the client's needs.

It should be noted that not all pornography exposure is deliberate. Some pornography exposure can be involuntary or accidental. I have had clients who were working on a school project when they typed in something benign like "box" or "fart," and suddenly their screen populated with inappropriate sexual images. I've also had several clients talk about clicking on links in the comments section of an age-appropriate video they watched, and suddenly, they were catapulted onto a pornographic website. Additionally, there are times when clients report involuntary exposure. This may come from a peer who is using pornography on the bus and showing peers around them, or perhaps pornography is used in the offenses perpetrated against them. This accidental or involuntary exposure can be upsetting or distressing for some children, whereas others might experience an increased curiosity. This type of exposure can generally be processed in session, and age-appropriate education around pornography can be provided at this time.

Additionally, there have been times that clients report their pornography use as a form of education. This is especially true for clients who identify as LGBTQIA+, as they report receiving minimal education specific to their identity. Given the lack of societal discourse around this topic, clients may seek out information and answers to their question via the internet, and ultimately, pornography. To support clients, and minimize pornography use, it is imperative that clinicians provide age-appropriate materials on sex and sexuality that meets the client's identity.

COMMON CHALLENGES THAT COME UP WHEN WORKING WITH THE FAMILIES OF CHILDREN WITH PROBLEMATIC SEXUAL BEHAVIORS

When working with children, you are inevitably working with family systems. This can be a rewarding experience; however, it does not come without some unique challenges. This is especially true when working on sensitive issues such as trauma, sexual abuse, or problematic sexual behaviors. Caregivers, just like everyone else, have their own biases, preconceived notions, and life experiences that can impact the way they view their child's behaviors. These views can affect the ways they engage with their child and their child's treatment, and at times may become a barrier that needs to be addressed. The way that caregivers view sexuality and their understanding or sexual development may also prove to be a topic that needs addressing. Ensuring that caregivers have accurate information about childhood development and sexuality is imperative to the treatment process. Having this information increases safety and protection within the home and community. Safety also comes from their understanding of technology, the way their child interacts with technology and their awareness around the material their child accesses. There are a variety of challenges that can come up when working with families, and the families of children with problematic sexual behaviors are no different. I detail some of the challenges I see most frequently, and the ways that I handle these challenges when they do come up.

Caregivers' Response

Inappropriate, appropriate, neutral, or a combination of all three, caregiver responses can run the gamut when problematic sexual behaviors are discovered. Often, we are meeting with families in a time of confusion, anger, fear, and uncertainty. Providing caregivers the space to communicate and express their experiences and thoughts, while also therapeutically challenging them at times, can be a delicate dance. It is important that caregivers feel validated and supported throughout the treatment process, but there will be times that they are asked to step out of their comfort zone, and this can be hard. It is likely that changes within the family system will be needed to foster a healthier and safer environment moving forward, and this can be a challenging experience for caregivers. At times these changes may look like creating more structure and regulation in the home, and at others it may look like helping caregivers build trust with their child so they can loosen their grip on structure and control. This is frequently dependent on the ways that problematic sexual behaviors are seen and handled within the family system. Family responses to problematic sexual behaviors fall along a continuum, and when caregivers are too far in one direction or another, it creates barriers to healthy change, and can impact the therapy process. This is seen when caregivers are hyperreactive or hyporeactive to their child's problematic sexual behaviors, and common challenges that come from both responses are discussed in further detail below.

Hyperreactive Response

At first glance, a hyperreactive response from caregivers may be deemed appropriate and protective. While this is true, a hyperreactive response that fails to shift as the child progresses in treatment can eventually lead to a host of issues. A hyperreactive response is usually rooted in fear, and though this is understandable, we do not want families to remain frozen in this state. Increased supervision, safety plans, and potential restructuring of room placements in the home are protective changes that are frequently made when problematic sexual behaviors are first discovered. Caregivers typically feel less fearful and more in control once these changes have been implemented, their child has been engaged in treatment for some time, and they are starting to see shifts in their child's behaviors and awareness of boundaries. If caregivers do not experience this shift, or become even more controlling of dynamics in the home, this may indicate to the therapist that a discussion is warranted. Discussing the ways that caregivers view their child's problematic sexual behaviors, and whether these behaviors are triggering for them, can help clinicians better understand where the caregivers' response is coming from, and how to best support them while facilitating shifts in the way they view their child and the problematic sexual behaviors.

Hyperreactive responses can lead to issues that impact the child's progress in treatment. Examples of this can look like spending an exorbitant amount of treatment time safety planning or strained relationships within the family system that requires constant treatment attention and repair. Unfortunately, children who engage in problematic sexual behaviors may become the "targeted child" within the family, a term used to describe a child within a family system that is singled out and mistreated, or treated in a significantly different manner, than the other children in the home. The child who engaged in problematic sexual behaviors may become the target of the fear, anger, resentment, and/or other challenging emotions the caregivers are experiencing. This negatively impacts the child and leaves the family's ability to grow, learn, and heal stunted and stuck. Some signs of a hyperreactive response include (1) caregivers' inability to see progress or shifts in their child's response to treatment; (2) caregivers' inability to, or significant challenges with, allowing their child to build back trust and earn developmentally appropriate privileges; (3) overly strict expectations and rules around safety that fail to shift as the child progresses in treatment; (4) punitive punishments when the child makes developmentally appropriate mistakes; and (5) pulling the child out of school, prosocial activities, or the community, due to caregivers' own anxiety regarding their child being around others.

It is important that the therapist acknowledge the caregivers' concerns and provides compassion; however, the therapist must also provide the appropriate education and redirection needed for caregivers to move past these challenges so they can begin repairing the trust and relationship with their child. If a caregiver is experiencing significant challenges with making a shift from their initial fear response to a response that is proportional to the progress their child has made, I may refer them to their own therapy so they can work past these blocks.

Hyporeactive Response

At first glance, a hyporeactive response from caregivers may be seen as unsafe and could look like they are unconcerned with their child's behaviors. Though this could be the case, often a hyporeactive response is indicative of shame and embarrassment or highlights a lack of appropriate education regarding the seriousness of these behaviors. When a family presents with a hyporeactive response it's important to offer immediate education around safety, age-appropriate behaviors, and ways to foster safety in their home. If this has been addressed but there is not an appropriate shift in responsiveness, this is when a hyporeactive response becomes worrisome.

A hyporeactive response not only impacts the child's progress in treatment but also impacts their safety and the safety of others both inside and outside of the home. When a hyporeactive response occurs, therapists must address the significant risks and concerns that accompany this inappropriately relaxed response. Again, a hyporeactive response can be indicative of the caregivers' shame or lack of understanding, thus it is important to hold space for their experiences while also fostering the support they need to make appropriate changes.

If a therapist has provided the appropriate education, clearly discussed expectations regarding safety and rules that should be implemented, and there is still little change, this may be grounds for a more intensive intervention, such as a call to Child Protective Services (CPS) or a suspension from treatment until a treatment contract regarding engagement can be created and agreed upon. This may feel extreme, but if a child is engaging in problematic sexual behaviors and appropriate safeguards are not in place, even though the caregivers are aware of their child's safety concerns, it is creating the opportunity for more problematic sexual behaviors and victimization to occur. We, as clinicians, do not want to be in a situation where our lack of intervention is enabling harmful behaviors to continue. Some signs of a hyporeactive response include the following. (1) Lax supervision: Supervision will look different throughout the stages of treatment; however, if problematic sexual behaviors are discovered, the immediate response should be sight-and-sound supervision at all times the child is around other children. If a child is new in treatment and is continuing to have unsupervised alone time with other children, this is a huge red flag and needs to be addressed immediately. The same is true for animals. If the child's problematic sexual behaviors involve animals, or if the child has been unsafe around animals and there are concerns of the child enacting problematic sexual behaviors with animals, animals should not be left alone with the child. (2) Denial of problematic sexual behaviors or minimizing behaviors by the family to normalize the problematic sexual behaviors that have occurred: Initially, denial may be present, but if the caregivers are unable to shift this viewpoint, even with sufficient evidence that problematic sexual behaviors occurred, this becomes a treatment concern. (3) Allowing the child with problematic sexual behaviors to continue sharing a room with another child: This can be tricky, as lower-resourced families may not feel like they can separate kids or have the space for everyone to have their own bedroom. Clinicians can help explore and problem-solve potential solutions. This may mean that the child with problematic sexual behaviors, or a younger sibling, is moved into the caregiver's room for the time being. Or perhaps the child with problematic sexual behaviors sleeps in the living room and door alarms are placed on the other bedrooms so caregivers are alerted if someone is entering or leaving a room. (4) Unlimited and unsupervised internet access: Internet access should be monitored via sight-and-sound supervision until a more detailed discussion about past technology use has been had. Regardless of whether the child has struggled with using pornography, parental controls should be activated on all devices that children in the home have access to. (5) Allowing the child with problematic sexual behaviors to be in the position of watching over, or caring for, other children in the home:

A child who has engaged in problematic sexual behaviors should not be left alone with children and should not be placed in a position of power over other children, period. This is tremendously unsafe, as it creates the potential for continued engagement in problematic sexual behaviors toward others. If this dynamic is occurring, it needs to be addressed and stopped immediately, and this scenario likely warrants a CPS call.

Helping caregivers grasp the seriousness of safety, supervision, and minimizing the chances for problematic sexual behaviors to continue is very important. Caregivers play a particularly crucial role in creating an environment that is conducive to healthy change, and supporting their child in discontinuing any problematic sexual behaviors is a major part of this.

Technology Literacy

Let's face it, technology is advancing at a monumental pace, and it can be hard to keep up. Children today have more access to the internet than ever before, and we are seeing that they are being exposed to inappropriate content at earlier and earlier ages (DeLago et al., 2019). Unfortunately, with this increase in technology access, there does not seem to be an equal increase in education around safe technology use. I often see a certain level of naïvety among adults when it comes to the way they view technology and how they think children are utilizing it. Many believe that inappropriate content, like pornography, can be avoided with the use of parental blockers for sites like Pornhub. This gives caregivers a false sense of security and they feel confident about letting their child have unsupervised access on devices. What caregivers may not know is that inappropriate content is no longer sequestered to certain sites, it is *everywhere*. This content is easily and readily accessible. It can be linked in the comment section of a popular video, accessed via social media, or visited through a QR code scanning app. Providing adequate education around technology use is a part of the treatment work we do with problematic sexual behavior clients, but it should also be a part of the work we do with caregivers. Helping them understand the sheer amount of inappropriate content that's available one click away, and the tools they can use to limit this access, is a critical step in teaching healthy technology use.

I will generally start this conversation by asking caregivers about the role that technology plays in their household. This response varies widely, and some caregivers may already have a good understanding of the perils present and have appropriate measures in place to ensure safe internet use in their home. Others may think that their child is "too young" to access inappropriate or unsafe material, therefore they have minimal rules or guidelines in place to regulate internet use. The caregiver's response will help me discern the level of psychoeducation needed, and the level of support they may need in creating a plan to ensure safe internet use at home.

If caregivers already have a good understanding of internet safety and have plans in place, I have them walk me through the ways that internet is regulated in their home. We discuss different parental controls they utilize, the level of direct supervision their child has while on devices, the level of access their child has to different technology devices, and how much time their child spends on technology. If caregivers do not seem to have a good understanding of internet safety, or present as relaxed in their views regarding technology use, a more comprehensive discussion will be had.

If caregivers are less discerning when it comes to technology and the variety of ways kids can use it, I provide a thorough review of the ways technology can be misused, the risks present, and how they can further educate themselves to become proficient in technology safety. I've found that most caregivers understand that the internet can be unsafe but aren't aware of the different ways it can be so. They are aware that their child should not be on pornography sites, but may not think about their child entering chatrooms, playing inappropriate games, or video-chatting with strangers. For this reason, I typically recommend that all internet access be sight-and-sound supervised, at least at the beginning of treatment. This provides the opportunity and time for conversations that will help the caregiver better understand the role they play in healthy internet use and how to help their children build skills to be safe and smart internet users.

Sight-and-sound supervision should continue until appropriate tools are put in place, like supervision software that can alert the caregiver to content their child is accessing. Even with this in place, supervision should remain high at the beginning and slowly shift as the child demonstrates healthy and safe choices as their treatment progresses. This continuum of supervision is dependent on particulars like the child's age and history of inappropriate internet use. Depending on their specific needs, rules around internet use and supervision may remain relatively strict or shift markedly as therapy continues.

For an older child, like a twelve-year-old, who has minimal history of inappropriate internet use, this may look like starting off with direct sight-and-sound supervision and their caregiver sitting next to them. As the child engages in treatment and has conversations around internet and technology expectations, perhaps they start to use technology while in the living room with their caregiver present; however, the caregiver is no longer directly next to them. Then, perhaps the child can wear headphones while on the internet in the living room, that way their parent is present but can't hear what they are accessing. This progression continues until the child can use technology without direct supervision and demonstrates consistent healthy and responsible choices. Tools should be in place, like random checks of the search history, to act as a safety net should the child struggle with safe and appropriate choices. If this becomes the case, these challenges are addressed in therapy, and internet privileges revert back to the current needs of the child at that time. Again, plans will look different for each child and these plans are often dependent on factors such as their age, their needs, and their history with technology. For example, the plan for a six-year-old will differ drastically compared to the plan created for the twelve-year-old discussed above. Developmentally, a six-year-old should have supervision when on the internet and has little need to access this on their own. They will continue to build age-appropriate skills and a developmentally appropriate understanding of safe technology use while under the guidance of their caregivers.

The goal of providing technology literacy to children and their caregivers is to help them develop a healthy understanding of technology and how to utilize it in safe and effective ways. It is also to help caregivers understand the dangers present on the internet, the ease in which inappropriate materials can be accessed, and the importance of proper supervision. The goal is not to avoid all technology use or internet access, in fact, quite the opposite. Technology is being used more and more, whether it is in the classroom or during extracurricular activities, so it's important our clients and their caregivers learn how to utilize technology well.

Lack of Knowledge Around Sexual Development

We can't expect caregivers to provide what they don't have. Some caregivers had access to age-appropriate sexual education while growing up, and others did not. Some caregivers may have grown up in a home where sexual education and body awareness were topics that were openly discussed, while others did not. Some caregivers grew up in households where boundaries were appropriate and respected; again, others did not. All of this to say that each family you work with will differ, and their understanding of sexual development is no exception. Some caregivers have had access to this education and have a strong understanding of what is, and is not, age-appropriate behaviors or conversations for their child. Others may have very little knowledge around what should be, or should not be, expected regarding their child's development, which can lead to labeling appropriate behaviors as abnormal or inappropriate behaviors as normal.

If it seems that caregivers have some gaps in their understanding or knowledge of sexual development, I will take some time to run through the different developmental stages, and some of the typical behaviors we see children engage in during these periods. I will also discuss any age-appropriate education that should occur during this developmental period and explore with caregivers how they want this information presented to their child. In addition to discussing these details, I encourage caregivers to use the anatomical names for body parts in their home and inform them that this will be the language used throughout therapy. They may need a brief overview of the names for these body parts and some brief education around why using anatomical names is important. I normalize the discomfort this may bring up initially and reiterate the positives of normalizing this language in their home.

On occasion, I come across caregivers who have strong convictions regarding sexual education and feel very uncomfortable with their child engaging in age-appropriate sexual education while in treatment. They may hold specific beliefs that are rooted in religion or have internalized inaccurate information from their own upbringing. I make it clear that it is not my intention to undermine their beliefs or experiences, and I address this challenge through an educational lens. I assure them that the information I intend to share about these topics is not rooted in my own beliefs or morals; rather, it is rooted in the research present within the field. I place a strong emphasis on the increased safety that comes from this education and the benefits that come from having a shared language and understanding of these concepts moving forward. When I provide this perspective, caregivers often appear less alarmed and are more willing to engage in the education they may need to support their child. This also affords me the opportunity to engage in age-appropriate sexual education with their child throughout the therapeutic process. I find that talking with caregivers ahead of time about the sexual education that will be discussed in treatment is helpful. This gives them a heads-up and provides them the opportunity to express any concerns or questions they may have about this topic. When they are aware of what's being discussed, it also allows them to prepare for potential questions their child may have and can help them keep an eye out for any shifts in their child's behaviors.

Caregivers are some of the most influential people in their child's life, thus, their ability to have conversations with their child about sexual education is important. The education and comfort level caregivers have regarding discussions about age-appropriate sexual education may vary drastically. Some caregivers you work with will be comfortable discussing this topic with their child, but often, my experience is that caregivers are either over or under communicative around this topic. Some parents may provide too much information, struggling to understand what is and is not age-appropriate for their child. Others may avoid the topic altogether and report significant struggles with initiating these conversations or knowing how to answer questions their child may have. Providing caregivers with scaffolding around this topic can help them feel more comfortable and confident having regular conversations around sexual education and healthy sexual development. This may also mean providing caregivers with accurate sexual education if this is something they've never received.

I find it easiest to have educational conversations about sexual development and education with both the child and caregivers at the same time. This can help the caregivers feel less self-conscious or uncomfortable about their own potential lack of knowledge, and model how to have these conversations with their child moving forward. These conversations provide the shared language and foundation for future conversations that may occur in the therapy room, or outside of it.

Caregiver's Own Trauma

The way a caregiver responds to the discovery of problematic sexual behaviors can be indicative of their own trauma history. The topic of problematic sexual behaviors can be jarring in and of itself, however, when someone has their own history of trauma related to sexual abuse, it can be even more unsettling. Given the prevalence of sexual violence in the United States, it is likely that you will encounter caregivers of children with problematic sexual behaviors who also have a victimization history of their own. The Centers for Disease Control and Prevention (CDC) affirms that sexual violence in the United States is common. The data shows that more than half of women and nearly one in three men will experience "sexual violence involving physical contact" within their lifetime (CDC, 2022, "How Big Is the Problem" section, para. 2). Given how common sexual violence is, clinicians need to be ready to work with caregivers who have been the victims of sexual violence. Though the caregiver is not our identified client, it is still important to have an idea of how to support the caregiver, because not doing so can negatively impact their child's treatment.

As we know, trauma, and the ways that people deal with trauma, varies drastically. Some caregivers with their own sexual trauma history may be triggered by their own child and the discovered behaviors, struggling to cope with the memories or feelings that are coming up for them. On the opposite end of the spectrum, we may encounter caregivers who are in a state of denial, as acknowledging their child's behaviors is too arduous and distressing. Regardless, their trauma is real and will play a role in the ways they are able to show up for their child and their child's problematic sexual behavior–specific treatment. How we address this will depend on the way the caregivers are presenting.

If a caregiver is forthright about their own trauma history, I can provide therapeutic space for them to process any feelings or thoughts coming up for them in relation to their child's problematic sexual behaviors. If a caregiver is being flooded by memories and emotions related to their own abuse, I inquire about their own therapy. If they have a therapist, I may ask for a release of information, that way I can contact their therapist and discuss the ways that their trauma is showing up in their child's therapeutic work. We can collaborate on how to best support the caregiver in processing their own trauma response to the problematic sexual behaviors, while also providing support and care to their child. If the caregiver does not have a therapist, I often acknowledge the challenges that come with caring for a child with problematic sexual behaviors, on top of managing their own trauma from past experiences, and discuss how helpful adding in their own therapeutic support can be. If a caregiver is deeply struggling, I may also add family sessions without the client into our treatment. Though this is not intended to act as the caregiver's own therapy, it can be helpful to process their current experience with their child and the different ways the problematic sexual behaviors are impacting areas of their life. Better understanding this can help me support the larger family system by referring to appropriate resources and creating intentional plans around respite for the caregivers.

There are times when caregivers will not disclose a history of sexual victimization, but there are strong indications that this is present. If the caregivers are presenting as overwhelmed, I take the same approach discussed above. Even if their victimization history is not acknowledged, they can benefit from the same education, referrals, and recommendations. Occasionally, caregivers with a victimization history present in a drastically different way from the caregivers who are inundated by their own feelings and memories—they will present as numb and avoidant, and in more extreme cases may inadvertently enable dynamics that are exacerbating the problematic sexual behaviors that are occurring.

Some of the caregivers you encounter may come from homes where abuse was common and poor boundaries were normalized. They may not have received adequate support to process and heal from their victimization, thus internalizing some of their experiences as "normal" or minimizing their trauma. Growing up in this environment may have distorted their understanding of healthy and typical boundaries, and without intervention they may unintentionally perpetuate these same beliefs and actions in their own home. This presents as a uniquely challenging dynamic to address, as pointing out and asking caregivers to acknowledge and change these unhealthy beliefs or dysfunctional dynamics is also asking them to acknowledge that they did not get the appropriate support they needed when experiencing trauma. If they are not in a stable position to do so, this can be disorienting, and they may be resistant to this change, sometimes unable to see dynamics in their home as unhealthy or enabling problematic behaviors.

Responding to caregivers who minimize unsafe behaviors starts with assuring them that you are not there to judge them or their past; you are there to provide additional information that may help them make alternative choices in the future. This can be a slow process, but their presence and choice to engage their child in therapeutic services shows that there is a piece of them that wants something different for their child, perhaps something they didn't have. This is the piece that you water and encourage to grow. During this process, I've had caregivers open up about their trauma history, sometimes for the first time in their lives. I hold space for this, and also encourage them to seek out their own therapist. When this happens, I've also witnessed caregivers who experience tremendous amounts of guilt and shame. I reiterate to the caregiver that they did the best they could with the information they had at the time, again, acknowledging that they cannot give what they did not have. I then point out that they are now actively working on creating a safer and more appropriate environment for their child. They are choosing to create a different path, one that they were not afforded. This is where we see generational traumas shift, and we can applaud the caregivers for having the strength to do so. We can reinforce their efforts and hard work, continuing to motivate them to make the changes necessary to support their child in discontinuing any problematic sexual behaviors.

COMMON STRUGGLES AND ISSUES EXPERIENCED WHEN WORKING WITHIN LARGER SYSTEMS WHILE TREATING PROBLEMATIC SEXUAL BEHAVIORS

Problematic sexual behaviors do not happen in a vacuum. At times we may have clients who present with challenges that appear straightforward and easy to treat, or work with families who are high functioning and well resourced. Yes, these clients may appear uncomplicated on the surface, but they still exist within the larger context of societal systems. For better or worse, all clinicians working with children who have engaged in problematic sexual behaviors are doing so within larger systems. At times we may feel like these systems support our clients and their families, and at other times we may feel confined by their parameters or let down by their lack of response or resources. Whether it be entities like licensing boards or the lack of societal discourse around healthy sexuality, living within and under these larger systems impacts the work we do with clients. Below, I discuss some of the challenges I experience when working within the parameters of larger systems and ways that our society can impact the work we do with clients.

Mandatory Reporting

If you're working with children who are engaging in problematic sexual behaviors, you will also be making mandatory reports. It's not a matter of if, it's a matter of when. I find myself making mandatory reports for three main reasons: my client discloses sexual behaviors with another child, my client discloses that someone has abused them, or historical abuse that hasn't been reported. I will walk through each of these three scenarios, discuss the challenges that may come up in each, and how I handle these situations.

Client Discloses Sexual Behaviors With Another Child

When children are identified as having problematic sexual behaviors, it is clear that an adult in their life has identified atypical or problematic behaviors or has discovered the child's engagement in problematic sexual behaviors. This report might originate with a teacher at school, a caregiver, or a coach. These behaviors are identified, and the child is brought in for services. Once you begin working with this child, and you begin discussing their past behaviors, you may find that there is more than one instance of problematic sexual behaviors, or more than one child they have engaged in problematic sexual behaviors with. If other children are involved, this constitutes a mandatory report. These reports are important to make because, ideally, it will identify the other child as needing services and connect them with such. Though these behaviors are reportable, in my experience, CPS will commonly state they are closing the report at screening—meaning that the incident will not be investigated. These reports are often closed at screening due to the client's age. The report itself is not challenging, it's the impact this report can have on your client and your therapeutic rapport. I handle this with transparency and frequent reminders about my role as a mandatory reporter. I will have this conversation and remind them about the limits of confidentiality before engaging in treatment work that could bring up new information that hasn't been previously disclosed. When new reportable information is disclosed, I address it in the session immediately. I speak with my client about how they'd like to move forward, giving them the opportunity to be present for the report, or letting them know I can do it on my own. I also let them know that we need to inform their caregivers of this new information and ask how they'd like to do this.

Client Discloses Abuse Perpetrated Against Them

When abuse is discovered, protocol is followed, and a mandatory report is made. In this circumstance, it may feel less nerve-racking for clients, as it is not their behaviors being reported, rather it's behaviors that others have done to them. When they disclose that another child, adolescent, or adult has engaged in abusive behaviors toward them, I discuss the reporting process and inform them that this information will be shared with a CPS worker. I then make the report and follow up with my client in their next session. I also ask them how they'd like to go about sharing this information with their care-giver. Sometimes they invite the caregiver into session to share the details, other times they ask if I can provide this information. I let them know that I will but that at some point we will need to come together as a team to discuss the disclosure. This process gets tricky when the report of abuse is against a current caregiver.

In such cases, safety and imminent risk need to be assessed. If the immi-nent risk to safety is high, and the client discloses significant abuse that is current or ongoing, such as sexual abuse by a caregiver, the client is not able to leave my office with their caregiver and emergency plans are made. If safety and imminent risk have been assessed as low, and the client discloses an abusive behavior such as a caregiver spanking them with a belt, they can be released to their caregiver after the session, but the abuse still needs to be reported. I let the client know that I will need to report the information they shared and discuss this process. Occasionally, clients seem unfazed, however, much of the time they appear anxious about the impact this disclo-sure is going to have on their family. I validate these feelings, process their concerns, and assure them that they have done nothing wrong. After making the report, I ask the CPS worker I'm speaking with whether I can talk with the caregivers about the report I made. Sometimes they say no, but generally they say yes. If they say that I can discuss this with the caregiver, I call and debrief the caregiver(s) on the report I made and provide any details the CPS worker shared regarding the follow-up process. After speaking with them, I offer a follow-up session to process any thoughts or feelings that are coming up for them, and share the role that the disclosure will, or will not, play in their child's therapy.

Historical Abuse That Hasn't Been Reported

There have been times when I've attempted to follow up on reports of his-torical abuse but discover that it was not previously reported. In my opinion, these are the easiest mandatory calls to make. They do not involve current dynamics and, at times, the client and caregivers have already discussed this situation. In these instances, reports often have minimal impact on therapeutic rapport. I handle these reports the same way as others, but they often require less follow-up with caregivers and clients usually experience less distress.

Lack of Discourse Around Sexuality as a Society

Let's face it, we as a country need to get better at talking about sex. Sexual education is fundamental to healthy sexual development; however, within the United States, requirements around sexual education vary from state to state, and the content being addressed also varies drastically. Breuner and Mattson's (2016) gathering of research on evidence-based sexual health education speaks to the numerous health organization and their recommendations for comprehensive sex education to best support healthy development. They highlight that "developing a healthy sexuality is a key developmental milestone for all children and adolescents that depends on acquiring information and forming attitudes, beliefs, and values about consent, sexual orientation, gender identity, relationships, and intimacy" (p. 2). If we are not talking with children about this topic and providing age-appropriate sexual education, we are doing a disservice to their healthy development.

It can be uncomfortable to think of children as sexual beings, and when discussions around this topic come up, therapists and caregivers alike may experience a level of uneasiness. Some caregivers will avoid these topics altogether, assuming that the child's school will educate them on all things related to sexual education. Given the state of sexual education nationwide, and the lack of practical information and education being shared in these settings, it is safer to provide our clients with age-appropriate information to ensure they are getting the information they need. This responsibility falls squarely on us, and we should be prepared to assess and provide this information when providing problematic sexual behavior–specific treatment. In addition to educating our clients, we should also work on addressing these topics with caregivers, which was discussed earlier in this chapter. Ultimately, the lack of regulation and mandates in the United States leaves tremendous levels of disparity regarding the sexual education our clients are receiving. Comprehensive information is not often provided but absolutely needed, therefore, we need to fill this educational void.

Lack of Training Specific to Working with Problematic Sexual Behaviors and Clinicians Working Outside of Their Scope of Practice

As discussed at the beginning of this book, specializing in the treatment of youth who have engaged in illegal sexual behaviors is a niche specialty, and when it's further limited to clinicians who specialize in treating children twelve and under who struggle with problematic sexual behaviors, the number of clinicians grows even smaller. Research shows that finding adequate training, consultation, and supervision for working with this population remains a challenging issue for practitioners, further creating a shortage of qualified therapists (Hackett et al., 2005). This in and of itself is an issue, but it becomes a larger issue when clinicians are working with limited to no training around how to work with these children. Working with this population requires extensive training, and one way to limit the amount of work being done by practitioners who lack training is to produce a formal accreditation process. This could ensure clinicians working in this area of the field have accredited and advanced training and are therefore not working outside of their scope of practice.

Within this profession, there is discourse around practicing within one's scope for good reason. Not doing so can lead to many unfavorable outcomes, ranging from ineffective treatment to actively harming a client. It is unlikely that therapists entering the field want to do more harm than good, but when clinicians practice outside of their scope, this can absolutely happen. Just like there are specialties within the medical field, there are specialties within the therapy field. There are different associations connected with these specialties such as the Association for Play Therapy, who is responsible for credentialing registered play therapists. There are certifications one must possess before practicing within a specialty, such as becoming eye movement desensitization and reprocessing (EMDR) certified prior to utilizing this recall-based therapy modality. These associations and certifications help ensure that a clinician is well trained and practicing within their scope and provides clinicians with structured and detailed instructions on how to become certified within these specialties. Unfortunately, there are no associations, credentialing processes, or certified best practices when it comes to treating children with problematic sexual behaviors. This leads to confusion around who is most qualified to work with these children and what kind of training is needed prior to rendering these specialized services. There is a distinct need for some type of regulation as the number of children being referred to treatment for sexual behavior problems continues to grow.

Hackett et al. (2005) highlights the conundrum of needing to ensure practitioners are well trained in this complex area of practice, while also acknowledging that creating a formal accreditation process may further heighten the practitioner shortage within this area of the field. They identify the need for consultation, supervision, and training as being ever-present, acknowledging the fact that specialist services have greater access to resources like consultation, supervision, and training, compared to workers who are in more generalized settings, yet these supports are still lacking. In the end of their study, they recommend that "consideration should be given to the development and identification of different levels of accredited training in order to improve standards of practice" (p. 148). Even though regulation practices, like requiring accreditation, can have an initial negative impact on practitioner numbers, the importance of adequate training cannot be overstated.

Through the course of working with young children with problematic sexual behaviors, I have seen an unfortunate pattern of delayed intervention. Children and families have shared their experience of seeking out therapeutic support for problematic sexual behaviors only to end up with a clinician who has little training within this specialty. Rather than referring out, this clinician will meet with the child until they realize the child needs more specialized treatment and will then refer out. Unfortunately, these prior services can be detrimental to discontinuing the identified problematic sexual behaviors, and not receiving specialized care potentially allows for these unhealthy and inappropriate behaviors to continue and/or worsen.

Clinicians can inadvertently cause more harm if they attempt to treat these behaviors without the right training, as they may not fully understand what needs to be addressed when working toward extinguishing problematic sexual behaviors. To highlight the harm that insufficient training can have when working with these children, I've provided an example below. This example is based on a mixture of experiences I've had when working with children who did not receive specialized treatment initially and the complications that followed. Names and details have been altered, and this example is a composite of several accounts, and does not represent a specific client or instance.

Tony, a nine-year-old male, was referred to me for significant problematic sexual behaviors. He was identified by several systems as being high risk, and had prior contact with systems and resources such as the local child advocacy center, CPS, community mental health services, and Wraparound care. Tony had been involved in mental health therapy for years. He'd met with several therapists during this time, and even though they were aware of his problematic sexual behaviors, and reportedly worked on goals related to the problematic sexual behaviors, these behaviors persisted. As I started working with Tony, I spoke with his caregivers about their experiences with past services and clinicians who had engaged in treatment with Tony. During this time, I learned that the first therapist, who was meeting with Tony around the age of seven, became aware of sexualized behaviors, but believed them to be age-appropriate. These behaviors, however, were not developmentally typical, but because this therapist did not have the appropriate training, they were misidentified as age-appropriate and were not further addressed. As they continued meeting, Tony's behaviors started to escalate, and at this time his therapist also left the field, referring Tony to another therapist within this setting. During this transition, Tony's caregivers discussed their growing concerns regarding his behaviors, and the new therapist assured them that the behaviors would be addressed in their treatment together. This clinician viewed the behaviors as symptoms of trauma and early attachment wounds. Though their case conceptualization addressed Tony's attachment and early childhood trauma, it did not involve other factors that led to, and worsened, the problematic sexual behaviors. They only focused on the child's caregiver connection, and though this is very important, it is not sufficient for treating and extinguishing problematic sexual behaviors. Initially, the caregiver reported that they were seeing shifts in Tony's behaviors at home, and their relationship was improving, but it was discovered that Tony was sneaking onto devices at home and watching pornography. This issue was not further explored with Tony, rather the therapist spoke with the caregivers and implemented a plan around supervised internet use. Soon after, the caregivers received a call from his school and learned that Tony was increasingly initiating sexualized conversations with peers. The therapist became aware of these concerns and utilized this opportunity to speak with Tony about school-appropriate conversations and practice social skills. Though this conversation was important to have, and these skills important to learn, again, it did not address the larger root of these behaviors, as the therapist continued to focus on attachment. This therapist did not have the appropriate training and understanding of how to treat problematic sexual behaviors, so it created a challenging dynamic not unlike a game of Whac-A-Mole— behavioral concerns were targeted when they came up while other behaviors continued to go unchecked and fly under the radar, since the therapeutic goals were around strengthening caregiver attachment. By this time, Tony was now nearly nine years old and had been involved in therapy for nearly two years, seemingly to address his problematic sexual behaviors, but he was continuing to struggle with these behaviors. Tony had been meeting with his current therapist for 1.5 years, but had engaged in minimal discussions directly related to sexual behaviors. It was discovered that, for the past six months, Tony had been sneaking into his little brother's room and engaging in sexual behaviors with him. Devastated by this discovery, Tony's caregivers decided that the therapy he had been receiving was not adequately addressing the sexual behavior concerns they'd initially sought out therapy for; instead, they felt that the behaviors had gotten worse. At this time, they pulled Tony from his current services and asked for a referral to the clinic I work at, as we specialize in treating survivors and perpetrators of sexual abuse. This is how Tony ended up on my caseload.

In looking at this example, we can see how important specialized training is when working with children who have problematic sexual behaviors. Tony did not receive adequate treatment for his problematic sexual behaviors, as both previous therapists were practicing outside of their scope. They did not have the appropriate training to adequately address Tony's therapeutic needs, thus the behaviors persisted and worsened. This not only delayed appropriate support and intervention for Tony and his family but also enabled sexualized behaviors to worsen to the point of harming his younger brother. Treating problematic sexual behaviors is much more than safety planning around technology, addressing attachment, or processing past trauma. Yes, it involves these elements, but it also involves appropriate psychoeducation for the child and caregivers, understanding the multilayered factors that impact engagement in problematic sexual behaviors, and much more. Simply treating these struggles as attachment issues or trauma does not provide the nuanced and multisystem approach needed to address the multifaceted issues of problematic sexual behaviors.

Who Should Work With Children That Are Engaging in Problematic Sexual Behaviors?

So, since there isn't a certification process, or an organization in charge of providing guidelines and protocol for the effective treatment of children engaging in problematic sexual behaviors, who should provide these therapeutic services? Well, depending on who you ask, the answer may differ drastically. I don't have the answer to this question, but I am able to provide some of the varied viewpoints present within the research, and the discussions happening within the field.

Child Advocacy Centers

First, let's look at the role that child advocacy centers (CACs) can play in the treatment of these children. It can be argued that CACs are in a unique position to respond to children engaging in problematic sexual behaviors. They are already mandated to support children who have been victimized and already utilize a multidisciplinary model for their work with victimized children. Research emphasizes the importance of a multifaceted approach when treating children with problematic sexual behaviors, and the multidisciplinary approach used by CACs allows for focused intervention within a number of areas, including family work, increasing caregiver involvement and engagement, providing preventative education and mental health services to process trauma while also addressing problematic behaviors, and identifying additional community resources the child may need (Harris et al., 2023).

With their mandate to support children who have been victimized and their focus on family work and increasing caregiver engagement, they are in a unique position to help children who have engaged in problematic sexual behaviors. One reason for this is that CACs regularly see cases of sibling sexual abuse (Taylor et al., 2021; Tener et al., 2020). About one-quarter of children who experience sexual abuse do so at the hands of someone they are related to, such as a cousin or sibling (Finkelhor et al., 2009). Allardyce and Yates (2021) define sibling sexual abuse as a sibling engaging in "behaviour that causes sexual, physical and emotional harm, including sexually abusive behaviour which involves violence" (p. 15). It is difficult to establish the prevalence of sibling sexual abuse due to the secretive nature of these behaviors and the underreporting of sexual abuse in general, but in my experience working with this population, there are times where most of my caseload consists of children who have engaged in problematic sexual behaviors with their siblings. Given this fairly common dynamic and the high rate of stress within the family unit (Gray et al., 1999), it makes sense for CACs to meet with the child who was victimized, as well as the child who engaged in problematic sexual behaviors. This allows for optimal collaboration between therapists, as both clients are being seen within the same organization. It also provides a level of ease for the caregivers, as they do not need to travel to two different clinics when both children are being seen in the same location. This collaborative approach, and providing specialized services to the family, can help lead to optimal outcomes.

CACs not only use a collaborative approach but also have specialized training in treating victims of abuse and maltreatment, a nearly universal experience of children engaging in problematic sexual behaviors (Gray et al., 1999; Finkelhor et al., 2007; Szanto et al., 2012; Vizard et al., 2007). They have specific training around sexual abuse, regularly work with victims of sexual abuse, have experience working with family systems, and often have connections to varied resources in the community, many of which children with problematic sexual behaviors may need referrals to. Currently, the only issue I'm aware of when it comes to CACs treating children who have problematic sexual behaviors is that their focus is often on the victim who experienced harmful sexual behaviors rather than the child who engaged in these behaviors.

CACs in the United States often refer the child who has engaged in problematic sexual behaviors to appropriate therapeutic interventions but do not typically treat the child unless they are young (Tener et al., 2019). That being said, there is significant overlap seen in children who engage in problematic sexual behaviors and those who have been victimized themselves, and in these cases, it is possible for CACs to work with these children (Tener et al., 2019). So, with a few tweaks of the already-present protocols and systems within CACs, it can be argued that they are in a prime position to support these children (Harris et al., 2023; Sites & Widdifield, 2020). If they can expand their ability to meet with children who are engaging in problematic sexual behaviors, regardless of whether the child has experienced their own sexual abuse or not, they could arguably be one of the best providers to meet with these children given their specialized training, role within the community, and current work with children who have been victimized.

Clinicians Who Are Certified in Working With Juveniles Who Have Engaged in Harmful Sexual Behaviors

Though there is no specific certification for working with children engaging in problematic sexual behaviors, there are certifications for clinicians working with juveniles and adults who have engaged in sexual offending behaviors. It has been argued that clinicians who hold these certifications may be in the best position to serve children with problematic sexual behaviors since they already have specialized training relevant to sexual abuse–specific treatment and evaluation. The Colorado Sex Offender Management Board (SOMB, 2023) published a white paper report addressing current best practices. They stated that the assessment and treatment of a child with problematic sexual behaviors would be "best conducted by an experienced, licensed clinician with specialized training in children's problematic sexual behavior in order to ethically perform such an evaluation," as they acknowledge the need to have "advanced expertise not offered in traditional graduate course work" (SOMB, 2023, p. 24). The state of Oregon holds a similar stance, and since I live in Oregon, I'll provide an example of Oregon's specific boards and statutes and how this relates to the treatment of children with problematic sexual behaviors.

In the state of Oregon, we have the Sex Offense Treatment Board, which is housed within the Health Licensing Office. The Sex Offense Treatment Board oversees the practice standards and guidelines for the evaluation and treatment of juveniles who have engaged in sexually abusive behaviors. To work with this population in a clinical capacity, it is mandated by the board that you be certified. The certification process requires a minimum number of hours dedicated to formal training applicable to sexual abuse evaluation and treatment, direct clinical contact with clients, direct supervision, and meeting minimum education requirements. To illustrate the level of specialized training and education needed to be a certified clinical sexual offense therapist in the state of Oregon, I've provided a list of the requirements taken from the Sex Offense Treatment Board certification information page:

> a minimum of a master's degree in behavioral science, an active Oregon mental health professional license, a minimum of at least 2,000 hours of direct clinical contact with clients within a six year period prior to the application for certification and must include 1,000 hours of direct treatment services, 500 hours of evaluations, and 500 hours of treatment-plan related activity, and lastly, a minimum of 60 hours of formal training applicable to sexual abuse specific treatment and evaluation within six years prior to applying for certification. (Oregon Health Authority, n.d., "Education and Training section, para. 1)

Becoming a certified clinical sexual offense therapist clearly requires extensive training within this specialization, and for this reason, some may argue that therapists that hold this certification are best qualified to meet with children engaging in problematic sexual behaviors.

Within Oregon, this is the argument made by the Sex Offense Treatment Board. The Sex Offense Treatment Board's (2020) definition of "juvenile" includes anyone under the age of eighteen at the time they engaged in their sexually harmful behaviors. This means that to work with children engaging in problematic sexual behaviors, you must obtain Sex Offense Treatment Board certification as a clinical, secondary clinical, associate, or intern therapist. Working with this population without the appropriate certification is seen as working outside the scope of professional practice and can result in a board complaint. Therefore, in the state of Oregon, it can be argued that the only clinicians who should be working with children engaged in problematic sexual behaviors should be Sex Offense Treatment Board certified. Even though that's what the statutes state, I believe that this outlook is problematic.

A clinician who has the certification of clinical sexual offense therapist (CSOT) may have incredible training when it comes to treating a sixteen-year-old who has been charged with sexual offenses, but that does not mean they have the appropriate training to work with a seven-year-old who has been engaging in problematic sexual behaviors. The treatment protocols for an adjudicated sixteen-year-old and a seven-year-old are drastically different, but the Oregon Sex Offense Treatment Board's definition of what makes someone qualified to work with both cases would be the same. Best practices for treating problematic sexual behaviors identifies the need to individualize the child's treatment to respond to the vastly diverse behaviors, contexts, and factors that led to the problematic sexual behaviors. The research acknowledges that juveniles who engage in sexual offenses are different than adults who engage in sexual offenses, thus they should be treated differently, and the evolution of juvenile sex offense–specific treatment reflects this (Creeden, 2020; Hackett, 2014; McPherson et al., 2023). The research also acknowledges that children engaging in problematic sexual behaviors are different than juveniles who engage in sexual offenses, however, the Sex Offense Treatment Board's definition of who should be treating children with problematic sexual behaviors does not reflect this.

Though I can appreciate the Sex Offense Treatment Board's attempt to regulate and ensure only qualified clinicians are providing services to this unique population, it can cause harm to lump the treatment of children with problematic sexual behaviors into the same regulations required to treat juveniles with illegal sexual behaviors. Someone who is only trained in working with adjudicated juveniles may provide problematic sexual behavior treatment that is over the top or not developmentally appropriate for young kids. Depending on the training, it could be argued that a child and family therapist could be more qualified than a CCSOT clinician to address problematic sexual behaviors, as they have the background and subsequent training needed to effectively work with families, a crucial component of problematic sexual behavior treatment.

Licensed Marriage and Family Therapists

St. Amand et al. (2008) reviewed eleven treatment outcome studies that examined eighteen different types of treatment when addressing problematic sexual behaviors, and the element that was most strongly correlated with the reduction in problematic sexual behaviors was parental involvement and training. For this reason, it could be argued that a licensed marriage and family therapist (LMFT) may be well suited to treat children with problematic sexual behaviors. LMFTs receive comprehensive training in family counseling, and this education, coupled with additional training to better understand problematic sexual behaviors, could enable an LMFT to provide effective treatment from a systems approach. LMFTs possess great skills when it comes to family work, and should they participate in additional training related to problematic sexual behaviors, they could be strong candidates for treating problematic sexual behaviors in a holistic manner.

They may also serve as a good choice if the problematic sexual behaviors are less invasive and more related to environmental factors. The research shows that growing up in homes where there is exposure to sexual activity, nudity, pornography, domestic violence, physical abuse, and poor boundaries increases the chances of a child's engagement in problematic sexual behaviors (; Curwen et al. 2014; Friedrich et al., 2003; Levesque et al., 2010; Mesman et al., 2019). Given that these behaviors may stem from dynamics occurring at home, or within the family, licensed marriage and family therapists may be best equipped to address the family-specific shifts that need to occur to decrease the chances of future problematic sexual behaviors occurring.

CONCLUSION

Regardless of who provides the treatment, be it a therapist from a child advocacy center, a certified clinical sexual offense therapist, or a licensed marriage and family therapist, the research is clear: a multisystem approach involving family-based interventions should be emphasized when treating children with problematic sexual behaviors. Having specialized training, such as the training needed to be a clinical sex offense therapist, is incredibly important given the complex nature of these behavioral problems. Not only is it important to be trained in treating problematic sexual behaviors, but it is also necessary to have specialized training in working with young children, facilitating family therapy, and utilizing both psychoeducation focused therapies (cognitive behavioral therapy [CBT], problematic sexual behavior-CBT [PSB-CBT]), and expressive dynamic therapies to best serve this unique population.

Ambiguity Around National Response, Certifications, and Protocol

Though treating problematic sexual behaviors in children is a highly specialized focus within the mental health field, there is no overarching entity, organization, or credentialing process that ensures clinicians rendering these services are doing so with the appropriate education and specialized training needed. This creates a host of issues including clinicians practicing outside of their scope, lack of understanding around best practices, minimal supervision when working with this highly vulnerable population, and minimal checks to ensure educational foundations are in place for working with these nuanced behavioral struggles. Without this oversight it is much easier for these children to fall through the cracks and for more harm to occur.

Children who engage in problematic sexual behaviors are frequently both the victims of harm, as well as the perpetrators of harm. This challenges the current dichotomy seen in sex offense–specific work where there is a designated "offender" and "victim," thus creating challenges around who should be working with these children. On one hand, a child who has experienced sexual abuse and/or maltreatment may receive therapeutic support via a child advocacy center (CAC), however if this same child is also engaging in harmful behaviors, are they still an appropriate fit for receiving services at a CAC? If not, should they be referred to a community agency or a private practice? If so, it may be difficult to find clinicians with adequate and appropriate training to both understand and treat the nuances of problematic sexual behaviors. So how do we know if a clinician has the necessary training to treat a child with problematic sexual behaviors? Well, that's the issue. There is no agreed-upon definition of what makes a clinician certified to work with this population and no overarching board or protocol to lean on when uncertainty arises.

There are many clinical specialties within the broader mental health field. A clinician can specialize in sex therapy, the treatment of eating disorders, working with addictions, and so on. Each of these distinct specializations require certifications. To be a practicing sex therapist in the United States, you must be certified through the American Association of Sexuality Educators, Counselors, and Therapists (AASECT). Specializing in the treatment of addictions often requires a clinician to obtain the distinction as a certified alcohol and drug counselor (CADC). A licensed therapist who has completed a high level of training to specialize in the treatment of eating disorders is certified through the International Association of Eating Disorders Professionals Foundation as a certified eating disorders specialist (CEDS). Each of these specialties requires intensive training, specialized education, and specific supervision to ensure that the treatment being rendered is based on best practices. This should be no different for the clinicians working with problematic sexual behaviors. Certification ensures clinicians are practicing within their scope and providing clients with the best care possible. Given the increase in national discourse regarding the identification and treatment of problematic sexual behaviors, it seems that establishing protocols for specializing with this population is overdue.

As discussed earlier, when clinicians lack the appropriate training to treat problematic sexual behaviors, these behaviors may persist, be cast off as "normative," or simply be ignored out of discomfort. The mishandling of these behaviors creates a ripple effect of possible negative outcomes. A child engaging in problematic sexual behaviors who is not being treated appropriately may continue to engage in these behaviors, inflicting more sexual harm and leading to more identified victims. A clinician who does not understand the crucial role family therapy plays in the treatment of problematic sexual behaviors may focus on the child's behaviors but miss the necessary family work needed to aid the child in discontinuing these behaviors. A clinician who specializes in treating adjudicated youth may have the specialization needed to treat sexually abusive behaviors but miss the steps needed to address the child's own history of sexual abuse and maltreatment. All of this is to say that as the focus on treating children with problematic sexual behaviors grows, there is a definitive need to provide clinicians with an idea of what exactly is needed to ensure they are prepared to work with this population.

In my opinion, there is a need for the United States to develop a national strategy to identify children with problematic sexual behaviors, create a nationwide policy around appropriate protocols to address these behaviors, and create regulations around who and how interventions and services should be rendered. Creating this oversight can help ensure children exhibiting these behaviors are not overlooked; rather, they can appropriately intervene and provide treatment so that these behaviors do not escalate. This can help prevent further future contact from systems like CPS or the juvenile justice systems. We as a nation can take a preventative approach to problematic sexual behaviors rather than a reactive approach, ultimately leading to a decrease in problematic sexual behaviors, sexual abuse, and victimization, while increasing safety within communities.

Additionally, there is a need to address the inconsistencies present among agency responses to these behaviors. When reporting harmful sexual behaviors by adolescents, they are often followed up on, frequently leading to contact with the juvenile justice system. This connects them with a system that can link them with the appropriate services and highlights recommendations and protocols for moving forward with the treatment of these identified harmful sexual behaviors. When reporting a child who has engaged in harmful sexual behaviors, the follow-up, if there is any, is much less certain. As we know from the research, children exhibiting problematic sexual behaviors are more likely to have had previous contact with child welfare services, sometimes even prior to the development of problematic sexual behaviors (Hackett, 2014). If we know that these children are often being identified by child welfare agencies, we can deduce that they play a meaningful role in intervening on problematic sexual behaviors and successfully identifying children who need intervention. If there is a lack of agreement across agencies around what constitutes atypical or typical sexual behaviors in children, we can infer that there will also be inconsistencies in how these reports are handled, therefore, discrepancies in how often children are appropriately referred to therapeutic services.

There have been times, when making hotline calls about similar cases, that one case was handled differently from the other. The different handling of these reports could be based on a number of factors, such as the training the hotline workers received, their level of understanding around sexual behaviors in children, potential biases in their view of typical versus atypical sexual behaviors in children, and so on. Regardless of the reason these calls were handled differently, these inconsistencies can drastically impact the treatment of problematic sexual behaviors. How these cases are handled can have a direct impact on whether the child and their family is connected to appropriate resources and information that assists them in intervention. When there is ambiguity around how to best identify and intervene on these cases, there are inconsistencies in sharing effective information, which can ultimately lead to hyperreactive or hyporeactive responses when problematic sexual behaviors are reported. Creating consistency among the many elements that go into successfully identifying problematic sexual behaviors—such as training, education, and protocol—will aid in early intervention and better detection on a system wide level.

Chapter 11

Furthering the Field

As interest in this population grows, it is important to look forward and assess the needs to best serve this population. In the beginning of this book, I engaged in an extensive literature review regarding the treatment of problematic sexual behaviors for children ages twelve and younger. While conducting this review, it became abundantly clear that there is a general need for more research and, even more so, research that addresses the diversity seen among this population. There is a need for research regarding the treatment of gender-nonconforming and gender-diverse children who engage in problematic sexual behaviors. There is a need for further research regarding the neurodiverse and developmentally delayed children who are engaging in problematic sexual behaviors. There is a need to ensure the presence of equity and equality when providing problematic sexual behavior–specific treatment. Continuing research that focuses on this population is important, but it is equally important to address the ways clinicians can provide ethical and effective care for such a diverse population.

In addition to the needs we see in research, there is a significant lack of assessment tools specific to this population. I provide a list of assessments that clinicians can use, most of which address trauma. This is important given the trauma that most of these clients have experienced; however, there is a need for more tools specific to problematic sexual behaviors. Assessment tools can help verify that the treatment being provided is effective. We need tools that will establish and substantiate the improvements clients experience after engaging in problematic sexual behavior–specific treatment. My hope is that the increased awareness and interest in this population, in addition to furthering the research, will enable the creation of such tools.

LACK OF RESEARCH

A significant barrier that I, and anyone working with this population, come up against is the relative lack of research present in this area of the field. In the broadest sense, the research available regarding the treatment of children with problematic sexual behaviors is limited. When it comes to the research available that addresses the *diversity* among children presenting with problematic sexual behaviors, the available research becomes even scarcer. This scarcity is seen when looking for research specific to the treatment of problematic sexual behaviors in females, gender-diverse children, and youth with developmental disabilities (Campbell et al., 2016; Hackett, 2014; McPherson et al., 2023). Additionally, historical context or responses to problematic sexual behaviors is often missing from the research. Harris and colleagues (2023) examined the historical responses to problematic sexual behaviors from the 1940s to the present day (2024). They highlight the growth this field has seen when it comes to societal views on gender and sexuality; however, they also acknowledge the importance of recognizing that "historically, problematic sexual behavior concerns were influenced by white supremacy, homophobia, heterosexism, and firm gender binaries," and it is likely that these factors continue to influence the research and treatment children experience today (Harris et al., 2023, "A Review of Historical Responses to Problematic Sexual Behavior" section, para. 1).

Below, I've highlighted these areas, along with others, that are poorly represented within the research. Further research is required to establish effective interventions for children that present with problematic sexual behaviors and hold one or more of the following identities.

Race and Ethnicity

Ethnicity is not something that is often recorded in the research of youth's engagement in harmful sexual behaviors (Finkelhor et al., 2009; Hackett et al., 2014; McPherson et al., 2023). Hackett (2014) cites his earlier work, where he writes about the lack of recognition regarding ethnicity within the research and suggests a potential reason being that the problematic sexual behaviors being researched were seen as the primary focus, whereas the ethnicity of the youth was seen as secondary. This is clearly problematic as ethnicity plays a major role in an individual's lived experience and informs the appropriate approaches, interventions, and models clinicians should use. He cites the research done by Mir and Oktie (2002) that highlights these differences and asserts the importance of rejecting the view that Western approaches and models are equally applicable to all youth, regardless of ethnic background. Additionally, DeLamater and Friedrich (2002) highlight that sexual development and sexual behaviors are significantly influenced by the social context a child grows up within. This means that the sociocultural environments children grow up in will have a distinct influence on their sexual understanding, development, and behaviors.

More research regarding the treatment of problematic sexual behaviors and the intersection of ethnicity and culturally informed care is needed. There is little evidence of movement within policies and assessments that address the specific needs of subgroups within this population (Hackett et al., 2005). This need has been identified for decades, but further research into the subgroups of young people engaging in problematic sexual behaviors—like young people with learning disabilities, ethnic and racial minorities, and females—continues to be inadequate.

In 2022, Colorado's Sex Offender Management Board conducted a state-wide survey of board-approved providers. This report, published in 2023, documented that children being treated for problematic sexual behaviors were from all racial/ethnic identities; however, most providers reported that the children they were treating for problematic sexual behaviors were white. Over half of the respondents also reported that they worked with some children who were African American and Hispanic (SOMB, 2023). Though this report was specific to Colorado, it highlights the reality that children from every racial/ethnic background engage in problematic sexual behaviors but a large portion of the children receiving services are white. Within the research, it's common for the studies of treatment and control groups to be predominantly white (Allen, 2023; Carpentier et al. 2006). We know that all ethnicities and races are accounted for when looking at which children engage in problematic sexual behaviors, however, providers are reporting that the majority of the clients they are serving are white, and the research being done frequently uses white males as the sample group. This dynamic points to a glaring disparity in the services being provided and research being done. There is no doubt that this inequality impacts the research and the treatment that minority children receive.

Not only does addressing race and ethnicity within research enable us to view our clients through a holistic lens, addressing these elements is necessary, as race and ethnicity actively impact our clients' lived experiences. Thigpen (2009) identifies both race and ethnicity as being important sociocultural factors that impact sexual behaviors. The lack of racial diversity present in the research highlights the possibility that current findings and understandings of sexual behaviors in children may not be representative of African American children (Gordon & Schroeder, 1995) or other minority children. The lack of research that addresses the influence that race and ethnicity have on sexual development can have harmful effects, such as mislabeling behaviors that minority children engage in, since the normative standard of behaviors are pulled from predominantly white male children (Thigpen et al., 2003).

There is also a lack of research examining the impact that racism has on sexual development and discussions around sexuality in general. Ward (2005) and West (2001) hypothesize that there is still fear within African American communities when it comes to openly discussing sexuality. They pose that this stems from historically racist views and stereotyping of African American sexuality, like the narrative created by whites that African Americans could not control their sexual appetites. Racism and oppression cannot be ignored, and further research should explore the impact it has on sexual development and in turn, the impact it could have on children's engagement in problematic sexual behaviors.

Girls and Gender-Diverse Children

Another area lacking research is the intersection of problematic sexual behaviors and gender identity. While the research, and the mental health field as a whole, is beginning to recognize that girls also engage in sexually harmful behaviors, female-specific studies are still rare. Several studies cite that problematic sexual behaviors in children are approximately equal between both sexes, but as children age, boys become more likely to engage in problematic sexual behaviors (Bonner et al., 2000; Szanto et al., 2012). Though girls engage in problematic sexual behaviors at approximately the same rate as boys during childhood, the research available indicates that there are distinct gender differences between boys and girls who act out sexually.

Girls engaging in problematic sexual behaviors tend to be younger (Finkelhor et al., 2009), have higher rates of having experienced sexual abuse (Hackett et al., 2013), and engage in more noninvasive problematic sexual behaviors compared to boys (DeLago et al., 2019). Though there are clear gender differences present between boys and girls who engage in these behaviors, research regarding effective interventions specific to girls is lacking. There is, however, research regarding the differing views around female and male displays of sexuality and the impact that gender roles may have on identifying normative and nonnormative sexual behaviors. When looking at research, adults tend to experience increased anxiety and concern regarding girls and their engagement in sexual behaviors, and these views and biases may result in girls inhibiting their sexual expression and hiding sexual behaviors and adults pathologizing normative sexual development and behaviors (Borneman, 1990; Goldman & Goldman, 1982). Though this information clarifies the impact that biases have in the way we view girls and their sexual behaviors, it does not discuss the impact these biases have on the problematic sexual behaviors they engage in or effective treatment for these behaviors.

Specific studies addressing the nuances between gender and problematic sexual behaviors are few and far between, but even rarer is literature focusing on gender-nonconforming and nonbinary youth who have engaged in problematic or sexually harmful behaviors. I was unable to find any studies or literature discussing the treatment of gender-diverse youth, only studies that highlight the tremendous lack of information and interventions currently available for these youth (Hackett, 2014; McPherson et al., 2023).

Additional research is required to help clinicians better understand the inherent differences between boys, girls, and nonbinary children presenting with problematic sexual behaviors, as well as direction regarding best practices when treating gender-diverse children engaging in problematic sexual behaviors. It can be argued that the lack of attention to gender within the current research produces treatment implications and research results that are unrepresentative, and lack generalizability, for children who do not identify as male. An approach that acknowledges the different experiences that female youth, gender-nonconforming youth, and nonbinary youth have while living in an androcentric society is needed.

Developmental Differences (Developmental Delays)

In addition to the sparse research and studies that address the different identities discussed above, there is also a need for additional research that focuses on the treatment of young children engaging in problematic sexual behaviors who also have learning disabilities and developmental delays. Within the last decade or so, there has been an increase in the referral of youth who have engaged in problematic sexual behaviors who also have learning disabilities (Hackett, 2005; 2014).

Children with developmental differences present with their own specific needs and vulnerabilities. They may experience heightened impulsivity and present as highly opportunistic, they may have varying social skill deficits, they may present as highly concrete in their cognitive processes, and so on (Timms & Goreczny, 2002). These differences could impact their engagement in problematic sexual behaviors, as they may not be aware of social norms around sexual behaviors, problematic sexual behaviors may be overlooked because they are wrongfully viewed as not being sexual beings in the same way their non-delayed peers are, and their needs around accessing developmentally appropriate sexual education may go unrecognized.

This population deserves treatment that addresses their specific needs and vulnerabilities. Unfortunately, the research is underdeveloped, and this population has historically been underserved. There is little empirical research that addresses the treatment needs of adolescents who have learning disabilities or delays and have also engaged in harmful sexual behaviors (Timms &

Goreczny, 2002). The absence of literature and research addressing these intersecting identities grows even larger when looking at young children who have delays and have engaged in problematic sexual behaviors. Research within this area is underdeveloped and, should this continue, there are not only concerns that the distinct needs of these children will go unnoticed but also that the treatment they receive will fail to address either their vulnerabilities or the specific care and education needed to encourage healthy sexuality and development. Additional research addressing practice guidance, specific treatment needs, and how to best serve this population is greatly needed.

ASSESSMENTS

Assessment is often an important part of the treatment process. It supports the clinician in gathering and understanding the current challenges, struggles, and areas that a client may need additional support in. It also acts as a tool to demonstrate treatment efficacy via measurable improvements. There are several assessment tools available for children under the age of twelve; however, many of the tools created to assess the risk and needs related to harmful sexual behaviors were created for youth ages twelve and older. An example of an assessment that would be relevant for children with problematic sexual behaviors, but was created for adolescents, is the protective and risk observations for eliminating sexual offense recidivism (PROFESOR). This assessment was created by Worling in 2017, for youth twelve to twenty-five years of age. I am unaware of any assessment tool designed to evaluate the risk of a child reengaging in problematic sexual behaviors, apart from the latency age–sexual adjustment and assessment tool (LA-SAAT). Though this tool assesses the risk for continued problematic sexual behaviors, it is specifically for males ages eight to thirteen years, therefore the applicability remains semi-limited. It appears that with increased awareness of children engaging in problematic sexual behaviors, there has also been some interest in creating helpful assessments.

Curwen et al. (2014) conducted a study identifying variables that attempted to differentiate children who had been reprimanded by an adult for problematic sexual behaviors but continued these behaviors from those who discontinued these behaviors after receiving a reprimand. One of the inclusion criteria for this study was that the child had to have been under the age of twelve when they engaged in their problematic sexual behaviors, demonstrating the specific focus on children as opposed to adolescents. The study investigated thirty-three potential risk variables and found that eight of these risk variables differentiated children who had been reprimanded but repeated problematic sexual behaviors from those who did not. This was the first study of its kind and points to hopes for the creation of an assessment that addresses risk of repeated problematic sexual behaviors for kids under the age of twelve years. While this is exciting, I'll switch focus to assessment tools and measures that do exist and can prove beneficial for the treatment of children with problematic sexual behaviors.

Child sexual behavior inventory (CSBI). This is a questionnaire for caregivers that asks about thirty-eight different sexual behaviors and the frequency of these behaviors. This caregiver report is specifically for children from the ages of two to twelve years.

Trauma symptom checklist for young children (TSCYC). This is a ninety-item questionnaire to be completed by the caregiver. It evaluates a wide variety of trauma-related symptoms in children and is specifically for children ages three to twelve years.

Child trauma screen (CTS). This is a free ten-item screening tool that measures exposure to trauma and subsequent posttraumatic stress disorder symptoms. This tool is specifically for youth ages six to seventeen years and can be administered via self-report or caregiver report.

Child behavior checklist (CBCL). This is a form completed by caregivers to screen for behavioral, social, and emotional problems. The questions are associated with the following eight categories: withdrawn/depressed, social problems, anxious/depressed, attention problems, thought problems, somatic complaints, aggressive behavior, and rule-breaking behavior. This assessment tool is appropriate to use with youth ages six to eighteen years.

Strengths and difficulties questionnaire (SDQ). This is a brief, twenty-five-item screening questionnaire that's broken into five subscales, with five questions within each subscale. The subscales are emotional symptoms subscale, prosocial behavior subscale, hyperactivity/inattention subscale, conduct problems subscale, and peer relationships subscale. There are currently three versions of this tool, one that can be completed by individuals eighteen years of age and older, one that can be completed by youth ages eleven to seventeen years, and another that can be completed by a caregiver or teacher of the identified child who falls between the ages of two to seventeen years.

Latency age-sexual adjustment and assessment tool (LA-SAAT). This is designed to assess the risk for continued harmful sexual behaviors in males ages eight to thirteen years. This is utilized by clinicians to form a professional judgment in assessing the likelihood of repeated problematic sexual behaviors.

Appendix

Activity Worksheets and Examples

BOUNDARIES

Boundaries Example

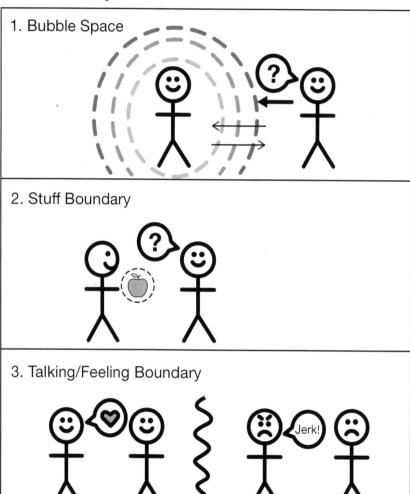

TYPES OF TOUCH

Appendix

Types of Touch Example

1. Good (or Safe) Touch

2. Bad (or Unsafe) Touch

3. Secret (or Sexual) Touch

FEELINGS FACES

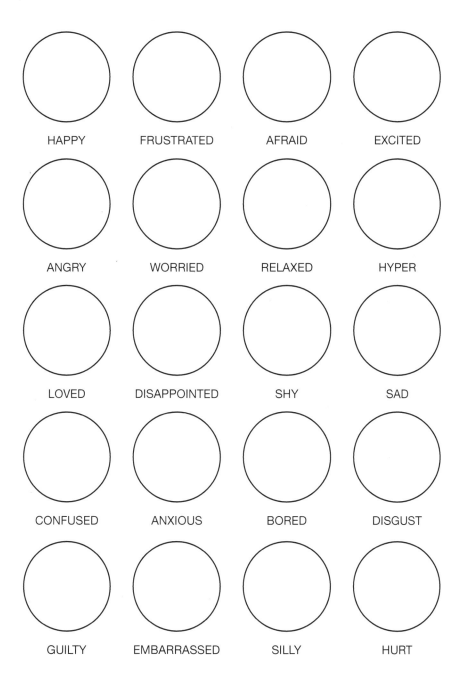

HAPPY   FRUSTRATED   AFRAID   EXCITED

ANGRY   WORRIED   RELAXED   HYPER

LOVED   DISAPPOINTED   SHY   SAD

CONFUSED   ANXIOUS   BORED   DISGUST

GUILTY   EMBARRASSED   SILLY   HURT

Feelings Faces Example

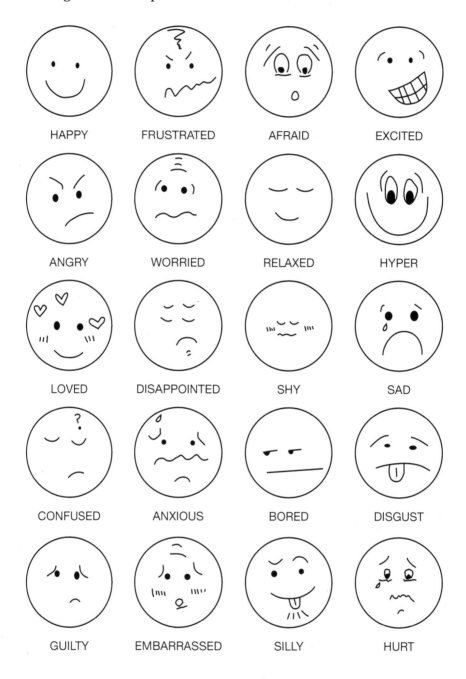

HAPPY · FRUSTRATED · AFRAID · EXCITED

ANGRY · WORRIED · RELAXED · HYPER

LOVED · DISAPPOINTED · SHY · SAD

CONFUSED · ANXIOUS · BORED · DISGUST

GUILTY · EMBARRASSED · SILLY · HURT

FEELINGS CHAIN

1. Triggers/Sensations:

2. Feelings:

3. Thoughts:

4. Actions:

Feelings Chain Example 1

1. Triggers/Sensations:

Smelling hot pizza/stomach growling

2. Feelings:

Hungry

3. Thoughts:

"Mmm that smells delicious"
"I'm going to go into the kitchen
and grab a slice."

4. Actions:

Walking into the kitchen, getting
a slice of pizza, and eating it.

Feelings Chain Example 2

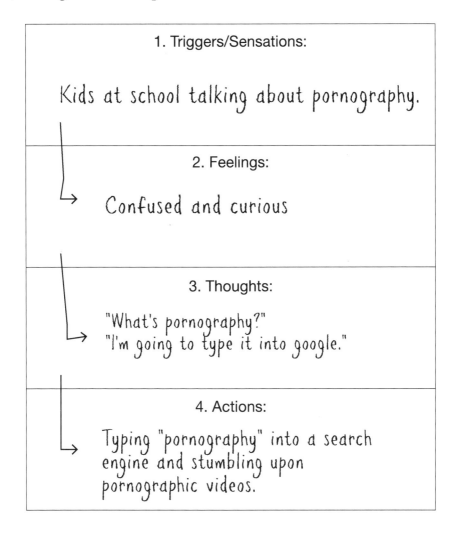

TROUBLE THOUGHTS

Thought Type: These are thought patterns we use when we are trying to avoid getting into trouble. These are also thought patterns that often tend to get us into more trouble.	Definition:
Making excuses	Rather than facing an uncomfortable conversation or feelings we make excuses and avoid responsibility.
Blaming	Assigning responsibility for something bad to someone or something else.
Minimizing	Making something seem smaller/less important/less impactful than it actually is.
Changing the subject	When someone starts talking about something or someone else to avoid the initial conversation.
Denying/Lying by omission	Refusing to admit when you've done or said something. Lying by not sharing all the details.
Avoiding	Keeping away from a topic or purposefully ignoring it to avoid responsibility or discussions about it.
Assuming	When you are making a guess, but treating it like a fact.
Playing the victim	Stating, or acting, like you are hurt when you're really the one who caused the hurt.

TROUBLE THOUGHTS: MIX AND MATCH

Directions. Cut out the different "trouble thoughts" and create your own examples of each below. Mix them up and have your therapist/caregiver/sibling identify which example goes with which pattern of thinking.

Pro tip. If developmentally appropriate, you can go a step further and have your client create examples for each of the thought types. Then they can mix up the examples and thought types and have you match the thought pattern to the appropriate example.

Making excuses	
Blaming	
Minimizing	
Changing the subject	
Denying/Lying by omission	
Avoiding	
Assuming	
Playing the victim	

Trouble Thoughts: Mix and Match Example

Directions. Cut out the different "trouble thoughts" and examples below. Mix them up and have your client identify which example goes with which pattern of thinking.

Thought Type	Example
Making excuses	Larry's mom asked him why he didn't do his chores when he got home from school, and Larry said he was going to but got too tired.
Blaming	Rosa wore her aunt's bracelet to school and lost it. When her aunt noticed, she said her sister was the one who borrowed it.
Minimizing	Lewis's dad noticed a candy bar in his backpack, and when his dad asked if he took it from the store, Lewis replied, "Yeah, but this is the only thing I stole. It's not even a big deal."
Changing the subject	River got an "F" on their math test. When their mom asked how their math test went, they told her that they got a leading part in the school play.
Denying/Lying by omission	Jessica and her sister took $5 from the counter and went to the park and then store without asking. When their parents asked about the $5, Jessica stated that they didn't take it and that they'd just gone to the park.
Avoiding	Trenton's father was lecturing him about taking things from his brother's room without asking. Trenton put his fingers in his ears and yelled, "La, la, la."
Assuming	When Cole smiled at Lucy, Lucy took that as Cole liking her and leaned over to kiss him on the cheek.
Playing the victim	Ryan pushed his sister. When she fell over and started crying, he looked around, fell to the ground, and started crying, stating that she hurt him.

STAIRCASE ACTIVITY

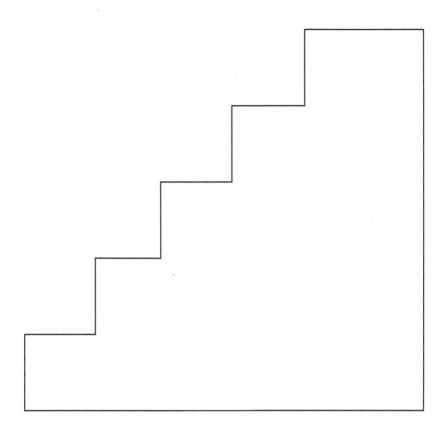

Staircase Activity Example

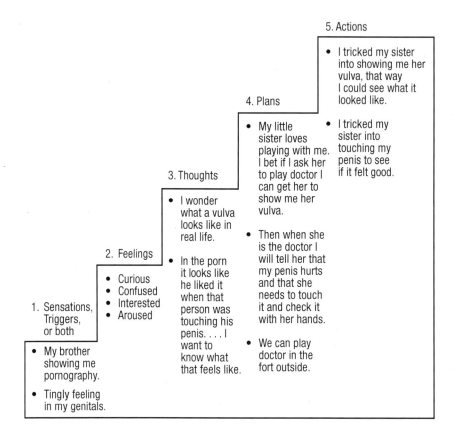

5. Actions

- I tricked my sister into showing me her vulva, that way I could see what it looked like.

4. Plans

- My little sister loves playing with me. I bet if I ask her to play doctor I can get her to show me her vulva.

- Then when she is the doctor I will tell her that my penis hurts and that she needs to touch it and check it with her hands.

- We can play doctor in the fort outside.

- I tricked my sister into touching my penis to see if it felt good.

3. Thoughts

- I wonder what a vulva looks like in real life.

- In the porn it looks like he liked it when that person was touching his penis. . . . I want to know what that feels like.

2. Feelings

- Curious
- Confused
- Interested
- Aroused

1. Sensations, Triggers, or both

- My brother showing me pornography.

- Tingly feeling in my genitals.

WEED ACTIVITY

Weed Activity Example

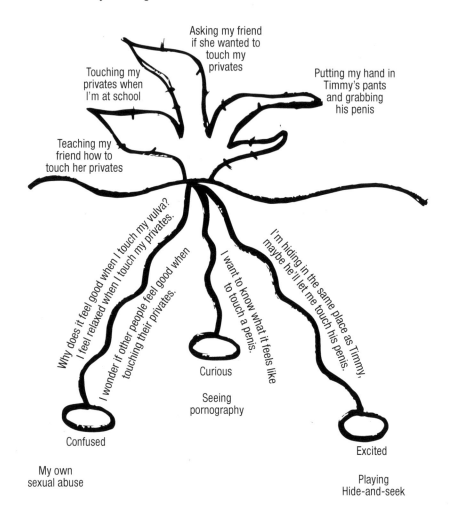

Asking my friend if she wanted to touch my privates

Touching my privates when I'm at school

Putting my hand in Timmy's pants and grabbing his penis

Teaching my friend how to touch her privates

Why does it feel good when I touch my vulva?
I feel relaxed when I touch my privates.

I wonder if other people feel good when touching their privates.

I want to know what it feels like to touch a penis.

I'm hiding in the same place as Timmy, maybe he'll let me touch his penis.

Curious

Seeing pornography

Confused

Excited

My own sexual abuse

Playing Hide-and-seek

FLOWER ACTIVITY

Flower Activity Example

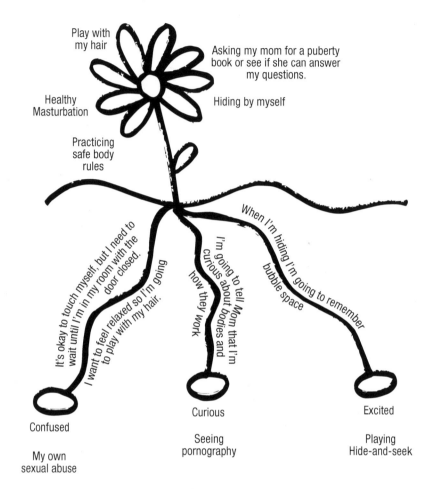

Play with my hair

Asking my mom for a puberty book or see if she can answer my questions.

Healthy Masturbation

Hiding by myself

Practicing safe body rules

It's okay to touch myself, but I need to wait until I'm in my room with the door closed.

I want to feel relaxed so I'm going to play with my hair.

I'm going to tell Mom that I'm curious about bodies and how they work

When I'm hiding I'm going to remember bubble space

Confused

My own sexual abuse

Curious

Seeing pornography

Excited

Playing Hide-and-seek

ROCK AND RIPPLE ACTIVITY

Rock and Ripple Activity Example

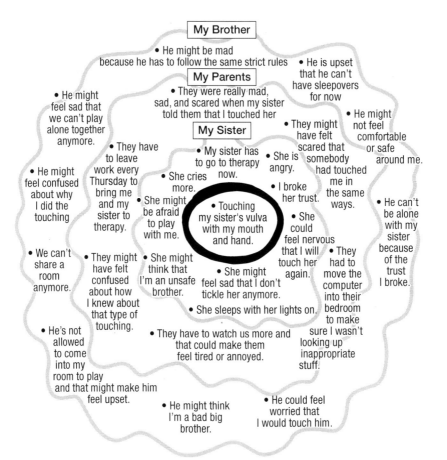

LETTER OF GROWTH

Here are some prompts that can get you started:

1. Acknowledging that sexual touch happened.
2. How you feel about the touches you did.
3. How it might have made _____ feel.
4. Why you are in therapy.
5. What you've learned in therapy that will help you stay safe and keep others safe.
6. How you've learned to acknowledge the touching and not do it again.

SAFE-PLAY PLAN

Home

- I will only use safe touch.
  - Safe touch is touch that is appropriate and safe, like a special handshake, hugs, and high fives.
  - I will *not* do unsafe touch to others (hurtful touch or sexual touch).
- I will follow the rules that my caregivers made.
  - Some of these rules are no kicking the ball inside, playing nicely, and asking before I get a snack.
- I will practice good privacy.
  - I will change by myself and in private (if my sibling is in the room, I will change in the bathroom or wait for them to leave the room).
  - I will use the bathroom with the door closed.
  - I will only shower or take a bath by myself, and I will be the only one in the bathroom.
  - I will have my own blanket, my own pillow, and my own bed.
- If I want to touch myself in a sexual way, I will do so safely.
  - This means, I will go to the bathroom, or my bedroom, and lock the door. I will also be completely alone.
  - I will not touch other people.
  - I will not touch myself in front of other people or in shared spaces like the living room.

School

- I will keep treating people nicely.
  - This means I'll keep practicing safe touch and using kind words.
- I will use bubble space at school.
- If someone is bullying me or asking me to do unsafe things I will tell my teacher immediately. I deserve to feel safe and comfortable at school!
- I can let my caregiver know about homework so that they can support me if I need help finishing it.
  - I will also ask my caregiver for support with any projects or studying I need to do.

Community

- I will not *ever* leave with a stranger!
  - If a stranger tries to get me to leave, or tries to take me, I will scream for help. If a stranger asks if I want to see something cool, like their dog, I will get the adult I'm with and we can go together.

- I will not walk off wherever I want.
  - If I want to go somewhere, I will ask before leaving.
- If someone is trying to give me something, I will not take it.
  - No matter what it is. Even if it's something cool like a four-wheeler.
- If someone is fighting in front of me, I will tell an adult I trust.
- If I see a little kid walking off with a stranger, or walking away, I will yell and tell an adult immediately.
- I will practice good boundaries by keeping my hands to myself.
- If I want to touch someone or their stuff, I will use consent before getting in their bubble. I will only use safe touch.
  - If someone is asking me to do unsafe/sexual touch, I will tell them, "No!" and tell a trusted adult right away.
- I will talk appropriately.
  - This means I will not share important details, like my address, with strangers.
  - I will not say inappropriate things to others, and I will do my best not to use swear words.

Health

- Mental/emotional:
  - If I notice I'm having unhealthy thoughts (like wanting to hurt myself or touch other people in unsafe ways) I can talk to my caregivers, or another trusted adult.
  - I will keep working on building trust so I can feel really good about myself.
  - I will only watch appropriate things.
    - If people are doing inappropriate things, like sexual touching or using drugs, I will get off and tell an adult.
    - If I'm tempted to watch pornography, I will tell an adult so they can help me.
- Physical:
  - I will not engage in unsafe or secret touches.
  - I will keep moving my body in ways that I like.
  - I will wear certain clothing when doing activities to keep myself safe.
    - I will wear pants while four-wheeling. I will wear a helmet while riding a bike. I will wear swim trunks while swimming.

SAFE-PLAY PLAN

Home
School
Community
Health

TREATMENT REVIEW

Boundaries

- **feeling/talking boundary:** How our behaviors make people feel.
  - Example: We don't want to talk to someone in a way that makes them feel uncomfortable, or sad, or mad.
  - How we feel sometimes makes us talk a certain way, and how we talk makes people feel a certain way.
- **stuff boundary:** Treating our stuff, and other people's stuff in a nice way.
  - We should *always ask* before touching someone's stuff, and touch in a respectful and safe way.
  - People should ask us before touching our things too.
- **bubble boundary:** Our personal space boundary, body boundary, and how comfortable we are with people being close to us.
  - We protect our bubble space, and respect other people's bubble space by listening to them.
  - We *always ask* before getting into someone's bubble.
  - We protect our bubble space by speaking up and letting people know if they are too close to us.
    - If they don't move, or don't get consent to enter my bubble, we will tell an adult.

Types of Touch

- **secret touch:** Touching someone, or getting touched, on private parts.
  - If someone tells us to keep a touch a secret, we should *definitely* tell an adult and *not* keep it a secret.
- **bad touch:** Touch that hurts people and their bodies.
  - Example: punching someone, kicking someone, or pushing someone.
  - Bad touch can also be when we don't get consent and still touch someone (like hugging without asking).
- **good touch:** Touch that is safe and healthy.
  - Example: hugs, fist bumps, and high fives.
  - We *always* get consent before touching.

Feelings Chain

1. Sensations/Triggers
2. Feelings
3. Thought
4. Action

Trouble Thoughts

Ways of thinking that allow us to avoid responsibility. That may seem good at first, but when we avoid responsibility after doing something we shouldn't have, we actually make things worse and feel worse afterward. The best way to avoid trouble thoughts is to simply tell the truth. Telling the truth will help more than lying about it.

- making excuses
- blaming
- minimizing
- changing the subject
- denying/lying by omission
- avoiding
- assuming
- playing the victim

Healthy Relationships: CERTS

- **C**onsent
  - Getting Permission. We need to ask and listen to their answer.
- **E**qual
  - That both people have the same power, similar age, same knowledge.
- **R**espect
  - Treating people with kindness, respecting their boundaries, and not being mean.
- **T**rust
  - Building trust takes time. We need to show people that they can trust us. Our actions and choices either build or break trust.
- **S**afety
  - Treating people safely. This means we respect their boundaries, and we don't hurt them or their feelings.

Healthy Consent: FRIES

- **F**reely given
  - They say yes because they want to say yes. We are not bribing, threatening, or tricking anyone into saying yes.
- **R**eversible
  - We can always take our consent back. This means we are always able to change our mind at any time.
- **I**nformed
  - This means the person knows what we are talking about. If they understand what we are saying and know what it means, then they are informed.
- **E**xcited
  - We are excited to do the thing we are saying yes to. No one is forcing us or making us feel guilted into saying yes.
- **S**pecific
  - We know the details.

INITIAL TREATMENT SAFETY PLAN

I, _____, and my caregiver(s) _____, agree to follow the rules below. This plan is to help keep me, and others around me safe. If any of the rules below are broken, we will be honest with our therapist so we can process what happened and come up with steps to avoid safety breaches in the future. This plan should be provided to all adults who oversee supervision, and they should agree to follow the rules below.

Home

- All members of the family will be dressed when in shared spaces.
- All members of the family will shower and use the bathroom with the door closed.
- I will change alone, either in my room or in the bathroom. I will not change in front of others.
- I will have my own bed and sleep alone in this bed.
- I will not share blankets or pillows with anyone.
- I will knock on doors before entering, and people will knock on my door before entering my room.
- I will not touch others unless it is appropriate (like a hug or high five), and I will always get their permission first. Family members should also get my permission before touching me.
- I will have sight-and-sound supervision if on the internet.
- I will only watch age-appropriate shows, and my caregivers will supervise and let me know if a show is inappropriate.

Community

- I will have sight-and-sound supervision at all times.
- If I need to use the restroom while in the community, I will try my best to use a single-stall restroom. If I can't, then a caregiver will do their best to accompany me in the larger bathrooms.
- I will not talk with strangers. If I'm at the park, I can talk to new kids, but if I'm talking to new people, an adult I trust will be nearby.

School

- I will have sight-and-sound supervision while on the internet.
- I will have, at a minimum, sight supervision while at recess.
- I will not touch others, unless it is appropriate touch (high fives, fist bumps, and maybe hugs) and I have the other person's permission.
- I will not be left alone with peers. There should always be an adult present.

Transportation

- I will sit in the back seat of my caregiver's car, or the front two seats of the bus.
- I will wear my seat belt if one is provided.
- I will not distract the driver.
- I will have a seat to myself, and I will stay seated.

References

Abel, G. G., Becker, J. V., Mittelman, M. S., Cunningham-Rathner, J., Rouleau, J. L., & Murphy, W. D. (1987). Self-report sex crimes of nonincarcerated paraphiliacs. *Journal of Interpersonal Violence*, *2*, 3–25.

Alissar El-Murr. (2017). *Problem sexual behaviours and sexually abusive behaviours in Australian children and young people*. Australian Institute of Family Studies. https://aifs.gov.au/sites/default/files/publication-documents/46_problem_sexual _behaviours_0.pdf

Allardyce, S., & Yates, P. (2018). *Working with children and young people who have displayed harmful sexual behaviour*. Dunedin Academic Press.

Allen, B. (2023). Etiological pathways to the emergence of preteen problematic sexual behavior: An exploratory mediational model. *Sexual Abuse*, *35*(4), 488–502. https://doi.org/10.1177/10790632221128313

American Psychological Association. (2023, November 15). *APA dictionary of psychology*. https://dictionary.apa.org/sexual-abuse

ARCH National Respite Network & Resource Center. (2013, December 10). *Resources for caregivers*. https://archrespite.org/caregiver-resources/

Blasingame G. (2018). Traumatic brain injury and sexually offensive behaviours. *Journal of Child Sexual Abuse*, *27*(8), 972–977. https://doi.org/10.1080/10538712 .2018.1510454

Bonner, B. L., Walker, C. E., & Berliner, L. (2000, March 2). Children with sexual behavior problems: Assessment and treatment. Final report, Grant No. 90-CA-1469, National Center on Child Abuse and Neglect, Administration for Children, Youth, and Families, US Department of Human Services.

Borneman, E. (1990). Progress in empirical research on children's sexuality. In M. E. Perry (Ed.), *Childhood and adolescent sexology: Handbook of sexology* (7), 201–210. Elsevier Science Ltd.

Breuner, C. C., & Mattson, G. (2016). Sexuality education for children and adolescents. *Pediatrics*, *138*(2). https://doi.org/:10.1542/peds.2016-1348

Briggs, F. (2014). Child sexual abuse in early-childhood care and education settings. *Early Child Development and Care, 184*(9–10), 1415–1435. https://doi.org/10.1080/03004430.2014.901011

Burton, D. L. (2000). Were adolescent sexual offenders children with sexual behavior problems? *Sexual Abuse: Journal of Research & Treatment, 12,* 37–48.

Burton, J., Rasmussen, L. A., Bradshaw, J., Christopherson, B. J., & Huke, S. C. (1998). *Treating children with sexually abusive behavior problems: Guidelines for child and parent intervention.* The Haworth Press, Inc.

Campbell F., Booth A., Hackett S., & Sutton A. (2020). Young people who display harmful sexual behaviours and their families: A qualitative systematic review of their experiences of professional interventions. *Trauma, Violence & Abuse, 21*(3), 456–469. https://doi.org/10.1177/1524838018770414

Campbell F., Booth A., Stepanova E., Hackett S., Sutton A., Hynes K, Sanderson J., & Rogstad J. (2016). *Harmful sexual behaviour in children: Evidence for identifying and assessing risk in children and young people who display harmful sexual behaviour.* https://www.nice.org.uk/guidance/ng55/documents/evidence-review

Cantwell, H. B. (1988). Child sexual abuse: Very young perpetrators. *Child Abuse and Neglect, 12,* 579–582.

Carpentier, M. Y., Silovsky, J. F., & Chaffin, M. (2006). Randomized trial of treatment for children with sexual behavior problems: Ten-year follow-up. *Journal of Counseling and Clinical Psychology, 74*(3), 482–488.

Centers for Disease Control and Prevention (CDC). (2022, June). *Fast facts: Preventing sexual violence.* https://www.cdc.gov/violenceprevention/sexualviolence/fastfact.html#:~:text=Sexual%20violence%20is%20common.&text=One%20in%204%20women%20and,penetrate%20someone%20during%20his%20lifetime

Chaffin, M., Berliner, L., Block, R., Johnson, T. C., Friedrich, W., Louis, D., Lyon, T. D., Page, J., Prescott, D., & Silovsky, J. F. (2008). Report of the ATSA task force on children with sexual behavior problems. *Child Maltreatment, 13*(2), 199–218.

Creeden, K. (2018). Adjusting the lens. In A. R. Beach, A. J. Carter, R. W. Mann, & Pia Rotshtein (Eds.) *The Wiley-Blackwell handbook of forensic neuroscience* (pp. 783–811). Wiley-Blackwell. https://doi.org/10.1002/9781118650868.ch30

Creeden, K. (2020). Trauma and young people who display sexually harmful behaviour. In H. Swaby, B. Winder, R. Lievesley, K. Hocken, N. Blagden, & P. Banyard (Eds.) *Sexual crime and trauma* (pp. 85–111). Palgrave Macmillan. https://doi.org/10.1007/978-3-030-49068-3_4

Cunningham, C., & MacFarlane, K. (1996). *When children abuse: Group treatment strategies for children with impulse control problems.* Safer Society Press

Curwen, T., Jenkins, J. M., & Worling, J. R. (2014). Differentiating children with and without a history of repeated problematic sexual behavior. *Journal of Child Sexual Abuse, 23*(4), 462–480. https://doi.org/10.1080/10538712.2014.906529

Davies, S. L., Glaser, D., & Kossoff, R. (2000). Children's sexual play and behavior in pre-school settings: staff's perceptions, reports, and responses. *Child Abuse & Neglect, 24*(10), 1329–1343. https://doi.org/10.1016/s0145-2134(00)00184-8

Deblinger, E., Lippman, J., & Steer, R. A. (1996). Sexually abused children suffering from post-traumatic stress symptoms: Initial treatment outcome findings. *Child Maltreatment, 1,* 310–321.

Deblinger, E., Steer, R. A., & Lippmann, J. (1999). Two-year follow-up study of cognitive behavioral therapy for sexually abused children suffering post-traumatic stress symptoms. *Child Abuse & Neglect, 23*(12), 1371–1378.

DeLago, C., Schroeder, C. M., Cooper, B., Deblinger, E., Dudek, E., Yu, R., & Finkel, M. A. (2019). Children who engaged in interpersonal problematic sexual behaviors. *Child Abuse & Neglect.* DOI:10.1016/j.chiabu.2019.104260.

DeLamater, J., & Friedrich, W. (2002). Human sexual development. *Journal of Sex Research, 39,* 10–14. https://doi.org/10.1080/00224490209552113

Department of Human Services. (n.d.). *Chapter VI-Family Support Services.* http://www.dhs.state.or.us/caf/safety_model/procedure_manual/ch06/ch6-section1.pdf

Elkovitch, N., Latzman, R. D., Hansen, D. J., & Flood, M. F. (2009). Understanding child sexual behavior problems: A developmental psychopathology framework. *Clinical Psychology Review, 29,* 586–598. https://doi.org/10.1016/j.cpr.2009.06.006

Elliott, M., Browne, K., & Kilcoyne, J. (1995). Child sexual abuse prevention: What offenders tell us. *Child Abuse & Neglect, 19*(5), 579–594. https://doi:10.1016/0145-2134(95)00017-3

Evertsz, J., & Kirsner, J. (2003). *Issues for intellectually disabled children with problem sexual behaviours: Literature review and research report.* Australian Childhood Foundation/ Department of Human Services, Melbourne.

Ey, L. A., & McInnes, E. (2017). Educators' observations of children's display of problematic sexual behaviors in educational settings. *Journal of Child Sexual Abuse, 27*(1), 88–105. https://doi.org/10.1080/10538712.2017.1349855

Farmer, E., & Pollock, S. (2003). Managing sexually abused and/or abusing children in substitute care. *Child & Family Social Work, 8*(2), 101–112. https://doi.org/10.1046/j.1365-2206.2003.00271.x

Finkelhor, D., Ormrod, R., & Chaffin, M. (2009). *Juveniles who commit sex offenses against minors.* Office of Juvenile Justice and Delinquency Prevention (OJJDP), US Department of Justice. https://www.ojp.gov/pdffiles1/ojjdp/227763.pdf

Finkelhor, D., Ormrod, R. K., & Turner, H. A. (2007). Polyvictimization and trauma in a national longitudinal cohort. *Development and Psychopathology, 19,* 149–166. https://doi.org/10.1017/s0954579407070083

Flood, M. (2009). The harms of pornography exposure among children and young people. *Child Abuse Review, 18*(6), 384–400. https://doi.org/10.1002/car.1092

Friedrich, W. N. (1990). *Psychotherapy of sexually abused children and their families.* W.W. Norton & Company.

Friedrich, W. N., & Luecke, W. J. (1988). Young school-age sexually aggressive children. *Professional Psychology, 19,* 155–164.

Friedrich, W. N., Davies, W. H., Feher, E., & Wright, J. (2003). Sexual behavior problems in preteen children. *Annals of the New York Academy of Sciences, 989*(1), 95–104. https://doi.org/10.1111/j.1749-6632.2003.tb07296.x

Garcia, G. (2017). *Listening to my body.* Skinned Knee Publishing.

Gil, E. (1991). *The healing power of play: Working with abused children.* The Guilford Press.

Gil, E., & Shaw, J. (2014). *Working with children with sexual behaviour problems.* The Guilford Press.

Glasgow, D., Horne, L., Calam, R., & Cox, A. (1994). Evidence, incidence, gender, and age in sexual abuse of children perpetrated by children: Towards a developmental analysis of child sexual abuse. *Child Abuse Review, 3*, 196–210.

Goldman, R., & Goldman, J. (1982). *Children's sexual thinking.* Routledge & Kegan Paul Books Ltd.

Gordon, B. & Schroeder, C. (1995). *Sexuality: A developmental approach to problems.* Springer.

Gray, A., Busconi, A., Houchens, P., & Pithers, W. D. (1997). Children with sexual behavior problems and their caregivers: Demographics, functioning, and clinical patterns. *Sexual Abuse: A Journal of Research and Treatment, 9*(4), 267–290. https://doi.org/10.1177/107906329700900402

Gray, A., Pithers, W. D., Busconi, A., & Houchens, P. (1999). Developmental and etiological characteristics of children with sexual behavior problems: treatment implications. *Child Abuse & Neglect, 23*(6), 601–621. https://doi.org/10.1016/s0145-2134(99)00027-7

Griggs, D. R., & Boldi, A. (1995). Parallel treatment of parents of abuse reactive children. In M. Hunter (Ed.), *Child survivors and perpetrators of sexual abuse* (pp. 147–165). Sage Publications.

Hackett, S. (2014). *Children and young people with harmful sexual behaviours.* Dartington. https://tce.researchinpractice.org.uk/wp-content/uploads/2020/05/children_and_young_people_with_harmful_sexual_behaviours_research_review_2014.pdf

Hackett, S., Masson, H., & Phillips, S. (2005). *Services for young people who sexual abuse: A report on mapping and exploring services for young people who have sexually abused others.* Youth Justice Board for England and Wales. https://core.ac.uk/download/pdf/4157311.pdf

Hackett, S., Phillips J., Masson, H., & Balfe, M. (2013) Individual, family and abuse characteristics of 700 British child and adolescent sexual abusers. *Child Abuse Review, 22*(4), 232–245. https://doi.org/10.1002/car.2246

Hanson, R. K., & Slater, S. (1988). Sexual victimization in the history of sexual abusers: A review. *Annals of Sex Research, 1*, 485–499.

Harris, M., Lanni, D., & Svendsen, S. (2023). A conceptual analysis of system responses to the issue of problematic sexual behaviors in children and recommendations for future work in children's advocacy center multidisciplinary teams. *Frontiers in Psychiatry, 14*, 1266463. https://doi.org/10.3389/fpsyt.2023.1266463

Health Share of Oregon. (2024). *Wraparound care.* https://www.healthshareoregon.org/health-equity/wraparound

Heiman, M. (2002). Helping parents address their child's sexual behavior problems. *Journal of Child Sexual Abuse, 10*(3), 35–57. https://doi.org/10.1300/j070v10n03_03

James, B. (1989). *Treating traumatized children: New insights and creative interventions.* Lexington Books.

Jenkins, C., Grimma, J., Shierb, E., van Doorena, S., Ciesara, E., & Reid-Quiñonesa, K. (2020). Preliminary findings of problematic sexual behavior-cognitive-behavioral therapy for adolescents in an outpatient treatment setting. *Child Abuse and Neglect, 105.* https://doi.org/10.1016/j.chiabu.2020.104428

Johnson, T. C. (1988). Child perpetrators—children who molest other children: Preliminary findings. *Child Abuse & Neglect, 12*(2), 219–229. https://doi.org/10.1016/0145-2134(88)90030-0

Johnson, T. C., & Berry, C. (1989). Children who molest. *Journal of Interpersonal Violence, 4*(2), 185–203. https://doi.org/10.1177/088626089004002004

Kaeser, F., DiSalvo, C., & Moglia, R. (2000). Sexual behaviors of young children that occur in schools. *Journal of Sex Education and Therapy, 25*(4), 277–285. https://doi.org/10.1080/01614576.2000.11074361

Katz, M. (1997). *On playing a poor hand well: Insights from the lives of those who have overcome childhood risks and adversities.* New York: W. W. Norton.

Kenny, M. C., Capri, V., R., R., Thakkar-Kolar, Ryan, E. E., & Runyon, M. K. (2008). Child sexual abuse: from prevention to self-protection. *Child Abuse Review, 17*(1), 36–54. https://doi.org/10.1002/car.1012

Kor, K., Simpson, H., & Fabrianesi, B. (2023). Strengthening schools' responses to students' harmful sexual behaviors: A scoping review. *Trauma, Violence, & Abuse, 24*(4), 2726–2742. https://doi.org/10.1177/15248380221111483

Kurtuncu, M., Akhan, L. U., Tanir, İ. M., & Yildiz, H. (2015). The sexual development and education of preschool children: Knowledge and opinions from doctors and nurses. *Sexuality and Disability, 33*(2), 207–221. https://doi.org/10.1007/s11195-015-9393-9

Lane, S. (1997). The sexual abuse cycle. In G. Ryan & S. Lane (Eds.), *Juvenile sexual offending: Causes, consequences, and correction* (Rev. ed., pp. 77–121). Jossey-Bass.

Lee, A. M. (n.d.). *The 13 disability categories under IDEA.* Understood. https://www.understood.org/en/articles/conditions-covered-under-idea

Lévesque, M., Bigras, M., & Pauzé, R. (2010). Externalizing problems and problematic sexual behaviors: same etiology? *Aggressive Behavior, 36*(6), 358–370. https://doi.org/10.1002/ab.20362

Marshall, W. L., Barbaree, H. E., & Eccles, A. (1991). Early onset and deviant sexuality in child molesters. *Journal of Interpersonal Violence, 6,* 323–335.

Martinson, F. M. (1981). Eroticism in infancy and early childhood. In D. S. Bromberg & W. T. O'Donohue (Eds.), *Children and sex: Findings, new perspectives* (pp. 22–35). Elsevier Academic Press.

McDowell, R., Dunklin, R., Schmall, E., & Pritchard, J. (2023, November 29). Hidden horror of school sex assaults revealed by AP. AP News. https://apnews.com/article/sports-only-on-ap-sexual-misconduct-sexual-harassment-1b74feef88df4475b377dcdd6406ebb7

McGrath, J., Cumming, G. F., & Burchard, B. (2003). *Current practices and trends in sexual abuser management: The Safer Society 2002 Nationwide Survey.* Safer Society Press.

McKibbin, G., & Humphreys, C. (2023). Frontline workers' response to harmful sexual behavior: Building blocks for promising practice. *Trauma, Violence & Abuse, 24*(2), 597–612. https://doi.org/10.1177/15248380211036077

McPherson, L., Vosz, M., Gatwiri, K., Hitchcock, C., Tucci, J., Mitchell, J., Fernandes, C., & Macnamara, N. (2023). Approaches to assessment and intervention with children and young people who engage in harmful sexual behavior: A scoping review. *Trauma, Violence, & Abuse, 25*(2). https://doi.org/10.1177/15248380231189293

Meiksans, J., Bromfield, L., & Ey, L. (2017, December). *A continuum of responses for harmful sexual behaviours: An issues paper for Commissioner for Children and Young People Western Australia.* Australian Centre for Child Protection, University of South Australia. https://www.ccyp.wa.gov.au/media/2973/a-continuum-of-responses-for-harmful-sexual-behaviours-australian-centre-for-child-protection-april-2018.pdf

Mesman, G. R., Harper, S. L., Edge, N. A., Brandt, T. W., & Pemberton, J. L. (2019). Problematic sexual behavior in children. *Journal of Pediatric Health Care.* https://doi.org/10.1016/j.pedhc.2018.11.002

Miller, S., Nunnally, E. W., & Wackman, D. B. (1975). *Alive and aware: Improving communication in relationships.* Interpersonal Communication Programs, Inc.

Multnomah County. (2024). *Wraparound.* https://www.multco.us/behavioral-health/wraparound

National Center on the Sexual Behavior of Youth (NCSBY). (2024). *Children: Child sexual development.* https://www.ncsby.org/children

National Children's Alliance. (2024a). *Fact sheet: About NCA and CACs* [Fact Sheet]. https://www.nationalchildrensalliance.org/media-room/nca-digital-media-kit/fact-sheet/

National Children's Alliance. (2024b). *How the CAC model works.* https://www.nationalchildrensalliance.org/cac-model/

National Children's Alliance. (2024c). *NCA's national standards of accreditation.* https://www.nationalchildrensalliance.org/ncas-standards-for-accredited-members/

National Wraparound Initiative. (2024). *Wraparound basics or what is wraparound: An introduction.* https://nwi.pdx.edu/wraparound-basics/#whatisWraparound

Office of Juvenile Justice and Delinquency Prevention. (2022, April 18). *Statistical briefing book.* http://www.ojjdp.gov/ojstatbb/victims/qa02401.asp?qaDate=2014

Office of Juvenile Justice and Delinquency Prevention. (January 2024). *In focus: Children's advocacy centers* [Fact Sheet]. https://ojjdp.ojp.gov/publications/in-focus-childrens-advocacy-centers.pdf

Oregon Health Authority. (n.d.). *Sexual Offense Treatment Board–Certification information.* https://www.oregon.gov/oha/PH/HLO/Pages/Board-Sex-Offender-Treatment-License.aspx

Oregon Laws. (2021, June 8). *OAR-413-020-0070: Voluntary placement agreement limitations.* https://oregon.public.law/rules/oar_413-020-0070

Ovelmen, K. (2021). *Clarification and reunification: Guidebook for working with youth and families impacted by sexual abuse.*

Pithers, W. D., & Gray, A. S. (1993). *Pre-adolescent sexual abuse research project: Research grantees status report.* National Center on Child Abuse and Neglect.

Pithers, W. D., Gray, A., Busconi, A., & Houchens, P. (1998a). Caregivers of children with sexual behavior problems: Psychological and familial functioning. *Child Abuse & Neglect, 22*, 129–142.

Pithers, W. D., Gray, A., Busconi, A., & Houchens, P. (1998b). Children with sexual behavior problems: Identification of five distinct child types and related treatment considerations. *Child Maltreatment, 3*(4), 384–406. https://doi.org/10.1177/1077559598003004010

Planned Parenthood. (2024). *Sexual consent.* https://www.plannedparenthood.org/learn/relationships/sexual-consent

Rasmussen, L. A. (2002). Integrating cognitive-behavioral and expressive therapy interventions: Applying the trauma outcome process in treating children with sexually abusive behavior problems. *Journal of Child Sexual Abuse, 10*(4), 1–29. https://doi.org/10.1300/j070v10n04_02

Ray, J., Smith, V., Peterson, T., Gray, J., Schaffner, J., & Houff, M. (1995). A treatment program for children with sexual behavior problems. *Child and Adolescent Social Work Journal, 12*(5), 331–343.

Sex Offender Management Board (SOMB). (2023, April 17). *Children with sexual behavior resource document* [White Paper]. https://cdpsdocs.state.co.us/dcj/DCJ%20External%20Website/SOMB/Research.Reports/WhitePaper/Children%20with%20Problematic.pdf

Sexual Offense Treatment Board. (2020, January 1). *Practice standards and guidelines for the evaluation, treatment, and management of juvenile sexual abusers.* State of Oregon. https://www.oregon.gov/oha/PH/HLO/Documents/SOTB_Juvenile_Sexual_Abusers_Treatment_Standards.pdf

Shawler, P. M., Bard, E. M., Taylor, E. K., Wilsie, C., Funderburk, F., & Silovsky, J. F. (2018). Parent-child interaction therapy and young children with problematic sexual behavior: A conceptual overview and treatment considerations. *Children and Youth Services Review, 84*, 206–214. https://doi.org/10.1016/j.childyouth.2017.12.006

Shlonsky, A., Albers, B., Tolliday, D., Wilson, S., Norvell, J., & Kissinger, L. (2017, May 30). Rapid evidence assessment: Current best evidence in the therapeutic treatment of children with problem or harmful sexual behaviours, and children who have sexually offended (pp. 1–114). Royal Commission into Institutional Responses to Child Sexual Abuse. https://apo.org.au/sites/default/files/resource-files/2017-05/apo-nid92426.pdf

Silovsky, J. F., & Bonner, B. L. (2004). Sexual development and sexual behavior problems in children ages 2–12. National Center on the Sexual Behavior of Youth (NCSBY) [Fact Sheet.] Office of Juvenile Justice and Delinquency Prevention (OJJDP).

Silovsky, J. F., Hunter, M. D., & Taylor, E. K. (2018) Impact of early intervention for youth with problematic sexual behaviors and their caregivers. *Journal of Sexual Aggression, 25*(1), 4–15. https://doi.org/10.1080/13552600.2018.1507487

Sites, J., & Widdifield, J. (2020). Children with problematic sexual behavior: Recommendations for the multidisciplinary team and children's advocacy center response. Southern Regional Children's Advocacy Center and Oklahoma Commission on Children and Youth. https://files.calio.org/PSB_Multidisciplinary-Team_CAC _Response_Recommendations.pdf

Sneddon, H., Grimshaw, D. G., Livingstone, N., & Macdonald, G. (2020). Cognitive-behavioural therapy (CBT) interventions for young people aged 10 to 18 with harmful sexual behaviour. *Cochrane Database of Systematic Reviews, 6*(6), DOI: 10.1002/14651858.CD009829.pub2.

St. Amand, A., Bard, D. E., & Silovsky, J. F. (2008). Meta-analysis of treatment for child sexual behavior problems: Practice elements and outcomes. *Child Maltreatment, 13*(2), 145–166. https://doi.org/10.1177/1077559508315353

Stone, N., Ingham, R., & Gibbins, K. (2013). "Where do babies come from?" Barriers to early sexuality communication between parents and young children. *Sex Education, 13*(2), 228–240. https://doi.org/10.1080/14681811.2012.7377

Swisher, L. M., Silovsky, J. F., Stuart, J. R. H., & Pierce, K. (2008). Children with sexual behavior problems. *Juvenile and Family Court Journal, 59*(4), 49–69. https://doi.org/10.1111/j.1755-6988.2008.00021.x

Szanto, L., Lyons, J. S., & Kisiel, C. (2012). Childhood trauma experience and the expression of problematic sexual behavior in children and adolescents in state custody. *Residential Treatment for Children & Youth, 29*(3), 231–249. https://doi.org /10.1080/0886571x.2012.702519

Taylor, E. K., Tener, D., Silovsky, J. F., & Newman, A. (2021). Comparison of children's advocacy center responses to harmful sexual behavior among siblings: An international perspective. *Child Abuse Neglect, 122*. https://doi.org/10.1016/j .chiabu.2021.105371

Tempest, B. (2017, October 24). Parenting children or youth who are sexually reactive. Families Rising. https://nacac.org/resource/parenting-children-or-youth-who -are-sexually-reactive/#:~:text=Sexual%20reactivity%20is%20when%20a

Tener, D., Newman, A., Yates, P., & Tarshish, N. (2020). Child advocacy center intervention with sibling sexual abuse cases: cross-cultural comparison of professionals' perspectives and experiences. *Child Abuse Neglect, 105*, 104259. https:// doi.org/10.1016/j.chiabu.2019.104259

Thigpen, J. W. (2009). Early sexual behavior in a sample of low-income, African American children. *Journal of Sex Research, 46*(1), 67–79. https://doi.org/10.1080 /00224490802645286

Thigpen, J., Pinkston, E., & Mayefsky, J. (2003). Normative sexual behavior of African American children: Preliminary findings. In J. Bancroft (Ed.) *Sexual development* (pp. 241–254). Indiana University Press.

Timms, S., & Goreczny, A. (2002) Adolescent sex offenders with mental retardation literature review and assessment considerations. *Aggression and Violent Behavior, 7*(1), 1–9. https://doi.org/10.1016/s1359-1789(00)00031-8

US Department of Education. (2023, July). *Free appropriate public education for student with disabilities: Requirements under section 504 of the rehabilitation act of 1973.* https://www2.ed.gov/about/offices/list/ocr/docs/edlite-FAPE504.html

Vizard, E., Hickey, N., French, L., & McCrory, E. (2007). Children and adolescents who present with sexually abusive behaviour: A UK descriptive study. *Journal of Forensic Psychiatry & Psychology*, *18*(1), 59–73. https://doi.org/10.1080/14789940601056745

Ward, E. G. (2005). Homophobia, hypermasculinity and the US Black church. *Culture, Health, & Sexuality*, *7*, 493–504. https://doi.org/10.1080/13691050500151248

West, C. (2001). *Race matters*. Beacon Press.

Willey, K. (2017). *Breathe like a bear*. Rodale Kids.

Yates, P., & Allardyce, S. (2021). *Sibling sexual abuse: A knowledge and practice overview*. Centre of Expertise on Child Sexual Abuse. https://www.csacentre.org.uk/app/uploads/2023/09/Sibling-sexual-abuse-report.pdf

Zeng, G., Chu, C. M., & Lee, Y. (2015). Assessing protective factors of youth who sexually offended in Singapore: preliminary evidence on the utility of the DASH-13 and the SAPROF. *Sexual Abuse: A Journal of Research and Treatment*, *27*(1), 91–108. https://doi.org/10.1177/1079063214561684

Zolondek, S. C., Abel, G. G., Northey, W. F., & Jordan, A. D. (2001). The self-reported behaviors of juvenile sexual offenders. *Journal of Interpersonal Violence*, *16*, 3–85.

Index

AASECT. *See* American Association of Sexuality Educators, Counselors, and Therapists

accountability, 45–47

action: in feelings chain, 15, 28, 170; step in staircase activity, 48

ADHD. *See* attention deficit hyperactivity disorder

adjudicated youth, in juvenile justice system, 85, 91, 106, 136, 139

adolescent problematic sexual behaviors: child sexual abuse cases from, xviii; ERASOR assessment tool for, xx; impacting factors for, xix–xx; PROFESOR assessment tool for, xx, 146; unaddressed child problematic sexual behaviors and, xiv

adolescent sexual abuse treatment programs: limited published research on, xv; Safer Society survey on, xiv

adult problematic sexual behaviors, xiv; child and adolescent onset of, xv; child sexual abuse treatment reduction in, xviii

adult sexual abuse treatment programs: child sexual offense treatment evolved from, xiv; Safer Society survey on, xiv

adult sexual offenders, methods used to target children, xxvi–xxvii

adverse childhood experiences: children problematic sexual behaviors impacted by, xv, 104, 110; light switch metaphor and, 40; maltreatment and, xix, xxiv, 40, 104

age-appropriate sexual behaviors, xxix; defined, xxx–xxxi. *See also* normative sexual exploration

aggressive socialization exposure, problematic sexual behaviors impacted by, xix

American Association of Sexuality Educators, Counselors, and Therapists (AASECT), 138

American Psychological Association (APA), sexually abusive behaviors defined by, xxx

animals, child problematic sexual behaviors with, xix, xxxvii, xxxix, 119

APA. *See* American Psychological Association

arousal in treatment room, 113; codewords use for, 114

assessment: developmentally oriented approach in, xx–xxi; forensically oriented approach, xx; limited research on, xv, 141, 146–47 assessment tools, xv; CBCL, 147; CSBI, 147; CTS, 147; ERASOR, xx; LA-SAAT, 146, 147; PROFESOR, xx, 146; SDQ, 147; TSCYC, 147

Association for the Treatment of Sexual Abusers (ATSA) Task Force, 112; on problematic sexual behaviors definition, xxx

attachment challenges, 110–11

attention deficit hyperactivity disorder (ADHD), 112

atypical sexual knowledge, xxxii

autism spectrum disorder, 111, 112

Beach Ball Ice Breaker rapport-building activity, 8–9

behavioral intervention approaches, xxii

behavioral redirection, for child problematic sexual behavior minimization, xxv

behavioral response outcomes: emotion expression aid to healing, xxi; externalizing behaviors and abusive behaviors, xxi; internalizing emotions and self-destructive behaviors, xxi

bodily autonomy: bubble space boundary activity and, 15, 150, 170; "Consent for Kids" YouTube video for, 15

body awareness, xli, xlii, xliii; body parts, xxvi, xxvii, 31–35, 123; checking in, 23–26; coping skills and interventions, 29–31; disconnection as coping strategy, 23; emotional recognition and regulation, 26–29

body language, 17

body parts, 31; caregivers use of anatomical names for, xxvi, xxvii, 33, 123; children instruction on correct, xxvi, xxvii, 33, 123; healthy masturbation, 35; normalizing, 32; puberty talk, 34; safety and, 33

body rights activity, 17–18

body safety programs, xxviii

boundaries, 149; activities for, 15–16; appropriate touch education, xxvi–xxvii; body rights activity, 17–18; bubble space activity, 15, 150, 170; emotional/mental, 16–17, 150, 170; feelings charades activity, 17; physical, 14–16, 150, 170; promotion of privacy and healthy, xxvii; stuff activity, 15–16, 150, 170; talking/feeling activity, 16, 150, 170

brain, early childhood trauma impact on, xx–xxi

Breathe Like a Bear (Willey), 31

bubble breathing activity, 30–31

bubble space boundary activity, bodily autonomy and, 15, 150, 170

building rapport, xli, xlii, xliii, 3; answering initial questions, 4; with clients, 4–6; DHS open cases and, 4, 96; with family, 6; rapport-building activities, 7–9

bullying, xxxviii, 69, 172

CACs. *See* Child Advocacy Centers

CADC. *See* certified alcohol and drug counselor

Candy Land Color Game rapport-building activity, 8

caregiver response, to children with problematic sexual behaviors: hyperreactive response, 117–18; hyporeactive response, 118–20

caregivers: body parts anatomical names use by, xxvi, xxvii, 33, 123; CACs engagement with, 133; client history engagement by, 38; coaches and instructors communication from, 92–93; denial or minimization of problematic sexual behaviors, 123–24; guilt and shame of, 126; lack of knowledge around sexual development, 122–24; locker accompaniment by, 92; own trauma of, 124–26; psychoeducation regarding empathy, 72–73; ROI for

CACs by, 104; ROI for coach and school information, 88, 93; ROI for own therapist, 125; safe-play plan participation, 79; safety plan cooperation and input from, 13
case management, for child problematic sexual behaviors, xv
CBCL. *See* child behavior checklist
CBT. *See* cognitive behavioral theory
CDC. *See* Centers for Disease Control and Prevention
CEDS. *See* certified eating disorders specialist
Centers for Disease Control and Prevention (CDC), on sexual violence, 124
certifications, 140; of AASECT for sex therapy, 138; ambiguity around, 137–39; for CADC, 138; of CEDS, 138; for EMDR, 130; by Oregon Sex Offense Treatment Board, 135–36
certified alcohol and drug counselor (CADC), 138
certified eating disorders specialist (CEDS), 138
CERTS. *See* consent, equality, respect, trust, and safety
challenges: attachment, 110–11; mental health, 111–13; of pornography use, 114–16. *See also* children twelve years of age and younger, characteristics, barriers and challenges working with; families of children with problematic sexual behaviors, challenges for working with
checking in, with body awareness, 23; feelings chart check-in activity, 24–25; puppet check-in activity, 25–26
Child Advocacy Centers (CACs), 103; caregiver engagement and, 133; caregivers ROI for, 104; child problematic sexual behaviors referral by, 134, 138; collaborative approach of, 134; family work focus of, 133;

on forensic interviews and exams, 106; identified victim evaluation at, 105; mandate to support victimized children, 133; MDT model used by, 104, 133; National Children's Alliance National Standards of Accreditation, 104; sibling sexual abuse and, 133–34
child behavior checklist (CBCL), 147
childhood sexual development: categories for, xxxii; children ages five to nine, xxxi; children ages ten to twelve, xxxi; children ages zero to four, xxxi; developmental categories for, xxxi–xxxii
child problematic sexual behaviors, xiii; adolescent problematic sexual behaviors unaddressed, xiv; adverse childhood experiences impact on, xv, 104, 110; with animals, xix, xxxvii, xxxix, 119; barriers to working with, xv; case management for, xv; child sexual abuse cases from, xviii; DHS involvement for, 11; elements for minimization of, xxv; five to nine years of age, xxxvii; hyperreactive caregiver response to, 117–18; hyporeactive caregiver response to, 118–20; increase in, xvii; juvenile justice system not tracking, xvii; national response, certifications, protocol ambiguity, 138–40; offender and victim status for, 138; onset of adult problematic sexual behaviors, xv; out-of-home placement for, 12; parent or caregiver involvement to minimize, xxvi; ten to twelve years of age, xxxviii–xxxix; zero to four years of age, xxxv
child problematic sexual behaviors treatment: from CACs, 133–34; Colorado Sex Offender Management Board on assessment and, 134–35; multisystem approach to, 137

Child Protective Services (CPS), 11, 139; hands-on sexual contact with another youth disclosure to, 12–13; hyporeactive caregiver and call to, 119, 120; mandatory reporting to, 86, 126–28; report handling inconsistencies by, 140; school educators as mandatory reporters to, 86

children: adult sexual offenders methods used to target, xxvi–xxvii; normative sexual exploration by, xviii; open parent-child communication importance, xxvi; parent involvement in self-protection skills for, xxvi, xxviii; red-flag behaviors education, xxvii

children five to nine years of age: concerning sexual behaviors, xxxvi–xxxvii; normative sexual behaviors, xxxvi; normative sexual knowledge, xxxv; problematic sexual behaviors, xxxvii

children ten to twelve years of age: concerning sexual behaviors, xxxviii; normative sexual behaviors, xxxviii; normative sexual knowledge, xxxvii; problematic sexual behaviors, xxxviii–xxxix

children twelve years of age and younger, characteristics, barriers and challenges working with, 109; arousal in treatment room, 113–14; attachment challenges, 110–11; mental health challenges, 112–13; neurodivergence challenges, 111–12; pornography use, 114–16; uncertainty, anxiety and resistance of, 110

children zero to four years of age: concerning sexual behaviors, xxxiv–xxxv; normative sexual behaviors, xxxiv; normative sexual knowledge, xxxiii; problematic sexual behaviors, xxxv

child sexual abuse cases: child and adolescent perpetration of, xviii; from child problematic sexual behaviors, xviii; early treatment impact on, xviii

child sexual abuse treatment: adult problematic sexual behaviors reduction and, xviii; evolved from adult sexual offense treatment, xiv; family involvement in, xxiv–xxv; parental involvement and training importance in, xi, xxiv–xxv; referral increase for, xvii; Safer Society survey on, xiv

child sexual behavior inventory (CSBI), 147

child trauma screen (CTS), 147

Clarification and Reunification (Ovelmen), 106

clarification meeting, with survivor therapist, 106

client history: caregiver engagement in obtaining, 38; child reluctance to discuss, 38; gathering of, 38–41; life history and sexual history timeline activity, 39–41; shy client help for, 39; trouble thoughts in, 42–44; variables influencing obtaining, 37–38

clients, building rapport with, 4–6

clinical sexual offense therapist (CSOT), 136

clinicians: certification for working with juveniles with harmful sexual behaviors, 134–37; formal accreditation process for, 130; working outside scope of practice, 129–32, 139

codewords, for arousal in treatment room, 114

cognitive behavioral theory (CBT), xl; model of emotions and feelings chain, 26; PSB-CBT-A, xxii, 137; psychoeducation of, xxiv, 137; TF-CBT, xxiv

collaborative approach, of CACs, 134
Colorado Sex Offender Management
Board: on child problematic sexual
behaviors assessment and treatment,
134–35; on race and ethnicity, 143
community, 86; CACs, 103–4;
DHS, 4, 11, 96; ICC, 98–99,
101–2; respite services, 95, 102–3;
survivor therapist services, 105–7;
wraparound services, 96–101
concerning sexual behaviors, xxxii;
characteristics involving immediate
therapeutic services, xxxiii; children
five to nine years of age, xxxvi–
xxxvii; children ten to twelve years
of age, xxxviii; children zero to four
years of age, xxxiv–xxxv. *See also*
problematic sexual behaviors
conduct disorder, 112
consent: in CERTS, 54–55; FRIES
components of, 59–62
consent, equality, respect, trust,
and safety (CERTS), healthy
relationship components, 171;
consent description, 54–55; equality
description, 55; follow-up discussion,
57–58; respect description, 55–56;
safety description, 56–57; trust
description, 56
"Consent for Kids" YouTube video, for
bodily autonomy, 15
coping skills: disconnection as, 23;
maladaptive, 29; mindfulness cards
for deep breathing, 30–31; to sit with
feelings, 29–30
CPS. *See* Child Protective Services
criminal behaviors, within family, xix
CSBI. *See* child sexual behavior
inventory
CSOT. *See* clinical sexual offense
therapist
CTS. *See* child trauma screen

denial or minimization, by hyporeactive
caregiver, 119

Department of Human Services (DHS):
child problematic sexual behaviors
and involvement with, 11, 96; FSS
avenues with, 96; open cases with,
4, 96; safety plan and, 11. *See also*
Child Protective Services
developmental differences, limited
research on problematic sexual
behaviors for, 145–46
developmentally oriented approach, in
assessment, xx–xxi
DHS. *See* Department of Human
Services
dirt: in flower activity, 51; in weed
activity, 49
disconnection, as coping strategy, 23
domestic violence, xix
dynamic play therapy, xxiv

education: appropriate touch, xxvi–
xxvii; children red-flag behaviors,
xxvii; around normative and atypical
sexual behaviors, xiv; sexual abuse,
xxviii. *See also* psychoeducation; sex
education
elements for minimization, of child
problematic sexual behaviors:
adequate sex education, xxv;
behavioral redirection, xxv;
supervision, xxv; understanding of
underlying needs of behaviors, xxv
EMDR. *See* eye movement
desensitization and reprocessing
emotional/mental boundaries: body
language, 17; feelings charades
activity, 17; feelings chart activity,
16–17; talking-feeling boundary, 16,
150, 170
emotional recognition and regulation:
body awareness, 26–29; empathy
and, 69; feelings chain, 15, 26–28,
155, 156, 157, 170; locus of control,
28–29
emotion expression with aid to healing,
xxi

empathy and awareness: emotional recognition and, 69; empathy versus sympathy, 71–72; intent versus impact difference and, 69–71; listen, 72–73; modeling, 73; patience and practice for, 73; psychoeducation around impact, 74–77; psychoeducation for caregivers regarding, 72–73; victim awareness, xli, 73–75

empathy versus sympathy, 71–72

equality, in CERTS, 55

estimate of risk of adolescent sexual offense recidivism (ERASOR) assessment, for adolescents, xx

ethnicity. *See* race and ethnicity

expressive therapy, xl, 137; emotion expression in, xxiv

externalizing emotions with abusive behaviors, xxi

extracurricular activities, 86; locker rooms and, 92–94; movement-based activities, 92; non-movement-based activities, 94; as protective factor, 91; safety plan for, 91–92

eye movement desensitization and reprocessing (EMDR) certification, 130

families of children with problematic sexual behaviors, challenges for working with: caregiver own trauma, 124–26; caregiver response, 116–20; sexual development lack of knowledge, 122–24; technology literacy, 120–22

family: assessing level of support for, 85–86; building rapport with, 6; CAC focus on work with, 133; environment impact, xix; involvement in child sexual behaviors treatment, xxiv–xxv; wraparound services approach centered on, 96–97, 98

family dynamics exploration, in problematic sexual behaviors treatment, xx

family support services (FSS), within DHS: independent living programs, 96; in-home family support services, 96; post-assisted guardianship assistance, 96; post-legal adoption, 96; for pre-adjudicated delinquents by court order, 96; voluntary custody agreements, 96; voluntary placement agreements, 96

family system chronic distress, problematic sexual behaviors impacted by, xix

FASD. *See* fetal alcohol spectrum disorder

fear, as root of hyperreactive caregiver response, 117

feelings: in feelings chain, 27, 155, 170; learning to sit with, 29–30; step in staircase activity, 48

feelings chain: actions, 15, 28, 170; CBT model of emotions and, 26; examples, 156, 157; feelings, 27, 155, 170; sensations/triggers, 27, 155, 170; thoughts, 27–28, 155, 170

feelings charade activity, 17

feelings chart activity, 16–17

feelings chart check-in activity, 24–25

feelings faces activity, 153, 154

feeling/talking boundary activity. *See* talking/feeling boundary activity

female sexual offenders, xiii

fetal alcohol spectrum disorder (FASD), 111–12

504 plan, in school, 90

flower, in flower activity, 51

flower activity, for ownership, 50, 165; dirt, 51; example, 166; flower, 51; follow-up discussion for, 52; roots, 51; seeds, 51

flower game activity, 63

forensically oriented approach, in assessment, xx

forensic interview and exam, CAC and, 106

foundations of treatment, xli, xlii, xliii, 11–21

freely given, reversible, informed, enthusiastic, and specific (FRIES) components, 59–62, 171

FSS. *See* family support services

full treatment protocol: treatment modules, xli; type and age range of client for, xl–xli

future safety and finishing strong, xli, xliii; safe-play plan, 79–80; treatment review, 80–81

Garcia, Gabi, 26

gender-diverse children, problematic sexual behaviors limited research on, 144–45

girls, problematic sexual behaviors limited research on, 144–45

goals, within safety plan, 13

hands-on sexual contact with another youth: continued contact information, 12–13; disclosure to child's parents, 12; reported behaviors, 12

healthy relationships and appropriate sexuality, xli, xlii–xliii, 53; with caregiver, 57; CERTS components, 54–58; exploration of person engaged in problematic sexual behaviors, 58; flower game activity, 63; with friends, 57; helpful tools to teach CERTS and FRIES, 62–63; psychoeducation related to pornography, 64–68; safety in, 63–64

high-risk behaviors, mental health challenges and, 112–13

history, xli, xlii, xliii

home: functioning within, 95; natural supports within, 95; out-of-home placements, 12; respite care support, 95, 102–3; safety plan for, 12, 172; sexual victimization in, 86

hyperreactive response, of caregivers: fear root of, 117; signs of, 118; targeted child and, 118

hyporeactive response, of caregivers: child with problematic sexual behaviors childcare of others, 119–20; CPS call for, 119, 120; denial or minimization of problematic sexual behaviors, 119; lax supervision, 119; room sharing with another child, 119; shame and embarrassment in, 118; unlimited and unsupervised internet access, 119

ICC. *See* Intensive Care Coordination

IEP. *See* Individualized Education Program

illegal sexual behaviors (ISBs), xxxi, 106, 136

impacts: letter of growth activity, 76; psychoeducation around, 74–77; ripple and rock activity for, 75–76, 167, 168

independent living programs, of DHS FSS, 96

Individualized Education Program (IEP), 87; qualifications for, 89; resources for, 89–90

Individuals With Disabilities Education Act, IEP disability identification, 89

in-home family support services, of DHS FSS, 96

integrative model, for intervention approaches, xxiii–xxiv

Intensive Care Coordination (ICC), 98–99, 101–2

intent versus impact, 69; activity, 70–71

internalizing emotions with self-destructive behaviors, xxi

International Association of Eating Disorder Professionals Foundation, CEDS certification by, 138

internet: hyporeactive caregiver unlimited access to, 119; sight and sound supervision of, 121 intervention approaches, xv; behavioral, xxii; CBT, xxii, xxiv, xl, 26, 137; integrative model for, xxiii–xxiv; MST, xxii; social learning, xxii; specialist abuse-specific approaches, xxii; strength-based, xxii; trauma-informed approach, xxii. *See also* therapy specialties

ISBs. *See* illegal sexual behaviors

juvenile justice system: adjudicated youth and, 85, 91, 106, 136, 139; child problematic behaviors not tracked by, xvii; on ISBs of youth ages thirteen to eighteen, xxxi, 106; services for youth ages twelve to eighteen, xiii

juvenile with harmful sexual behaviors, clinicians work with: Colorado Sex Offender Management Board and, 134–35; LMFT for, 136–37; Oregon Sex Offense Treatment Board certification, 135–36

larger systems, struggles and issues with: clinicians working outside scope of practice, 129–32; clinicians working with juveniles engaged in harmful sexual behaviors, 134–39; lack of training to work with problematic sexual behaviors, 129–32; mandatory reporting, 86, 126–28; society lack of sexuality discourse, 128–29

latency age-sexual adjustment and assessment tool (LA-SAAT), 146, 147

lax supervision, of hyporeactive caregiver, 119

Lego house metaphor, for treatment, 14

letter of growth activity, for impact, 76–77, 169

LGBTQIA+ clients, pornography and, 116

licensed marriage and family therapist (LMFT), 137

life history and sexual history timeline activity, 39–40; string of plates timeline activity, 41; traditional timeline activity, 41

light switch metaphor, adverse childhood experiences and, 40

listening, empathy and, 72–73

Listening to My Body (Garcia), 26

LMFT. *See* licensed marriage and family therapist

locker rooms, in extracurricular activities: caregiver accompanying to, 92; coaches and instructors communication, 92–93; who-what-where-when-why conversation, 93–94

maladaptive coping skills, 29

maltreatment, xix, xxiv, 40, 104

mandatory reporting: for client disclosing abuse perpetrated against them, 127–28; for client disclosing sexual behaviors with another child, 127; historical abuse that hasn't been reported, 128; by school and educators, 86

MDT. *See* multidisciplinary team

media, sexually explicit content in, 115

mental health challenges: ADHD, 112; ATSA on, 112; autism spectrum disorder, 111, 112; conduct disorder, 112; high-risk behaviors of, 112–13; PTSD, 112

mindfulness cards for deep breathing: bubble breathing activity, 30–31; Willey *Breathe Like a Bear* book, 31

modeling, of empathy, 73

movement-based activities, in extracurricular activities, 92

MST. *See* Multi-Systemic Therapy

multidisciplinary team (MDT) model, for CACs, 104, 133

Multi-Systemic Therapy (MST), xxii

multisystem involvement, 85; for child problematic sexual behaviors treatment, 137; community, 86, 95–107; extracurricular activities, 86, 91–94; home, 86, 95; school, 86–91

Multnomah County Wraparound Eligibility Criteria, for wraparound services, 98

National Children's Alliance's National Standards of Accreditation, for CACs, 104

national response, ambiguity around, 137–40

neurodivergence, 141; autism spectrum disorder, 111, 112; categories of, 111; challenges for, 111; FASD diagnosis and, 111–12

non-movement-based activities, in extracurricular activities, 94

normalization, of body parts, 32

normative sexual behaviors, xxxii; children five to nine years of age, xxxvi; children ten to twelve years of age, xxxviii; children zero to four years of age, xxxiv

normative sexual exploration, by children: description of, xviii, xxxii–xxxiii; sexual play compared to, xviii

normative sexual knowledge, xxxii; children five to nine years of age, xxxvi; children ten to twelve years of age, xxxvii; children zero to four years of age, xxxiii–xxxiv

Oregon Sex Offense Treatment Board: on certification for treatment of juveniles with sexually abusive behaviors, 135–36; CSOT certification by, 136

out-of-home placements, for child problematic sexual behaviors, 12

Ovelmen, Keith, 106

ownership, xli; accountability and, 45–47; flower activity, 50–52; staircase activity, 47–49, 161, 162; weed activity, 49–50

parental controls, technology literacy and, 120, 121

parental involvement, in child sexual abuse treatment, xxiv–xxv, xl; child self-protection skills discussion, xxvi, xxviii; protective factors with, xxvi–xxvii

parental training, in child sexual abuse treatment, xi, xxiv–xxv

patient and practice, for empathy, 73

perpetrator-specific treatment, xxiii

physical boundaries, 14; bubble space boundary activity, 15, 150, 170; stuff boundary activity, 15–16, 150, 170

physical health, safety plan for, 173

plans step, in staircase activity, 48

play therapy, xxiii, xxiv; Association for Play Therapy credentialing, 130

pornography: ability to stop access to, 67–68; addictive qualities of, 66–67; CERTS and FRIES role in, 67; challenge of use of, 114–16; LGBTQIA+ clients and, 116; media sexually explicit content, 115; minimal exposure to, 65–66; problematic use of, 66–67; psychoeducation related to, 64–68; unrealistic dynamics and expectations in, 65–66

post-assisted guardianship assistance, of DHS FSS, 96

post-legal adoption, of DHS FSS, 96

posttraumatic stress disorder (PTSD), 112

pre-adjudicated delinquents court ordered services, of DHS FSS, 96

problematic sexual behavior-cognitive behavioral therapy (PSB-CBT), xxiii, 137

problematic sexual behavior-cognitive behavioral therapy for adolescents (PSB-CBT-A), xxii, 137

problematic sexual behaviors, xxxii; aggressive socialization and unhealthy relationships exposure impact on, xix; ATSA definition of, xxx; CBT versus dynamic play therapy study, xxiii; children five to nine years of age, xxxvii; children ten to twelve years of age, xxxviii–xxxix; children zero to four years of age, xxxv; defined, xxix; exploration of relationship with person engaged with, 58; family environment impact on, xix, xxiv; family system chronic distress impact on, xix; maltreatment impact on, xix, xxiv, 40, 104; multiple trauma experiences and, xx, xxiv; neurodivergent children overrepresentation for, 111; protective factor of positive activities with prosocial peers, 91; relapse prevention versus expressive therapy study, xxiii; school prevention of, 86–87; survival therapist and disclosure of another child with, 105; symptomatic of trauma, xxi; treatment protocol for younger children with, xli–xlii; treatment protocol for younger children with self-focused, xlii–xliii. *See also* adolescent problematic sexual behaviors; adult problematic sexual behaviors; child problematic sexual behaviors
problematic sexual behaviors treatment: delayed intervention for, 130–31; family dynamics exploration, xx; hyperreactive caregiver impact on, 117–18; hyporeactive caregiver impact on, 118–19; lack of training for, 129–32, 139; trauma work, xx; victim and perpetrator approach in, xxiv. *See also* adolescent sexual abuse treatment programs; adult sexual abuse treatment programs; child problematic sexual behaviors treatment

protective and risk observations for eliminating sexual offense recidivism (PROFESOR) assessment, for adolescents, xx, 146
protective factors, with extracurricular activities, 91
protective factors, with parental involvement: appropriate touch boundaries education, xxvi–xxvii; child education on red-flag behaviors, xxvii; child self-protection skills discussion, xxvi, xxviii; correct body parts names instruction, xxvi, xxvii, 33, 123; education about sexual thoughts, feelings, experiences, xxvi; open parent-child communication, xxvi
protocol for little kids: treatment modules, xliii; type and age range of client for, xliii
protocol for younger children with problematic sexual behaviors: treatment modules, xli–xlii; type and age range of client for, xli
protocol for younger children with self-focused problematic sexual behaviors: treatment modules, xlii–xliii; type and age range of client for, xlii
PSB-CBT. *See* problematic sexual behavior-cognitive behavioral therapy
PSB-CBT-A. *See* problematic sexual behavior-cognitive behavioral therapy for adolescents
psychoeducation: for caregivers regarding empathy, 72–73; of CBT, xxiv, 137; around impacts, 74–77; related to pornography, 64–68
PTSD. *See* posttraumatic stress disorder
puberty talk, 34
puppet check-in activity, 25–26

Question Jenga rapport-building activity, 7–8

race and ethnicity: Colorado Sex Offender Management Board on, 143; limited research on problematic sexual behaviors and, 142–44; sexual development impact from, 143–44

rapport-building activities: Beach Ball Ice Breaker, 8–9; Candy Land Color Game, 8; Question Jenga, 7–8; Talking While Drawing, 9

red-flag behaviors, children education on, xxvii

relapse prevention therapy, xxiv

release of information (ROI): by caregivers for CACs, 104; by caregivers for coach and instructor information, 88, 93; by caregivers for own therapist, 125; by caregivers for school information, 88

research: adolescent sexual abuse treatment programs limited, xv; limited assessment and intervention approaches, xv, 141, 146–47; of sexually acting out youth over age of 12, xiii

research, problematic sexual behaviors limited, xvii; on developmental differences, 145–46; on girls and gender-diverse children, 144–45; on race and ethnicity, 142–44

respect, in CERTS, 55–56

respite services, 95, 102–3

ripple and rock activity, for impact, 75–76, 167, 168

risk factors assessment, in Trauma Outcome Process, xxii

rock and ripple activity. *See* ripple and rock activity

ROI. *See* release of information

roots: in flower activity, 51; in weed activity, 50

safe/good touch, 18, 152, 170

safe-play plan, 80; caregiver participation in, 79

Safer Society survey, of adult, adolescent, and child sexual abuse treatment programs, xiv

safety: body parts and, 33; in CERTS, 57; level of comfort around strangers, 64; personal, 64; in relationships, 63–64

safety plan: appropriate supervisor identification, 13; basics of, 12–13; caregiver concerns identification for, 12; caregiver cooperation and input for, 13; community, 172–73; DHS involvement and, 11; for extracurricular activities, 91–92; goals within, 13; health, 173–74; home, 12, 172; information on hands-on sexual contact with another youth, 12–13; initial treatment example, 174–75; as living document, 13; mental/emotional health, 173; physical health, 173; for schools, 14, 90–91, 172

school: barriers to response to problematic sexual behaviors, 87; educators as mandatory reporters, 86; 504 plan, 90; harmful social norms in, 87; IEP plans, 87, 89–90; minimization of behaviors, 87; problematic sexual behaviors prevention, 86–87; problematic sexual behaviors themes, 87; safety plans for, 14, 90–91, 172; sexual victimization prevalence in, 86

school engagement, 87; caregiver ROI and, 88, 93; questions in process of, 88–89

SDQ. *See* strengths and difficulties questionnaire

seeds: in flower activity, 51; in weed activity, 49–50

sensations/triggers: in feelings chain, 27, 155, 170; step in staircase activity, 47–48

sex education: age-appropriate on boundaries and privacy, xxxi, 123;

caregivers age-appropriate discussion, 123–24; for child problematic sexual behavior minimization, xxv; for healthy sexual development, 128–29

sex offense treatment, xiii

sexual abuse: definitional problems on, xxix; education, xxviii; sibling, 133

sexual development, lack of knowledge around, 122–24; racism impact, 143–44

sexually abusive behaviors, xxix; APA definition of, xxx

sexually reactive behaviors, xxix; defined, xxx

sexually transmitted disease (STD) prevention, 57

sexually transmitted infection (STI) prevention, 57

sexual offending behaviors: adolescent invasive acts of sexual harm with unaddressed, xiv; adult sexual offenders methods used to target children, xxvi–xxvii; Colorado Sex Offender Management Board work with juvenile, 134–35; description of child, xviii–xix; female, xiii; lack of resources for youth under age of twelve, xiii; resources for youth ages twelve to eighteen, xiii

sexual play, normative sexual exploration compared to, xviii

sexual/secret touch, 19, 152, 170

sexual violence, CDC on, 124

social learning intervention, xxii

society, lack of sexuality discourse, 128–29

specialist abuse-specific intervention approach, xxii

staircase activity, for ownership, 161; actions step, 48; example of, 162; feelings step in, 48; follow-up discussion for, 49; plans step, 48; sensations/triggers step, 47–48; thoughts step, 48

STD. *See* sexually transmitted disease

STI. *See* sexually transmitted infection

strength-based intervention approaches, xxii; in PSB-CBT, xxiii

strengths and difficulties questionnaire (SDQ), 147

string of plates timeline activity, 41

stuff boundary activity, 15–16, 150, 170

supervision: for child problematic sexual behavior minimization, xxv; software for technology, 121

survivor therapist services, 107; Child Abuse hotline reporting, 105; clarification meeting with, 106; for disclosure of problematic sexual behaviors of another child, 105; identified victim and, 105

talking/feeling boundary activity, 16, 150, 170

Talking While Drawing rapport-building activity, 9

targeted child, hyperreactive caregiver response and, 118

technology literacy: inappropriate content accessibility, 120; internet sight and sound supervision, 121; parental controls, 120, 121; supervision software, 121

TF-CBT. *See* trauma-focused CBT

therapy specialties: AASECT, 138; CADC, 138; CBT, xxii, xxiv, xl, 26, 137; CEDS, 138; EMDR, 130; play therapy, xxiii, xxiv, 130; TF-CBT, xxiv

thoughts: in feelings chain, 27–28, 155, 170; step in staircase activity, 48

touch types, 151; further learning on, 19–20; safe/good touch, 18, 152, 170; sexual/secret touch, 19, 152, 170; types of touch activity, 20–21; unsafe/bad touch, 18–19, 152, 170

traditional timeline activity, 41

trauma: brain and early childhood, xx–xxi; problematic sexual behaviors

symptomatic of, xxi; problematic
sexual behaviors treatment
addressing, xx
trauma-focused CBT (TF-CBT),
xxiv
trauma-informed intervention approach,
xxii
Trauma Outcome Process model: on
behavioral response outcomes, xxi;
client self-awareness assessment,
xxii; emotional, behavioral, and
cognitive outcomes assessment, xii;
risk factors assessment, xxii; on
trauma response outcomes, xxi
trauma symptom checklist for young
children (TSCYC), 147
treatment curriculum, xv; building
rapport, xli, xlii, xliii, 3–9; Lego
house metaphor for, 14
treatment modules: for full treatment
protocol, xli; for protocol for little
kids, xliii; for protocol for younger
children with problematic sexual
behaviors, xli–xlii; for protocol for
younger children with self-focused
problematic sexual behaviors,
xlii–xliii
treatment protocol, xv, xxxix; full
treatment, xl–xli; for little kids,
xliii; for younger children with
problematic sexual behaviors,
xli–xlii; for younger children with
self-focused problematic sexual
behaviors, xlii–xliii
treatment review, 80–81, 170–71
trouble thoughts, in client history,
43–44, 158, 159, 160, 170–71
trouble thoughts mix-and-match activity,
43–44, 159, 160, 170–71
trust, in CERTS, 56

TSCYC. *See* trauma symptom checklist
for young children
types of touch activity, 20–21, 170

unhealthy relationships exposure,
problematic sexual behaviors
impacted by, xix
unsafe/bad touch, 18–19, 152, 170

victim, 138; awareness, xli, 73–75;
CACs and, 105, 133; child
perpetrator out-of-home placement
and, 12; problematic sexual
behaviors treatment and, xxiv;
-specific treatment, xxiii; survivor
therapist and identified, 105
violence: CDC on sexual, 124;
domestic, xix; exposure to, xx`
voluntary custody agreements, of DHS
FSS, 96
voluntary placement agreements, of
DHS FSS, 96

Washington County Wraparound
Eligibility Criteria, for wraparound
services, 97–98
weed, in weed activity, 50
weed activity, for ownership, 51–52,
163; dirt, 49; example, 164; follow-
up discussion for, 50; roots, 50;
seeds, 49–50; weed, 50
who-what-where-when-why
conversation, for locker room, 93–94
wraparound services, 101; family
centered approach in, 96–97, 98;
ICC referral and, 98–99; Multnomah
County Wraparound Eligibility
Criteria, 98; process example, 99,
100; Washington County Wraparound
Eligibility Criteria, 97–98

About the Author

Genevieve Naquin is a licensed professional counselor and lead therapist at Higher Ground Counseling, a clinic that specializes in working with those who have problematic sexual behaviors, illegal sexual behaviors, and who have experienced abuse and trauma. She is a certified clinical sexual offense therapist who started her time in the field working with adolescents who were adjudicated for sexual offenses. She has since developed expertise in working with young children who are engaging in problematic sexual behaviors, a specialization that closely aligns with her passion for sexual abuse prevention. Naquin has presented on this topic in both educational and conference settings.